APR 4 1969

ink scribblings noted 9-24-69

809.93   Deverson, H   J   comp.
D493   Journey into night; an anthology.
          Norton [1966]
            320p. illus. 12.50

          1. Literature - Collections. 2. English
        literature (Selections: Extracts, etc.)
        3. American literature (Selections: Ex-
        tracts, etc.) 4. Night in literature. I.
        Title.

                              3-14-68 yc

JOURNEY INTO NIGHT

An anthology compiled by

H. J. DEVERSON

W·W·NORTON & COMPANY · INC · NEW YORK

FOR RUBY

CONTENTS

Cover picture: Sunset on the Indus River:
GUY GRAVETT

NIGHT IS FOR BEGINNINGS

Night coming on	EUAN DUFF	14
From Genesis	SWINBURNE	15
Milk Wood under Night	DYLAN THOMAS	15
Acquainted With the Night	ROBERT FROST	17
Oblomovka	I. A. GONCHAROV	17
Winter Evening	WILLIAM COWPER	18
Night among the Pines		
	ROBERT LOUIS STEVENSON	19
Dover Beach	MATTHEW ARNOLD	22
At Night on the Beach Alone		
	WALT WHITMAN	22
Moonlight, Dover Beach	BILL BRANDT	23
Sunset in the Fens	DONALD MCCULLIN	24
In a Vale	ROBERT FROST	25
Night on the Hills	J. ARTHUR GIBBS	26
To Night	JOSEPH BLANCO WHITE	28
The Dark Woods	MICHAEL TAYLOR	29
Cat of Islington	THURSTON HOPKINS	30
Rhapsody on a Windy Night	T. S. ELIOT	31
Stopping by Woods on a Snowy Evening		
	ROBERT FROST	33
The Evening Knell	JOHN FLETCHER	34

NIGHT IS FOR STAR-GAZING

Sky Magic	SIR JAMES FRAZER	35
On Looking Up by Chance at the Constellations	ROBERT FROST	38
The Origin of the Milky Way		
	TINTORETTO	39
Comment by PHILIP HENDY		
Holy Night	LORD SNOWDON	40
Rome: the Sacred Pool	ROLOFF BENY	42
The fickle stars	ST AUGUSTINE	43
The Moon	SHELLEY	43
Night	WILLIAM BLAKE	44
Silver	WALTER DE LA MARE	44
who knows . . . ?	e. e. cummings	45
McGonagall's Moon		46

NIGHT IS FOR PLEASURE

The Night of the Volunteer Ball		
	GEORGE AND WEEDON GROSSMITH	47
Eastern Hospitality	MARCO POLO	50
Hostesses	ERICH AUERBACH	51
The Embassy Reception		
	ERICH AUERBACH	52
Below Stairs	BILL BRANDT	53
Lookers-on	PATRICK WARD	54
Dancing Trinidadians	PATRICK WARD	55
Monica Mason	MICHAEL PETO	56
Trapeze	PATRICK WARD	57
Raissa Struchkova	ROGER WOOD	57
Plisetskaya	ZOË DOMINIC	58
Bull Fight	THURSTON HOPKINS	59
Flamenco	THURSTON HOPKINS	59
Curtain Call	ROGER WOOD	60
Pub People	ROGER MAYNE	62
Bingo	ROGER MAYNE	64
Fairground at Night	W. SUSCHITZKY	65
Girl with a Future	ROGER MAYNE	66
Woman with a Past, Kyoto	ROLOFF BENY	67
Price Twenty Deutschmarks		
	OTTO KARMINSKI	68
The Women in the Windows		
	IAN FLEMING	69
Casanova in London		69
A Night with Samuel Pepys		70
Reasons for Being Late	RICHARD STEELE	71
Water-drinker	GREVILLE	71
Disraeli in the warm Moonlight		72

NIGHT IS FOR ADVENTURE

A Night with the Miller of Trumpington		
	GEOFFREY CHAUCER	73
How I Escaped from the Boers		
	WINSTON S. CHURCHILL	79
Night in the desert	CHARLES DOUGHTY	89
The Boy and the River	MARK TWAIN	90
Dickens at Sea	CHARLES DICKENS	92

Two More for the Skylark

        DONALD MCCULLIN   93

The Burning Longship   PATRICK WARD   93

Living Space   THURSTON HOPKINS   94

Radio Telescope   AXEL POIGNANT   96

Monday Nights in Space

   KONAROV, EGOROV AND FEOKTISTOV   97

Lost among the Stars

    ANTOINE DE SAINT-EXUPÉRY   100

The Kon-Tiki's First Nights at Sea

        THOR HEYERDAHL   103

NIGHT IS FOR THE CITY

Noises in the Night   ROBERT SOUTHEY   105

Night Song   JAMES MCNEILL WHISTLER   105

The Ant-heap   ALEXANDER HERZEN   105

Child Stripping   HENRY MAYHEW   106

London Magic   CHARLES LAMB   107

Impression de Nuit

    LORD ALFRED DOUGLAS   107

Journey to Westminster

     SIR ALAN HERBERT   108

Life Guards at Dusk   JOHN COWAN   109

Barrow Boy   DONALD MCCULLIN   110

London Fog   THURSTON HOPKINS   111

Owl of Westminster   BARNET SAIDMAN   112

Piccadilly Circus   FRANK HERRMANN   114

Mental Hospital Night Sister

     ERICH AUERBACH   116

Night Thoughts on Bedlam

     CHARLES DICKENS   117

Stow's London at Night   118

The Great Fire   JOHN EVELYN   122

Night in Soho   COLIN MACINNES   124

Nocturne, New York   GAY TALESE   126

New York: Prop of Love

     BRUCE DAVIDSON   129

New York: Central Park

     BRUCE DAVIDSON   130

The Lady of the Camellias   JOHN TIMBERS   132

NIGHT IS FOR LOVING

From Epithalamion   EDMUND SPENSER   133

Such harmony   SHAKESPEARE   135

Sleep, angry beauty   THOMAS CAMPION   136

And is it night?   ANON.   136

Bridal Song   GEORGE CHAPMAN   137

Bridal Song   FRANCIS BEAUMONT?   137

The Night-piece: To Julia

     ROBERT HERRICK   138

Come, gentle night   SHAKESPEARE   139

Meeting at Night   ROBERT BROWNING   140

Last Sonnet   JOHN KEATS   140

But One   LORD BYRON   141

A Proposale   DAISY ASHFORD   142

i like my body . . .   e. e. cummings   144

Body, remember . . .   C. P. CAVAFY   144

The body   OTTO KARMINSKI   145

Love in a Corridor   JOHN HOPKINS   146

Now winter nights enlarge

     THOMAS CAMPION   146

Dawn at the Hunt Ball   ERICH AUERBACH   147

The Waiter   DENNIS STOCK   148

NIGHT IS FOR OWLS

The Boy and the Owls   WORDSWORTH   150

Short-eared Owl   ERIC HOSKING   151

There was a young lady   EDWARD LEAR   151

Owl by Flashlight   ERIC HOSKING   152

Owls and Goblins   GILBERT WHITE   153

Sweet Suffolk Owl   ANON.   154

Owl   GEORGE MACBETH   155

NIGHT IS FOR MUSIC

Nightingale   IZAAK WALTON   156

The Dramatist   LEN HOWARD   156

Nightingale, Aggressive   ERIC HOSKING   157

The Viola   ERICH AUERBACH   158

Music at Night   ALDOUS HUXLEY   159

Promenade Concert

GODFREY MACDOMNIC & ERICH AUERBACH   160

Street Music

  GODFREY MACDOMNIC AND JOHN COWAN   162

Jazz Club   FRANK HERRMANN   163

All-night Rave   JOHN HOPKINS   164

Fiesta with Sleeping Child

     PATRICK WARD   166

NIGHT IS FOR BEDS

The Bed of Life   GUY DE MAUPASSANT   167

Byron's Bedroom   BILL BRANDT   168

The Night the Baby was Born

     JOSEPH MCKEOWN   169

Mother and Child   BARNET SAIDMAN   170

Time to Go to Bed   MICHAEL PETO   171

Time to Get Up   KELVIN BRODIE   172

How to lie in bed   ANDREW BOORDE   173
The Honeymoon   GREVILLE   174
When His Majesty locked the doors
    JOSEPH MEAD   174
A Full Bed   ROBERT SOUTHEY   175
The Celestial Bed   MARY EDEN AND
    RICHARD CARRINGTON   176
The Great Bed of Ware   MARY EDEN AND
    RICHARD CARRINGTON   178
The Lass that Made the Bed to Me
    ROBERT BURNS   179
Bedmate   DR JOHN BROWN   181
The Night the Bed Fell   JAMES THURBER   181
A Terribly Strange bed   WILKIE COLLINS   186
A Bed with a History
    ALEXANDER CORDELL   191
Inscription for an Old Bed
    WILLIAM MORRIS   193

NIGHT IS FOR SLEEP

The Golden Chain   THOMAS DEKKER   194
A Plea   SAMUEL DANIEL   194
The Seven Sleepers   EDWARD GIBBON   195
Michelangelo's 'Night'   196
Vishnu Sleeping on the Shesh Snake
    W. SUSCHITZKY   198
Sleeping Nymph   BILL BRANDT   199
Tobias and Sara   200
To Sleep   JOHN KEATS   201
Sleep   MARY COLERIDGE   201
Sleepers, by Greville   202
The Stuff that sleep is made of   JOHN DAVY   203
Parvenu   VACHEL LINDSAY   204
The Middle of the Night   THOM GUNN   205
Mystery of the Vanishing Shirts   206
Bed and Board   AUGUSTUS HARE   206

NIGHT IS FOR THE SLEEPLESS

The Eye Awake   SHAKESPEARE   207
Sonnet   WILLIAM DRUMMOND   207
Sleepless   WORDSWORTH   208
Watchyng or they that can nat slepe
    ANDREW BOORDE   208
Sheep on the Welsh Hills
    OTTO KARMINSKI   209
The Night Walker   THURSTON HOPKINS   210
Starlings   BARNET SAIDMAN   211
Guy the Gorilla   W. SUSCHITZKY   212

Dog Watch   WILLIAM COBBETT   213
Gorillas in their Nest
    GEORGE B. SCHALLER   213
Pillows of Stone   JOHN MARSTON   214
To his watch   LORD HERBERT OF CHERBURY   214
Uneasy Heads   SHAKESPEARE   215
The Other World   WILLIAM GOLDING   216

NIGHT IS FOR DREAMS

Jacob's Dream   GENESIS   217
Be cheerful, sir   SHAKESPEARE   217
Plato on Dreams   B. JOWETT   218
The Dream   JOHN DONNE   219
Golden Dreams
    JOHN DAVIES OF HEREFORD   220
The Terrors of the Night   THOMAS NASHE   220
Dreams are but interludes   JOHN DRYDEN   220
A Kind of Dreaming   DONALD MCCULLIN   221
Man of the Night   DONALD MCCULLIN   222
Porter, Victoria Station   MALCOLM AIRD   223
The Dream . . .   JOHN HEDGECOE   224
. . . and the Dreamer
    HENRI CARTIER-BRESSON   225
Girl from China   ZOË DOMINIC   226
Girl of the Gorbals   BERT HARDY   227
The Man Outside   JOHN CHILLINGWORTH   228
From Darkness   LORD BYRON   229
Abraham Lincoln's Dream   R. L. MEGROZ   230
On the Nightmare   ERNEST JONES   231
The Hand   ALISON UTTLEY   232
The Dreams of the Opium Eater
    DE QUINCEY   233
Dreams   PIRANESI   237
Pagoda in Burma   ROLOFF BENY   238
Wet Night, New Orleans
    THURSTON HOPKINS   239
Three in the Underground
    DONALD MCCULLIN   239
Prayer Meeting in Paddington
    MALCOLM AIRD   240
The Vision of the Cross   241
Ode on Melancholy   JOHN KEATS   243

NIGHT IS FOR GHOSTS AND WITCHES

The Woman who obeyed a Gang of
   Ghosts   R. L. MEGROZ   244
The Witches' Charms   BEN JONSON   246

Mary's Ghost	THOMAS HOOD	247
Ghosts on a Wet Night	GUY GRAVETT	249
Three Women of Dundee	MICHAEL PETO	250
Ghost Road	ALEXANDER LOW	252
Gymnasium	GUY GRAVETT	252
Haunted Houses	LONGFELLOW	253
Night-hag	JOHN MILTON	254
Come, seeling night	SHAKESPEARE	254

NIGHT IS FOR CONFLICT

The Night before Agincourt		
	SHAKESPEARE	255
Cortés and the Melancholy Night		
	W. H. PRESCOTT	257
Anthem for Doomed Youth		
	WILFRID OWEN	262
Bayonet Charge	TED HUGHES	263
Bombers over Berlin	VON STUDNITZ	264
A letter from the blitz	JIM	265
The Night of Hiroshima	JOHN HERSEY	267
The Night of King Lear	SHAKESPEARE	268
'King Lear'	ZOË DOMINIC	269
Night Bomber Bound for Berlin		
	FL-LT. PETER CLARK	270
Commando Attack, Norway		
	CAPT. REYNOLDS	270
London's Burning	BERT MASON	271
Pink and Green Sleepers	HENRY MOORE	271

NIGHT IS FOR CRIME

Thieves!	GEORGE CRUIKSHANK	272
A Visit to the Dens of Thieves		
	HENRY MAYHEW	273
The Hateful Night	SHAKESPEARE	275
The Murder of P.C. 43		277
The Cask of Amontillado		
	EDGAR ALLEN POE	280
Night	HOGARTH	285
Interrogation	JOHN COWAN	286
Night Beat	BILL BRANDT	287

NIGHT IS FOR ENDINGS

Sheep to the Slaughter		
	DONALD MCCULLIN	288
Homecoming	JOSEPH MCKEOWN	290
The Cardinal	ROLOFF BENY	292
From Murder in the Cathedral		
	T. S. ELIOT	293
Cruel Necessity	POPE	294
The Sadness of a King	HENRY VIII	295
The Sadness of a Queen	ANNE BOLEYN	295
Even such is time	SIR WALTER RALEGH	296
After the Shift	MICHAEL PETO	297
The End of the Road	MICHAEL PETO	298
sam	e. e. cummings	299
The Last Hours of Socrates		300
The Clock Strikes Twelve for Doctor Faustus	CHRISTOPHER MARLOWE	303
On the Death of an Epicure		
	RICHARD GRAVES	304
The Night they came for Guy Fawkes		
	HENRY GARNETT	305
Soliloquy of a Misanthrope	TED HUGHES	306
Remember, remember	BERT HARDY	307
Another Day	DONALD MCCULLIN	308
Hospital Bed	ROGER MAYNE	310
Uphill	CHRISTINA GEORGINA ROSSETTI	310
So, we'll go no more a roving		
	LORD BYRON	311
When thou must home to shades of underground	THOMAS CAMPION	311
The Night they Buried Grampa		
	JOHN STEINBECK	312
The Night has a Thousand Eyes		
	FRANCIS WILLIAM BOURDILLON	316

Acknowledgements	319

INTRODUCTION

A THOUSAND wanderers into the night will take a thousand different courses; one will not sense what is plain to another, will not see the same forms or hear the same voices. So it is with this attempt to put together some of the writings and pictures that touch upon night. It is a brief excursion into a vast hinterland: may that excuse it for leaving so much ground uncovered.

H. J. DEVERSON

JOURNEY
INTO
NIGHT

In the outer world that was before this earth,
That was before all shape or space was born,
Before the blind first hour of time had birth,
Before night knew the moonlight or the morn;

Yea, before any world had any light,
Or anything called God or man drew breath,
Slowly the strong sides of the heaving night
Moved, and brought forth the strength of life
and death . . .

From GENESIS, *by Swinburne*

DYLAN THOMAS

Milk Wood under Night

[SILENCE]

FIRST VOICE (*Very Softly*)

To BEGIN at the beginning:

It is spring, moonless night in the small town, starless and bible-black, the cobble-streets silent and the hunched, courters'-and-rabbits' wood limping invisible down to the sloeblack, slow, black, crowblack, fishingboat-bobbing sea. The houses are blind as moles (though moles see fine to-night in the snouting, velvet dingles) or blind as Captain Cat there in the muffled middle by the pump and the town clock, the shops in mourning, the Welfare Hall in widows' weeds. And all the people of the lulled and dumbfounded town are sleeping now.

Hush, the babies are sleeping, the farmers, the fishers, the tradesmen and pensioners, cobbler, schoolteacher, postman and publican, the undertaker and the fancy woman, drunkard, dressmaker, preacher, policeman, the webfoot cocklewomen and the tidy wives. Young girls lie bedded soft or glide in their dreams, with rings and trousseaux, bridesmaided by glow-worms down the aisles of the organplaying wood. The boys are dreaming wicked or of the bucking ranches of the night and the jollyrodgered sea. And

NIGHT COMING ON, *by Euan Duff*

the anthracite statues of the horses sleep in the fields, and the cows in the byres, and the dogs in the wetnosed yards; and the cats nap in the slant corners or lope sly, streaking and needling, on the one cloud of the roofs.

You can hear the dew falling, and the hushed town breathing. Only *your* eyes are unclosed to see the black and folded town fast, and slow, asleep. And you alone can hear the invisible starfall, the darkest-before-dawn minutely dewgrazed stir of the black, dab-filled sea where the *Arethusa*, the *Curlew* and the *Skylark*, *Zanzibar*, *Rhiannon*, the *Rover*, the *Cormorant*, and the *Star of Wales* tilt and ride.

Listen. It is night moving in the streets, the processional salt slow musical wind in Coronation Street and Cockle Row, it is the grass growing on Llaregyb Hill, dewfall, starfall, the sleep of birds in Milk Wood.

Listen. It is night in the still, squat chapel, hymning in bonnet and brooch and bombazine black, butterfly choker and bootlace bow, coughing like nannygoats, sucking mintoes, fortywinking hallelujah; night in the four-ale, quiet as a domino; in Ocky Milkman's loft like a mouse with gloves; in Dai Bread's bakery flying like black flour. It is to-night in Donkey Street, trotting silent, with seaweed on its hooves, along the cockled cobbles, past curtained fernpot, text and trinket, harmonium, holy dresser, watercolours done by hand, china dog and rosy tin teacaddy. It is night neddying among the snuggeries of babies.

Look. It is night, dumbly, royally winding through the Coronation cherry trees; going through the graveyard of Bethesda with winds gloved and folded, and dew doffed; tumbling by the Sailors Arms.

Time passes. Listen. Time passes.

Come closer now.

Only you can hear the houses sleeping in the streets in the slow deep salt and silent black, bandaged night. Only you can see, in the blinded bedrooms, the combs and petticoats over the chairs, the jugs and basins, the glasses of teeth, Thou Shalt Not on the wall, and the yellowing, dickybird-watching pictures of the dead. Only you can hear and see, behind the eyes of the sleepers, the movements and countries and mazes and colours and dismays and rainbows and tunes and wishes and flight and fall and despairs and big seas of their dreams.

From where you are, you can hear their dreams. . . .

From UNDER MILK WOOD, *by Dylan Thomas*

Acquainted With the Night

I have been one acquainted with the night.
I have walked out in rain – and back in rain.
I have outwalked the furthest city light.

I have looked down the saddest city lane.
I have passed by the watchman on his beat
And dropped my eyes, unwilling to explain.
I have stood still and stopped the sound of feet
When far away an interrupted cry
Came over houses from another street,

But not to call me back or say good-bye;
And further still at an unearthly height,
One luminary clock against the sky

Proclaimed the time was neither wrong nor right.
I have been one acquainted with the night.

SELECTED POEMS: *Robert Frost*

Oblomovka

DUSK BEGAN to fall. Once more a fire was kindled in the kitchen and there was a clatter of knives: supper was being cooked. The servants were assembled at the gate; sounds of the *balalaika* and laughter were heard there. They were playing catch-who-can. The sun was setting behind the copse, throwing off a few warm rays, which went through the wood like shreaks of fire, clothing the tops of the pines with brilliant gold. Then the rays faded one after the other; the last one lingered, piercing the thick branches like an arrow, but it, too, disappeared at last. Objects lost their shapes; everything was merged first into a grey and then into a black mass. The birds gradually stopped singing and at last were silent altogether, except one, which as though from sheer contrariness chirped monotonously at intervals amidst the general stillness; but the intervals grew longer and longer and finally it gave one last, low whistle, slightly rustled the branches around it . . . and dropped asleep. All was still. Only the grasshoppers chirped louder than ever. White mist rose from the ground and spread over the meadows and the river. The river, too, was quieter; something splashed in it for the last time, and it stirred no more. There was a smell of damp. It grew darker and darker. Clumps of trees loomed like some strange monsters; it was eerie in the wood; something creaked there suddenly, as though one of the monsters were changing its place and dried branches cracked under its feet. The first star, like a living eye, gleamed brightly in the sky, and lights appeared in the windows of the house.

It was the moment of solemn stillness in nature, when the creative mind works more actively, poetic thoughts glow more fervently, the heart burns with passion more ardently or suffers more bitter anguish, when the seed of a criminal design ripens unhindered in a cruel soul, when . . . everything in Oblomovka is peacefully and soundly asleep.

From OBLOMOV, *by I. A. Goncharov,* translated by Natalie Duddington

Winter Evening

Now stir the fire, and close the shutters fast,
Let fall the curtains, wheel the sofa round,
And, while the bubbling and loud-hissing urn
Throws up a steamy column, and the cups,
That cheer but not inebriate, wait on each,
So let us welcome peaceful evening in . . .

Oh Winter, ruler of th'inverted year, . . .
I love thee, all unlovely as thou seem'st,
And dreaded as thou art. Thou hold'st the sun
A prisoner in the yet undawning east,
Shortening his journey between morn and noon,
And hurrying him, impatient of his stay,
Down to the rosy west; but kindly still
Compensating his loss with added hours
Of social converse and instructive ease,
And gathering, at short notice, in one group
The family dispersed, and fixing thought,
Not less dispersed by day-light and its cares.
I crown thee king of intimate delights,
Fire-side enjoyments, home-born happiness,
And all the comforts that the lowly roof
Of undisturbed retirement and the hours
Of long uninterrupted evening know.

THE TASK, 1785, *William Cowper*

ROBERT LOUIS STEVENSON

Night among the Pines

'The bed was made, the room was fit,
By punctual eve the stars were lit;
The air was sweet, the water ran;
No need was there, for maid or man,
When we put up, my ass and I,
At God's green caravanserai.'

FROM BLEYMARD after dinner, although it was already late, I set out to scale a portion
of the Lozère. An ill-marked stony drove-road guided me forward; and I met nearly
half a dozen bullock-carts descending from the woods, each laden with a whole pine-
tree for the winter's firing. At the top of the woods, which do not climb very high
upon this cold ridge, I struck leftward by a path among the pines, until I hit on a dell
of green turf, where a streamlet made a little spout over some stones to serve me for a
water-tap. 'In a more sacred or sequestered bower – nor nymph nor faunus haunted.'
The trees were not old, but they grew thickly round the glade: there was no outlook,
except north-eastward upon distant hill-tops, or straight upward to the sky; and the
encampment felt secure and private like a room. By the time I had made my arrange-
ments and fed Modestine, the day was already beginning to decline. I buckled myself
to the knees into my sack and made a hearty meal; and as soon as the sun went down,
I pulled my cap over my eyes and fell asleep.

Night is a dead monotonous period under a roof; but in the open world it passes
lightly, with its stars and dews and perfumes, and the hours are marked by changes in
the face of Nature. What seems a kind of temporal death to people choked between
walls and curtains, is only a light and living slumber to the man who sleeps afield. All
night long he can hear Nature breathing deeply and freely; even as she takes her rest
she turns and smiles; and there is one stirring hour unknown to those who dwell in
houses, when a wakeful influence goes abroad over the sleeping hemisphere, and all the
outdoor world are on their feet. It is then that the cock first crows, not this time to
announce the dawn, but like a cheerful watchman speeding the course of night. Cattle
awake on the meadows; sheep break their fast on dewy hillsides, and change to a new
lair among the ferns; and houseless men, who have lain down with the fowls, open their
dim eyes and behold the beauty of the night.

At what inaudible summons, at what gentle touch of Nature, are all these sleepers
thus recalled in the same hour to life? Do the stars rain down an influence, or do we
share some thrill of mother earth below our resting bodies? Even shepherds and old
country-folk, who are the deepest read in these arcana, have not a guess as to the means
or purpose of this nightly resurrection. Towards two in the morning they declare the

thing takes place; and neither know nor inquire further. And at least it is a pleasant incident. We are disturbed in our slumber, only, like the luxurious Montaigne, 'that we may the better and more sensibly relish it'. We have a moment to look upon the stars, and there is a special pleasure for some minds in the reflection that we share the impulse with all outdoor creatures in our neighbourhood, that we have escaped out of the Bastille of civilisation, and are become, for the time being, a mere kindly animal and a sheep of Nature's flock.

When that hour came to me among the pines, I wakened thirsty. My tin was standing by me half full of water. I emptied it at a draught; and feeling broad awake after this internal cold aspersion, sat upright to make a cigarette. The stars were clear, coloured, and jewel-like, but not frosty. A faint silvery vapour stood for the Milky Way. All around me the black fir-points stood upright and stock-still. By the whiteness of the pack-saddle, I could see Modestine walking round and round at the length of her tether; I could hear her steadily munching at the sward; but there was not another sound, save the indescribable quiet talk of the runnel over the stones. I lay lazily smoking and studying the colour of the sky, as we call the void of space, from where it showed a reddish grey behind the pines to where it showed a glossy blue-black between the stars. As if to be more like a pedlar, I wear a silver ring. This I could see faintly shining as I raised or lowered the cigarette; and at each whiff the inside of my hand was illuminated, and became for a second the highest light in the landscape.

A faint wind, more like a moving coolness than a stream of air, passed down the glade from time to time; so that even in my great chamber the air was being renewed all night long. I thought with horror of the inn at Chasseradès and the congregated nightcaps; with horror of the nocturnal prowesses of clerks and students, of hot theatres and pass-keys and close rooms. I have not often enjoyed a more serene possession of myself, nor felt more independent of material aids. The outer world, from which we cower into our houses, seemed after all a gentle habitable place; and night after night a man's bed, it seemed, was laid and waiting for him in the fields, where God keeps an open house. I thought I had rediscovered one of those truths which are revealed to savages and hid from political economists: at the least, I had discovered a new pleasure for myself. And yet even while I was exulting in my solitude I became aware of a strange lack. I wished a companion to lie near me in the starlight, silent and not moving, but ever within touch. For there is a fellowship more quiet even than solitude, and which, rightly under-stood, is solitude made perfect. And to live out of doors with the woman a man loves is of all lives the most complete and free.

As I lay thus, between content and longing, a faint noise stole towards me through the pines. I thought, at first, it was the crowing of cocks or the barking of dogs at some very distant farm; but steadily and gradually it took articulate shape in my ears, until I became aware that a passenger was going by upon the highroad in the valley, and singing loudly as he went. There was more of goodwill than grace in his performance; but he trolled with ample lungs; and the sound of his voice took hold upon the hillside and set the air shaking in the leafy glens. I have heard people passing by night in sleeping cities; some of them sang; one, I remember, played loudly on the bagpipes. I have heard the rattle of a cart or carriage spring up suddenly after hours of stillness, and pass, for some minutes, within the range of my hearing as I lay abed. There is a romance about all who are abroad in the black hours, and with something of a thrill we try to guess their business. But here the romance was double; first, this glad passenger, lit internally with wine, who sent up his voice in music through the night; and then I, on the other hand, buckled into my sack, and smoking alone in the pine-woods between four and five thousand feet towards the stars.

When I woke again many of the stars had disappeared; only the stronger companions of the night still burned visibly overhead; and away towards the east I saw a faint haze of light upon the horizon, such as had been the Milky Way when I was last awake. Day was at hand. I lit my lantern, and by its glowworm light put on my boots and gaiters; then I broke up some bread for Modestine, filled my can at the water-tap, and lit my spirit-lamp to boil myself some chocolate. The blue darkness lay long in the glade where I had so sweetly slumbered; but soon there was a broad streak of orange melting into gold along the mountain-tops of Vivarais. A solemn glee possessed my mind at this gradual and lovely coming in of day. I heard the runnel with delight; I looked round me for something beautiful and unexpected; but the still black pine-trees, the hollow glade, the munching ass, remained unchanged in figure. Nothing had altered but the light, and that, indeed, shed over all a spirit of life and of breathing peace, and moved me to a strange exhilaration.

I drank my water chocolate, which was hot if it was not rich, and strolled here and there, and up and down about the glade. While I was thus delaying, a gush of steady wind, as long as a heavy sigh, poured direct out of the quarter of the morning. It was cold, and set me sneezing. The trees near at hand tossed their black plumes in its passage; and I could see the thin distant spires of pine along the edge of the hill rock slightly to and fro against the golden east. Ten minutes later, the sunlight spread at a gallop across the hillside, scattering shadows and sparkles, and the day had come completely.

I hastened to prepare my pack, and tackle the steep ascent that lay before me; but I had something on my mind. It was only a fancy; yet a fancy will sometimes be importunate. I had been most hospitably received and punctually served in my green caravanserai. The room was airy, the water excellent, and the dawn had called me to the moment. I say nothing of the tapestries or the inimitable ceiling, nor yet of the view which I commanded from the windows; but I felt I was in some one's debt for all this liberal entertainment. And so it pleased me, in a half-laughing way, to leave pieces of money on the turf as I went along, until I had left enough for my night's lodging. I trust they did not fall to some rich and surly drover.

From TRAVELS WITH A DONKEY IN THE CEVENNES,
by Robert Louis Stevenson (1850–1894)

Dover Beach

The sea is calm tonight,
The tide is full, the moon lies fair
Upon the straits; – on the French coast the light
Gleams and is gone; the cliffs of England stand,
Glimmering and vast, out in the tranquil bay.
Come to the window, sweet is the night-air!
Only, from the long line of spray
Where the sea meets the moon-blanched land,
Listen! you hear the grating roar
Of pebbles which the waves draw back, and fling,
At their return, up the high strand,
Begin, and cease, and then again begin,
With tremulous cadence slow, and bring
The eternal note of sadness in.

Matthew Arnold (1822–1888)

At Night on the Beach Alone

On the beach at night alone,
As the old mother sways her to and fro singing her husky song,
As I watch the bright stars shining, I think a thought of the clef of the universes and of
    the future.

A vast similitude interlocks all,
All spheres, grown, ungrown, small, large, suns, moons, planets,
All distances of place however wide,
All distances of time, all inanimate forms,
All souls, all living bodies though they be ever so different, or in different worlds,
All gaseous, watery, vegetable, mineral processes, the fishes, the brutes,
All nations, colors, barbarisms, civilizations, languages,
All identities that have existed or may exist on this globe, or any globe,
All lives and deaths, all of the past, present, future,
This vast similitude spans them, and always has spann'd,
And shall forever span them and compactly hold and enclose them.

Walt Whitman

MOONLIGHT, Dover Beach, *by Bill Brandt*

In a Vale

When I was young, we dwelt in a vale
   By a misty fen that rang all night,
And thus it was the maidens pale
I knew so well, whose garments trail
   Across the reeds to a window light.

The fen had every kind of bloom,
   And for every kind there was a face,
And a voice that has sounded in my room
Across the sill from the outer gloom.
   Each came singly unto her place,

But all came every night with the mist;
   And often they brought so much to say
Of things of moment to which, they wist,
One so lonely was fain to list,
   That the stars were almost faded away

Before the last went, heavy with dew,
   Back to the place from which she came –
Where the bird was before it flew,
Where the flower was before it grew,
   Where bird and flower were one and the same.

And thus it is I know so well
   Why the flower has odor, the bird has song.
You have only to ask me, and I can tell.
No, not vainly there did I dwell,
   Nor vainly listen all the night long.

SELECTED POEMS: *Robert Frost*

SUNSET IN THE FENS, *by Donald McCullin*

J. ARTHUR GIBBS

Night on the Hills

It is a pity mankind is so little addicted to being out of doors after sunset. Some of the most beautiful drives and walks I have ever enjoyed have been those taken at night. Driving out one evening from Cirencester, the road on either side was illuminated with the fairy lights of countless glow-worms. It is the female insect that is usually responsible for this wonderful green signal taper; the males seldom use it. Whereas the former is merely an apterous creeping grub, the latter is an insect provided with wings. Flying about at night, he is guided to his mate by the light she puts forth; and it is a peculiar characteristic of the male glow-worm, that his eyes are so placed that he is unable to view any object that is not immediately beneath him.

It is early in summer that these wonderful lights are to be seen; June is the best month for observing them. During July and August glow-worms seem to migrate to warmer quarters in sheltered banks and holes, nor is their light visible to the eye after June is out, save on very warm evenings, and then only in a lesser degree.

The glow-worms on this particular night were so numerous as to remind one of the fireflies in the tropics. At no place are these lovely insects more numerous and resplendent than at Kandy in Ceylon. Myriads of them flit about in the cool evening atmosphere, giving the appearance of countless meteors darting in different directions across the sky.

In the clear Cotswold atmosphere very brilliant meteors are observable at certain seasons of the year. Never shall I forget the strange variety of phenonema witnessed whilst driving homewards one evening in the autumn from the railway station seven miles away. There had been a time of stormy, unsettled weather for some weeks previously, and the meteorological conditions were in a very disturbed state. But as I started homewards the stars were shining brightly, whilst far away in the western sky, beyond the rolling downs and bleak plains of the Cotswold Hills, shone forth the strange, mysterious, zodiacal light, towering upwards into a point among the stars, and shaped in the form of a cone. It was the first occasion this curious, unexplained phenomenon had ever come under my notice, and it was awe inspiring in itself. But before I had gone more than two miles of my solitary journey, great black clouds came up behind me from the south, and I knew I was racing with the storm. Then, as 'the great organ of eternity began to play' and the ominous murmurs of distant thunder broke the silence of the night, a stiff breeze from the south seemed to come from behind and pass me, as if travelling quicker than my fast-moving nag. Like a whisper from the grave it rustled in the brown, lifeless leaves that still lingered on the trees, making me wish I was nearer the old house that I knew was ready to welcome me five miles on in the little valley, nestling under the sheltering hill. And soon more clouds seemed to spring up suddenly, north, south, east, and west, where ten minutes before the sky had been clear and starry. And the sheet lightning began to play over them with a continuous flow of silvery radiance, north answering south, and east giving back to west the reflected glory of the mighty electric fluid. But the centre of the heavens was still clear and free from cloud, so that there yet remained a large open space in front of me, wherein the stars shone brighter than ever. As I gazed forward and upward, and urged the willing horse into a twelve-mile-an-hour trot, the open space in the heavens revealed the glories of the finest display of fireworks I have ever seen. First of all two or three smaller stars shot across the hemisphere and disappeared into eternal space. But suddenly a brilliant light, like an enormous rocket, appeared in the western sky, far above the clouds. First it moved in a steady flight, hovering like a kestrel above us; then, with a flash which startled me out of my wits and brought my horse to a standstill, it rushed apparently towards us, and finally disappeared behind the clouds. It was some time before either horse or driver regained the nerve which had for a time forsaken them; and even then I was inclined to attribute this wonderful meteoric shower to a display of fireworks in a neighbouring village, so close to us had this last rocket-like shooting-star appeared to be. A meteor which is sufficiently brilliant to frighten a horse and make him stop dead is of rare occurrence. I was thankful when I reached home in safety that I had not only won my race against the storm, but that I had seen no more atmospheric phenonema of so startling a nature.

In addition to the wonders of the heaven there are many other interesting features connected with a drive or walk by the light of the stars or the moon. A Cotswold village seen by moonlight is even more picturesque than it is by day. The old, gabled manor houses are a delightful picture on a cold, frosty night in winter; if most of the rooms are lit up, they give one the idea of endless hospitality and cheerfulness when viewed from without. To walk by a stream such as the Coln on such a night is for the time like being in fairyland. Each eddy and ripple is transformed into a crystal stream, sparkling with a thousand diamonds. The sound of the waters as they gurgle and bubble over the stones on the shallows seems for all the world like children's voices plaintively repeating over and over again the old strain:

'I chatter, chatter as I flow
To join the brimming river,
For men may come and men may go,
But I go on for ever.'

Now is the time to discover the haunts of wild duck and other shy birds like the teal and the heron. In winter weather many of these visitors come and go without our being any the wiser, unless we are out at night. Before sunrise they will be far, far away, and will probably never return any more. Time after time we have been startled by a flight of duck rising abruptly from the stream, in places where by day one would never dream of looking for them. Foxes, too, may be seen within a stone's throw of the house on a moonlight evening. They love to prowl around on the chance of a dainty morsel, such as a fat duck or a semi-domestic moorhen. Nor will they take any notice of you at such a time.

I made a midnight expedition once last hunting season to see that the 'earths' were properly stopped in some small coverts situated on a bleak and lonely spot on the Cotswold Hills. On the way I had to pass close to a large barrow. Weird indeed looked the time-worn stone that has stood for thousands of years at the end of this old burial mound. A small wood nearby rejoices in the name of 'Deadman's Acre'. The moon was casting a ghastly light over the great moss-grown stone and the deserted wolds. The words of Ossian rose to my lips as I wondered what manner of men lay buried here. 'We shall pass away like a dream. Our tombs will be lost on the heath. The hunter shall not know the place of our rest. Give us the song of other years. Let night pass away on the sound, and morning return with joy.' Then, as the rustling wind spoke in the lifeless leaves of the beeches, the plain seemed to be peopled with strange phantasies – the ghosts of the heroes of old. And a voice came back to me on the whispering breeze:

'Thou, too, must share our fate; for human life is short.
Soon will thy tomb be hid, and the grass grow rank on thy grave.'

MACPHERSON'S *Ossian*.

From A COTSWOLD VILLAGE, *by J. Arthur Gibbs* (1868–1899)

To Night

Mysterious Night! when our first parent knew
Thee from report divine, and heard thy name,
Did he not tremble for this lovely frame,
This glorious canopy of light and blue?
Yet 'neath a curtain of translucent dew,
Bathed in the rays of the great setting flame,
Hesperus with the host of heaven came,
And lo! creation widened in man's view.
Who could have thought such darkness lay concealed
Within thy beams, O Sun! or who could find,
Whilst flow'r and leaf and insect stood revealed,
That to such countless orbs thou mad'st us blind?
  Why do we then shun Death with anxious strife?
  If Light can thus deceive, wherefore not Life?

Joseph Blanco White (1775–1841)

THE DARK WOODS, *by Michael Taylor*

T. S. ELIOT

Rhapsody on a Windy Night

Twelve o'clock.
Along the reaches of the street
Held in a lunar synthesis,
Whispering lunar incantations
Dissolve the floors of memory
And all its clear relations,
Its divisions and precisions,
Every street lamp that I pass
Beats like a fatalistic drum,
And through the spaces of the dark
Midnight shakes the memory
As a madman shakes a dead geranium.

Half-past one,
The street-lamp sputtered,
The street-lamp muttered,
The street-lamp said, 'Regard that woman
Who hesitates toward you in the light of the door
Which opens on her like a grin.
You see the border of her dress
Is torn and stained with sand,
And you see the corner of her eye
Twists like a crooked pin.'

The memory throws up high and dry
A crowd of twisted things;
A twisted branch upon the beach
Eaten smooth, and polished
As if the world gave up
The secret of its skeleton,
Stiff and white.
A broken spring in a factory yard,
Rust that clings to the form that the strength has left
Hard and curled and ready to snap.

Half-past two,
The street-lamp said,
'Remark the cat which flattens itself in the gutter,
Slips out its tongue
And devours a morsel of rancid butter.'
So the hand of the child, automatic,
Slipped out and pocketed a toy that was running along the quay.
I could see nothing behind that child's eye.
I have seen eyes in the street
Trying to peer through lighted shutters,
And a crab one afternoon in a pool,
An old crab with barnacles on his back,
Gripped the end of a stick which I held him.

Half-past three,
The lamp sputtered,
The lamp muttered in the dark.
The lamp hummed:
'Regard the moon,
La lune ne garde aucune rancune,
She winks a feeble eye,
She smiles into corners.
She smooths the hair of the grass.
The moon has lost her memory.
A washed-out smallpox cracks her face,
Her hand twists a paper rose,
That smells of dust and eau de Cologne,
She is alone
With all the old nocturnal smells
That cross and cross across her brain.'

The reminiscence comes
Of sunless dry geraniums
And dust in crevices,
Smells of chestnuts in the street,
And female smells in shuttered rooms,
And cigarettes in corridors
And cocktail smells in bars.

The lamp said,
'Four o'clock,
Here is the number on the door.

Memory!
You have the key,
The little lamp spreads a ring on the stair.
Mount.
The bed is open; the tooth-brush hangs on the wall,
Put your shoes at the door, sleep, prepare for life.'

The last twist of the knife.

COLLECTED POEMS 1909–1935: *T. S. Eliot*

Stopping by Woods on a Snowy Evening

Whose woods these are I think I know.
His house is in the village though;
He will not see me stopping here
To watch his woods fill up with snow.

My little horse must think it queer
To stop without a farmhouse near
Between the woods and frozen lake
The darkest evening of the year.

He gives his harness bells a shake
To ask if there is some mistake.
The only other sound's the sweep
Of easy wind and downy flake.

The woods are lovely, dark and deep.
But I have promises to keep,
And miles to go before I sleep,
And miles to go before I sleep.

SELECTED POEMS: *Robert Frost*

The Evening Knell

Shepherds all, and maidens fair,
Fold your flocks up, for the air
Gins to thicken, and the sun
Already his great course hath run.
See the dewdrops how they kiss
Every little flower that is,
Hanging on their velvet heads
Like a rope of crystal beads:
See the heavy clouds low falling,
And bright Hesperus down calling
The dead Night from under ground;
At whose rising, mists unsound,
Damps and vapours fly apace,
Hovering o'er the wanton face
Of these pastures, where they come,
Striking dead both blood and bloom:
Therefore, from such danger lock
Every one his lovèd flock;
And let your dogs lie loose without,
Lest the wolf come as a scout
From the mountain, and, ere day,
Bear a lamb or kid away;
Or the crafty thievish fox
Break upon your simple flocks.
To secure yourselves from these,
Be not too secure in ease;
Let one eye his watches keep,
Whilst the t'other eye doth sleep;
So you shall good shepherds prove,
And for ever hold the love
Of our great god. Sweetest slumbers,
And soft silence, fall in numbers
On your eye-lids! So, farewell!
Thus I end my evening's knell.

John Fletcher (1579–1625)

FRAZER

Sky Magic

THERE ARE some grounds for believing that the reign of many ancient Greek kings was limited to eight years, or at least that at the end of every period of eight years a new consecration, a fresh outpouring of the divine grace, was regarded as necessary in order to enable them to discharge their civil and religious duties. Thus it was a rule of the Spartan constitution that every eighth year the ephors should choose a clear and moonless night and sitting down observe the sky in silence. If during the vigil they saw a meteor or shooting star, they inferred that the king had sinned against the deity, and they suspended him from his functions until the Delphic or Olympic oracle should reinstate him in them. . . .

. . . Shooting stars and meteors are viewed with apprehension by the natives of the Andaman Islands, who suppose them to be lighted faggots hurled into the air by the malignant spirit of the woods in order to ascertain the whereabouts of any unhappy wight in his vicinity . . . The Turrbal tribe of Queensland thought that a falling star was a medicineman flying through the air and dropping his fire-stick to kill somebody; if there was a sick man in the camp, they regarded him as doomed . . . The Ngarigo of New South Wales believed the fall of a meteor to betoken the place where their foes were mustering for war . . . By some Indians of California meteors were called 'children of the moon', and whenever young women saw one of them they fell to the ground and covered their heads, fearing that, if the meteor saw them, their faces would become ugly and diseased . . . When the Laughlan Islanders see a shooting star they make a great noise, for they think it is the old woman who lives in the moon coming down to earth to catch somebody, who may relieve her of her duties in the moon while she goes away to the happy spirit-land . . . It is a Mohammedan belief that falling stars are demons or jinn who have attempted to scale the sky, and, being repulsed by the angels with stones, are hurled headlong, flaming, from the celestial vault . . . When the Wotjobaluk tribe of Victoria see a shooting star, they think it is falling with the heart of a man who has been caught by a sorcerer and deprived of his fat . . . The Wambugwe of eastern Africa fancy that the stars are men, of whom one dies whenever a star is seen to fall. The Lolos, an aboriginal tribe of western China, hold that for each person on earth there is a corresponding star in the sky . . .

Superstitions of the same sort are still commonly to be met with in Europe. Thus in some parts of Germany they say that at the birth of a man a new star is set in the sky, and that as it burns brilliantly or faintly he grows rich or poor; finally when he dies it drops from the sky in the likeness of a shooting star . . . In Belgium and many parts of France the people suppose that a meteor is a soul which has just quitted the body, some-

35

times that it is specially the soul of an unbaptised infant or of some one who has died without absolution. At sight of it they say that you should cross yourself and pray, or that if you wish for something while the star is falling you will be sure to get it . . . In the Punjaub, Hindoos believe that the length of a soul's residence in the realms of bliss is exactly proportioned to the sums which the man distributed to charity during his life; and that when these are exhausted his time in heaven is up, and down he comes. In Polynesia a shooting star was held to be the flight of a spirit, and to presage the birth of a great prince. The Mandans of north America fancied that the stars were dead people, and that when a woman was brought to bed a star fell from heaven, and entering into her was born as a child. On the Biloch frontier of the Punjaub each man is held to have his star, and he may not journey in particular directions when his star is in certain positions. If duty compels him to travel in the forbidden direction, he takes care before setting out to bury his star, or rather a figure of it cut out of cloth, so that it may not see what he is doing.

Which, if any, of these superstitions moved the barbarous Dorians of old to depose their kings whenever at a certain season a meteor flamed in the sky, we cannot say. Perhaps they had a vague general notion that its appearance signified the dissatisfaction of the higher powers with the state of the commonwealth; and since in primitive society the king is commonly held responsible for all untoward events, whatever their origin, the natural course was to relieve him of duties which he had proved himself to be incapable of discharging. But it may be that the idea in the minds of these rude barbarians was more definite. Possibly, like some people in Europe at the present day, they thought that every man had his star in the sky, and that he must die when it fell. The king would be no exception to the rule, and on a certain night of a certain year, at the end of a cycle, it might be customary to watch the sky in order to mark whether the king's star was still in the ascendant or near its setting. The appearance of a meteor on such a night – of a star precipitated from the celestial vault – might prove for the king not merely a symbol but a sentence of death. It might be the warrant for his execution. . . .

Whatever its origin may have been, the cycle of eight years appears to have coincided with the normal length of the king's reign in other parts of Greece besides Sparta. Thus Minos, king of Cnossus in Crete, whose great palace has been unearthed in recent years, is said to have held office for periods of eight years together. At the end of each period he retired for a season to the oracular cave on Mount Ida, and there communed with his divine father Zeus, giving him an account of his kingship in the years that were past, and receiving from him instructions for his guidance in those which were to come. The tradition plainly implies that at the end of every eight years the king's sacred powers needed to be renewed by intercourse with the godhead, and that without such a renewal he would have forfeited his right to the throne. We may surmise that among the solemn ceremonies which marked the beginning or the end of the eight years' cycle the sacred marriage of the king with the queen played an important part, and that in this marriage we have the true explanation of the strange legend of Pasiphae and the bull. It is said that Pasiphae, the wife of King Minos, fell in love with a wondrous white bull which rose from the sea, and that in order to gratify her unnatural passion the artist Daedalus constructed a hollow wooden cow, covered with a cow's hide, in which the love-sick queen was hidden while the bull mounted it. The result of their union was the Minotaur, a monster with the body of a man and the head of a bull, whom the king shut up in a labyrinth, a building full of such winding and intricate passages that the prisoner might roam in it for ever without finding the way out. The legend appears to reflect a mythical marriage of the sun and moon, which was acted as a solemn rite by the king and queen of Cnossus, wearing the masks of a bull and cow respectively. . . .

. . . The identification of Pasiphae, 'she who shines on all', with the moon was made long ago by Pausanias, who saw her image along with that of the sun in a sanctuary of that wild rocky coast of Messenia where the great range of Taygetus descends seaward in a long line of naked crags. The horns of the waxing or waning moon naturally suggest the resemblance of the luminary to a white cow; hence the ancients represented the goddess of the moon drawn by a team of white cattle. When we remember that at the court of Egypt the king and queen figured as god and goddess in solemn masquerades, where the parts of animal-headed deities were played by masked men and women, we need have no difficulty in imagining that similar dramas may have been performed at the court of a Cretan king, whether we suppose them to have been imported from Egypt or to have had an independent origin.

The stories of Zeus and Europa, and of Minos and Britomartis or Dictynna appear to be only different expressions of the same myth, different echoes of the same custom. The moon rising from the sea was the fair maiden Europa coming across the heaving billows from the far eastern land of Phoenicia, borne or pursued by her suitor the solar bull. The moon setting in the western waves was the coy Britomartis or Dictynna, who plunged into the sea to escape the warm embrace of her lover Minos, himself the sun. The story how the drowning maiden was drawn up in a fisherman's net may well be, as some have thought, the explanation given by a simple seafaring folk of the moon's reappearance from the sea in the east after she has sunk into it in the west. To the mythical fancy of the ancients the moon was a coy or wanton maiden, who either fled from or pursued the sun every month till the fugitive was overtaken and the lovers enjoyed each other's company at the time when the luminaries are in conjunction, namely, in the interval between the old and the new moon. Hence on the principles of sympathetic magic that interval was considered the time most favourable for human marriages. When the sun and moon are wedded in the sky, men and women should be wedded on earth. And for the same reason the ancients chose the interlunar day for the celebration of the Sacred Marriages of gods and goddesses. Similar beliefs and customs based on them have been noted among other peoples. It is likely, therefore, that a king and queen who represented the sun and moon may have been expected to exercise their conjugal rights above all at the time when the moon was thought to rest in the arms of the sun. However that may have been, it would be natural that their union should be consummated with unusual solemnity every eight years, when the two great luminaries, so to say, meet and mark time together once more after diverging from each other more or less throughout the interval. It is true that sun and moon are in conjunction once every month, but every month their conjunction takes place at a different point in the sky, until eight revolving years have brought them together again in the same heavenly bridal chamber where first they met.

From THE GOLDEN BOUGH *by Sir James Frazer*

On Looking Up by Chance at the Constellations

You'll wait a long, long time for anything much
To happen in heaven beyond the floats of cloud
And the Northern Lights that run like tingling nerves.
The sun and moon get crossed, but they never touch,
Nor strike out fire from each other, nor crash out loud.
The planets seem to interfere in their curves,
But nothing ever happens, no harm is done.
We may as well go patiently on with our life,
And look elsewhere than to stars and moon and sun
For the shocks and changes we need to keep us sane.
It is true the longest drouth will end in rain,
The longest peace in China will end in strife.
Still it wouldn't reward the watcher to stay awake
In hopes of seeing the calm of heaven break
On his particular time and personal sight.
That calm seems certainly safe to last tonight.

SELECTED POEMS: *Robert Frost*

THE ORIGIN OF THE MILKY WAY, *by Jacopo Tintoretto* (1518–1594)

THE BED-CURTAIN is hung over a cloud, for the scene of this commotion is the bedroom of Hera on Olympus. Zeus, her husband, has had an affair with Alcmene, the grand-daughter of Perseus, and the result has been the birth of little Heracles. Alcmene being mortal, Zeus wants immortality for their child, and has a scheme. While he presides in proxy, in the form of his eagle with a thunderbolt in its claws, his messenger Hermes puts the infant to the breast of his sleeping wife. Hera, however, averse to the child, awakens and jumps out of bed; and the immortal milk is spilt in the heavens. It becomes the Milky Way.

From THE NATIONAL GALLERY, LONDON, *by Philip Hendy.*

It is better to light a candle
than to curse the darkness.

CHINESE PROVERB

HOLY NIGHT, *by Lord Snowdon*

The fickle stars

St Augustine (354–430) in the course of his 'Confessions' relates that his friend Firminus was, like himself, once disposed to believe in the value of horoscopes cast by astrologers, but became sceptical for the following reason, given in his own words:

MY FATHER told me that, when my mother was expecting to be brought to bed of me, a female slave of his friend was also great with child, and this of course was known to her master, who used to register with the minutest care even the birth of his puppies. But while they were counting with laborious accuracy the days, hours and minutes, the one for his wife, the other for his bondswoman, it so fell out that both women were delivered at the same moment, so that they were compelled to make the same horoscope, down to the minutest particulars, for the son and for the baby slave . . . Neither could mark the least difference in the position of the stars or the natal influences. And yet I was born in a good position, advanced rapidly along the sunny paths of the world, grew in wealth, rose in rank; while that slave, as I was told by one who knew him, remained just what he was, without any relaxation of his yoke.

From A BOOK OF ANECDOTES, *by Daniel George*

The Moon

I
And, like a dying lady lean and pale,
Who totters forth, wrapp'd in a gauzy veil,
Out of her chamber, led by the insane
And feeble wanderings of her fading brain,
The moon arose up in the murky east
A white and shapeless mass.

II
Art thou pale for weariness
Of climbing heaven and gazing on the earth,
Wandering companionless
Among the stars that have a different birth,
And ever changing, like a joyless eye
That finds no object worth its constancy?

Percy Bysshe Shelley (1792–1822)

ROME: THE SACRED POOL, *by Roloff Beny*

Night

The sun descending in the west,
  The evening star does shine;
The birds are silent in their nest.
  And I must seek for mine.
    The moon, like a flower
    In heaven's high bower,
    With silent delight
    Sits and smiles on the night. . . .

William Blake (1757–1827)

Silver

Slowly, silently, now the moon
Walks the night in her silver shoon;
This way, and that, she peers, and sees
Silver fruit upon silver trees;
One by one the casements catch
Her beams beneath the silvery thatch;
Couched in his kennel, like a log,
With paws of silver sleeps the dog;
From their shadowy cote the white breasts peep
Of doves in a silver-feathered sleep;
A harvest mouse goes scampering by,
With silver claws, and silver eye;
And moveless fish in the water gleam,
By silver reeds in a silver stream.

Walter de la Mare

who knows . . . ?

who knows if the moon's
a balloon, coming out of a keen city
in the sky – filled with pretty people?
(and if you and i should

get into it, if they
should take me and take you into their balloon,
why then
we'd go up higher with all the pretty people

than houses and steeples and clouds:
go sailing
away and away sailing into a keen
city which nobody's ever visited, where

always
        it's
            Spring) and everyone's
in love and flowers pick themselves

e.e.cummings

McGonagall's Moon

Beautiful Moon, with thy silvery light,
Thou seemest most charming to my sight;
As I gaze upon thee in the sky so high,
A tear of joy does moisten mine eye.

Beautiful Moon, with thy silvery light,
Thou cheerest the Esquimau in the night;
For thou lettest him see to harpoon the fish,
And with them he makes a dainty dish.

Beautiful Moon, with thy silvery light,
Thou cheerest the fox in the night,
And lettest him see to steal the grey goose away
Out of the farm-yard from a stack of hay.

Beautiful Moon, with thy silvery light,
Thou cheerest the farmer in the night,
And makest his heart beat high with delight
As he views his crops by the light of the night.

Beautiful Moon, with thy silvery light,
Thou cheerest the eagle in the night,
And lettest him see to devour his prey
And carry it to his nest away.

Beautiful Moon, with thy silvery light,
Thou cheerest the mariner in the night
As he paces the deck alone,
Thinking of his dear friends at home.

Beautiful Moon, with thy silvery light,
Thou cheerest the weary traveller in the night;
For thou lightest up the wayside around
To him when he is homeward bound.

Beautiful Moon, with thy silvery light,
Thou cheerest the lovers in the night
As they walk through the shady groves alone,
Making love to each other before they go home.

Beautiful Moon, with thy silvery light,
Thou cheerest the poacher in the night;
For thou lettest him see to set his snares
To catch the rabbits and the hares.

by William McGonagall (1830–1902), described by
'Punch' as the greatest Bad Verse writer of his age

GEORGE AND WEEDON GROSSMITH

The Night of the Volunteer Ball

April 16. The night of the East Acton Volunteer Ball. On my advice, Carrie put on the same dress that she looked so beautiful in at the Mansion House, for it occurred to me, being a military ball, that Mr Perkupp, who, I believe, is an officer in the Honorary Artillery Company, would in all probability be present. Lupin, in his usual incomprehensible language, remarked that he had heard it was a 'bounders' ball'. I didn't ask him what it meant though I didn't understand. Where he gets these expressions from I don't know; he certainly doesn't learn them at home.

The invitation was for half-past eight, so I concluded if we arrived an hour later we should be in good time, without being 'unfashionable', as Mrs James says. It was very difficult to find – the cabman having to get down several times to inquire at different public-houses where the Drill Hall was. I wonder at people living in such out-of-the-way places. No one seemed to know it. However, after going up and down a good many badly-lighted streets we arrived at our destination. I had no idea it was so far from Holloway. I gave the cabman five shillings, who only grumbled, saying it was dirt cheap at half-a-sovereign, and was impertinent enough to advise the next time I went to a ball to take a 'bus.

Captain Welcut received us, saying we were rather late, but that it was better late than never. He seemed a very good-looking gentleman, though, as Carrie remarked, 'rather short for an officer'. He begged to be excused for leaving us, as he was engaged for a dance, and hoped we should make ourselves at home. Carrie took my arm and we walked round the rooms two or three times and watched the people dancing. I couldn't find a single person I knew, but attributed it to most of them being in uniform. As we were entering the supper-room I received a slap on the shoulder, followed by a welcome shake of the hand. I said: 'Mr Padge, I believe?' He replied: 'That's right.'

I gave Carrie a chair, and seated by her was a lady who made herself at home with Carrie at once.

There was a very liberal repast on the tables, plenty of champagne, claret, etc., and, in fact, everything seemed to be done regardless of expense. Mr Padge is a man that, I admit, I have no particular liking for, but I felt so glad to come across someone I knew, that I asked him to sit at our table, and I must say that for a short fat man he looked well in uniform, although I think his tunic was rather baggy at the back. It was the only supper-room that I have been in that was not over-crowded; in fact we were the only people there, everybody being so busy dancing.

I assisted Carrie and her newly-formed acquaintance, who said her name was Lupkin, to some champagne; also myself, and handed the bottle to Mr Padge to do likewise, saying: 'You must look after yourself.' He replied: 'That's right,' and poured out half a tumbler and drank Carrie's health, coupled, as he said, 'with her worthy lord and master'. We all had some splendid pigeon pie, and ices to follow.

The waiters were very attentive, and asked if we would like some more wine. I assisted Carrie and her friend and Mr Padge, also some people who had just come from the dancing-room, who were very civil. It occurred to me that some of the gentlemen knew me in the City, as they were so polite. I made myself useful, and assisted several ladies to ices, remembering an old saying that 'There is nothing lost by civility'.

The band struck up for the dance, and they all went into the ball-room. The ladies (Carrie and Mrs Lupkin) were anxious to see the dancing, and as I had not quite finished my supper, Mr Padge offered his arms to them and escorted them to the ball-room, telling me to follow. I said to Mr Padge: 'It is quite a West End affair,' to which remark Mr Padge replied: 'That's right.'

When I had quite finished my supper, and was leaving, the waiter who had been attending on us arrested my attention by tapping me on the shoulder. I thought it was unusual for a waiter at a private ball to expect a tip, but nevertheless gave a shilling, as he had been very attentive. He smilingly replied: 'I beg your pardon, sir, this is no good,' alluding to the shilling. 'Your party's had four suppers at 5s. a head, five ices at 1s., three bottles of champagne at 11s. 6d., a glass of claret, and a sixpenny cigar for the stout gentleman – in all £3 0s. 6d.!'

I don't think I was ever so surprised in my life, and had only sufficient breath to inform him that I had received a private invitation, to which he answered that he was perfectly aware of that; but that the invitation didn't include eatables and drinkables. A gentleman who was standing at the bar corroborated the waiter's statement, and assured me it was quite correct.

The waiter said he was extremely sorry if I had been under any misapprehension; but it was not his fault. Of course there was nothing to be done but to pay. So, after turning out my pockets, I just managed to scrape up sufficient, all but nine shillings; but the manager, on my giving my card to him, said: 'That's all right.'

I don't think I ever felt more humiliated in my life, and I determined to keep this misfortune from Carrie, for it would entirely destroy the pleasant evening she was enjoying. I felt there was no more enjoyment for me that evening, and it being late, I sought Carrie and Mrs Lupkin. Carrie said she was quite ready to go, and Mrs Lupkin, as we were wishing her 'Good-night', asked Carrie and myself if we ever paid a visit to Southend? On my replying that I hadn't been there for many years, she very kindly said: 'Well, why don't you come down and stay at our place?' As her invitation was so pressing, and observing that Carrie wished to go, we promised we would visit her the next Saturday week, and stay till Monday. Mrs Lupkin said she would write to us to-morrow, giving us the address and particulars of trains, etc.

When we got outside the Drill Hall it was raining so hard that the roads resembled canals, and I need hardly say we had great difficulty in getting a cabman to take us to Holloway. After waiting a bit, a man said he would drive us, anyhow, as far as 'The

Angel' at Islington, and we could easily get another cab from there. It was a tedious journey; the rain was beating against the windows and trickling down the inside of the cab.

When we arrived at 'The Angel' the horse seemed tired out. Carrie got out and ran into a doorway, and when I came to pay, to my absolute horror I remembered I had no money, nor had Carrie. I explained to the cabman how we were situated. Never in my life have I ever been so insulted; the cabman, who was a rough bully and to my thinking not sober, called me every name he could lay his tongue to, and positively seized me by the beard, which he pulled till the tears came into my eyes. I took the number of a policeman (who witnessed the assault) for not taking the man in charge. The policeman said he couldn't interfere, that he had seen no assault, and that people should not ride in cabs without money.

We had to walk home in the pouring rain, nearly two miles, and when I got in I put down the conversation I had with the cabman, word for word, as I intend writing to the *Telegraph* for the purpose of proposing that cabs should be driven only by men under Government control, to prevent civilians being subjected to the disgraceful insult and outrage that I had had to endure.

From THE DIARY OF A NOBODY, *by George and Weedon Grossmith*

MARCO POLO

Eastern Hospitality

... THE MEN (of Kamul) are addicted to pleasure, and attend to little else than playing upon instruments, singing, reading, writing, according to the practice of the country, and the pursuit, in short, of every kind of amusement. When strangers arrive, and desire to have lodging and accommodation at their houses, it affords them the highest gratification. They give positive orders to their wives, daughters, sisters, and other female relations, to indulge their guests in every wish, whilst they themselves leave their homes, and retire into the city, and the stranger lives in the house with the females as if they were his own wives, and they send whatever necessaries may be wanted; but for which, it is to be understood, they expect payment: nor do they return to their houses so long as the strangers remain in them. This abandonment of the females of their family to accidental guests, who assume the same privileges and meet with the same indulgences as if they were their own wives, is regarded by these people as doing them honour and adding to their reputation; considering the hospitable reception of strangers, who (after the perils and fatigues of a long journey) stand in need of relaxation, as an action agreeable to their deities, calculated to draw down the blessing of increase upon their families, to augment their substance, and to procure them safety from all dangers, as well as a successful issue to all their undertakings. The women are in truth very handsome, very sensual, and fully disposed to conform in this respect to the injunction of their husbands. It happened at the time when Mangu Khan held his court in this province, that the above scandalous custom coming to his knowledge, he issued an edict strictly commanding the people of Kamul to relinquish a practice so disgraceful to them, and forbidding individuals to furnish lodgings to strangers, who should be obliged to accommodate themselves at a house of public resort or *caravanserai*. In grief and sadness the inhabitants obeyed for about three years the command of their master; but finding at length that the earth ceased to yield the accustomed fruits, and that many unfortunate events occurred in their families, they resolved to despatch a deputation to the grand khan, in their names, to beseech him that he should be pleased to suffer them to resume the observance of a custom that had been so solemnly handed down to them by their fathers, from their ancestors in the remotest times; and especially as since they had failed in the exercise of these offices of hospitality and gratification to strangers, the interest of their families had gone progressively to ruin. The grand khan, having listened to this application, replied:- 'Since you appear to be so anxious to persist in your own shame and ignominy, let it be granted as you desire. Go, live according to your base customs and manners, and let your wives continue to receive the beggarly wages of their prostitution.' With this answer the deputies returned home, to the great delight of all the people, who, to the present day, observe their ancient practice.

THE TRAVELS OF MARCO POLO (1254–1324)

HOSTESSES AT THE DEBUTANTES' COMING-OUT PARTY, *by Erich Auerbach*

BELOW STAIRS, *by Bill Brandt*

LOOKERS-ON, *by Patrick Ward*

DANCING TRINIDADIANS, *by Patrick War*

PLISETSKAYA OF THE BOLSHOI in 'Swan Lake', *by Zoë Dominic*

Overleaf:

MONICA MASON in 'Rite of Spring'
by Michael Peto

TRAPEZE, *by Michael Ward*

RAISSA STRUCHKOVA in 'Romeo and Juliet'
by Roger Wood

BULL FIGHT, London night club
by Thurston Hopkins

FLAMENCO, Madrid night club
by Thurston Hopkins

Overleaf:

CURTAIN CALL after Ulanova's
first night at Covent Garden
by Roger Wood

Pub People

by Roger Mayne

BINGO, *by Roger Mayne*

FAIRGROUND AT NIGHT, *by W. Suschitzky*

GIRL WITH A FUTURE, *by Roger May*

WOMAN WITH A PAST, KYOTO, *by Roloff Be*

PRICE TWENTY DEUTSCHMARKS, *by Otto Karminski*

IAN FLEMING

The Women in the Windows

IF YOU are in search of sin or spectacle more solid than these naiveties [the night-life pleasures of the Reeperbahn in Hamburg], you walk across the broad street of the Reeperbahn and up Davidstrasse past the bogus Dutch block of the police station that cuts into the pretty façade of the St Pauli theatre. Fifty yards up this street on your right you will find a tiny alley protected from prying eyes by a tall wooden barrier bearing the words 'Adolescents forbidden'.

When you go through this you are greeted by a most astonishing sight – the brilliantly-lit alley, blocked also at the other end, is thronged, like a long stage or narrow piazza, with strolling men. At first sight, the neat, three-storied houses on both sides of the alley are like any others, except that they are all brightly lit as if for a gala occasion; but when you stroll down the alley you find that the bottom floors have been turned into wide show-cases elegantly furnished and decorated to resemble small parlours or drawing-rooms, and in each show-case, sitting in comfortable chairs or lounging on chaises-longues, are girls of varying ages and charms all scantily, though not immodestly, dressed. These girls are, to put it bluntly, 'for sale' at a price, I am reliably informed, of twenty Deutschmarks.

This street is no guilty hole-in-the-corner business, but a colourful, gay place. During my visit (purely in the interests of sociological research) there was not a drunken man to be seen, and if there had been I gather he would have been thrown out of the street by the two policemen who stand by the entrance.

Some of the girls in the show-cases looked pretty bored with the whole procedure, but most of them smiled and chatted away or got on with their knitting or petit-point with studied nonchalance. The street, I gather, operates throughout the twenty-four hours with a population of some 300 girls, who do six-hour shifts. The street and the houses are spotlessly clean, and medical supervision is very strict.

From EUROPE'S THRILLING CITIES, 1960, *by Ian Fleming*

I ALSO visited the bagnios where a rich man can sup, bathe and sleep with a fashionable courtesan, of which there are many in London. It makes a magnificent debauch and only costs six guineas.

CASANOVA IN LONDON, 1765

A Night with Samuel Pepys

Jan. 24, 1667 . . . And, anon, at about seven or eight o'clock, comes Mr Harris, of the Duke's playhouse, and brings Mrs Pierce with him, and also one dressed like a country-mayde with a straw hat on; which, at first, I could not tell who it was, though I expected Knipp: but it was she coming off the stage just as she acted this day in *The Goblins*; a merry jade. Now my house is full, and four fiddlers that play well. Harris I first took to my closet; and I find him a very curious and understanding person in all pictures and other things, and a man of fine conversation, and so is Rolt. So away with all my company down to the office, and there fell to dancing, and continued at it an hour or two, there coming Mrs Anne Jones, a merchant's daughter hard by, who dances well, and all in mighty good humour, and danced with great pleasure; and then sung and then danced, and then sung many things of three voices – both Harris and Rolt singing their parts excellently. Among other things, Harris sung his Irish song – the strangest in itself, and the prettiest sung by him, that ever I heard. Then to supper in the office, a cold, good supper, and wondrous merry. Here was Mrs Turner also, but the poor woman sad about her lodgings, and Mrs Markham: after supper to dancing again and singing, and so continued till almost three in the morning, and then, with extra-ordinary pleasure, broke up – only towards morning, Knipp fell a little ill, and so my wife home with her to put her to bed, and we continued dancing and singing; and, among other things, our Mercer unexpectedly did happen to sing an Italian song I know not, of which they two sung the other two parts to, that did almost ravish me, and made me in love with her more than ever with her singing. As late as it was, yet Rolt and Harris would go home to-night, and walked it, though I had a bed for them; and it proved dark, and a misly night, and very windy. The company being all gone to their homes, I up with Mrs Pierce to Knipp, who was in bed; and we waked her, and their I handled her breasts and did baiser la, and sing a song, lying by her on the bed, and then left my wife to see Mrs Pierce in bed to her, in our best chamber, and so to bed myself, my mind mightily satisfied with all this evening's work, and thinking it to be one of the merriest enjoyment I must look for in the world, and did content myself therefore with the thoughts of it, and so to bed; only the musique did not please me, they not being contented with less than 30s.

THE DIARY OF SAMUEL PEPYS

Reasons for Being Late

On Saturday night, 30th August 1707, Sir Richard Steele wrote this letter:

DEAR LOVELY MRS SCURLOCK, I have been in very good company, where your health, under the character of *the woman I loved best*, has been often drunk; so that I may say that I am dead drunk for your sake, which is more than *I die for you*.

RICH. STEELE

Six weeks later he wrote this letter to the same woman, who had now become his second wife:-

DEAREST BEING ON EARTH, Pardon me if you do not see me till eleven o'clock, having met a schoolfellow from India, by whom I am to be informed on things this night which expressly concern your obedient husband,

RICH. STEELE

WATER-DRINKER

November 7, 1836: . . . He [King William IV] was very angry at King Leopold's coming here, received him very coldly at Windsor, had no conversation with him on business, and on one occasion exhibited a rudeness even to brutality. It seems he hates water-drinkers; God knows why. One day at dinner Leopold called for water, when the King asked, 'What's that you are drinking, sir?' 'Water, sir.' 'G—— d—— it!' rejoined the other King; 'why don't you drink wine? I never allow anybody to drink water at my table.' Leopold only dined there, and went away in the evening. All this is very miserable and disgraceful.

THE GREVILLE MEMOIRS

Disraeli in the warm Moonlight

Young Benjamin Disraeli, later to become the great Tory Prime Minister, writes to his mother from Granada and describes the pleasures of the Spanish night in the year 1830:

. . . AFTER DINNER you take your siesta. I generally sleep for two hours. I think this practice conducive to health. Old people, however, are apt to carry it to excess. By the time I have risen and arranged my toilette it is time to steal out, and call upon any agreeable family whose Tertullia you may choose to honour, which you do, after the first time, uninvited, and with them you take your tea or chocolate. This is often *al fresco*, under the piazza or colonnade of the *patio*. Here you while away the time until it is cool enough for the *alameda* or public walk. At Cadiz, and even at Seville, up the Guadalquivir, you are sure of a delightful breeze from the water. The sea breeze comes like a spirit. The effect is quite magical. As you are lolling in listless languor in the hot and perfumed air, an invisible guest comes dancing into the party and touches them all with an enchanted wand. All start, all smile. It has come; it is the sea breeze. There is much discussion whether it is as strong, or whether weaker, than the night before. The ladies furl their fans and seize their mantillas, the cavaliers stretch their legs and give signs of life. All rise. I offer my arm to Dolores or Florentina (is not this familiarity strange?), and in ten minutes you are in the *alameda*. What a change! All is now life and liveliness. Such bowing, such kissing, such fluttering of fans, such gentle criticism of gentle friends! But the fan is the most wonderful part of the whole scene. A Spanish lady with her fan might shame the tactics of a troop of horse. Now she unfurls it with the slow pomp and conscious elegance of a peacock. Now she flutters it with all the languor of a listless beauty, now with all the liveliness of a vivacious one. Now, in the midst of a very tornado, she closes it with a whir which makes you start, pop! In the midst of your confusion Dolores taps you on the elbow; you turn round to listen, and Florentina pokes you in the side. Magical instrument! You know that it speaks a particular language, and gallantry requires no other mode to express its much subtle conceits or its most unreasonable demands than this slight, delicate organ. But remember, while you read, that here, as in England, it is not confined alone to your delightful sex. I also have my fan, which makes my cane extremely jealous. If you think I have grown extraordinarily effeminate, learn that in this scorching clime the soldier will not mount guard without one. Night wears on, we sit, we take a *panal*, which is as quick work as snapdragon, and far more elegant; again we stroll. Midnight clears the public walks, but few Spanish families retire till two. A solitary bachelor like myself still wanders, or still lounges on a bench in the *warm* moonlight. The last guitar dies away, the cathedral clock wakes up your reverie, you too seek your couch, and amid a gentle, sweet flow of loveliness, and light, and music, and fresh air, thus dies a day in Spain.

Adieu, my dearest mother, If possible, I write to my father from this place. 1,000 loves to all.

B. DISRAELI

GEOFFREY CHAUCER

A Night with the Miller of Trumpington

Surely one of the most eventful nights in literature is the one told of in The Reeve's Story, from Chaucer's 'Canterbury Tales'. John and Alan, needy students, have brought a sack of corn to the rascally Miller of Trumpington. After the miller has ground the corn he unlooses the students' horse, and while they are pursuing it across the fen, he steals some of their flour and gives it to his wife to cook. After a long chase John and Alan manage to catch the horse, and . . .

> Weary and wet, like cattle in the rain,
> Came foolish John and Alan back again.
> Said John, 'Alas the day that I was born!
> We've earned nowt here but mockery and scorn.
> Wor corn is stolen and they'll call us fools,
> Warden and all wor meäts in the Schools,
> And most of all the miller. What a day!'
> So back they went, John grousing all the way,
> Towards the mill and put the horse in byre.
> They found the miller sitting by the fire,
> For it was night, too late for going home,
> And, for the love of God, they begged a room
> For shelter and they proffered him their penny.
> 'A room?' the miller said. 'There isn't any.
> There's this, such as it is; we'll share it then,
> My house is small, but you are learned men
> And by your arguments can make a place
> Twenty foot broad as infinite as space.
> Take a look round and see if it will do,
> Or make it bigger with your parley-voo.'
> 'Well, Simon, you must have your little joke
> And, by St Cuthbert, that was fairly spoke!
> Well, people have a proverb to remind them
> To bring their own, or take things as they find them,'
> Said John. 'Dear host, do get us out the cup;

A little meat and drink would cheer us up.
We'll give ye the full payment, on my word.
No empty-handed man can catch a bird;
See, here's the silver, ready to be spent.'
   Down into Trumpington the daughter went
For bread and ale; the miller cooked a goose,
And tied their horse up lest it should get loose
Again, and in his chamber made a bed
With clean white sheets and blankets fairly spread,
Ten foot from his, upon a sort of shelf.
His daughter had a bed all by herself
Quite close in the same room; they were to lie
All side by side, no help for it, and why?
Because there was no other in the house.
   They supped and talked and had a fine carouse
And drank a lot of ale, the very best.
   Midnight or thereabout they went to rest.
   Properly pasted was this miller's head,
Pale-drunk he was, he'd passed the stage of red;
Hiccupping through his nose he talked and trolled
As if he'd asthma or a heavy cold.
To bed he goes, his wife and he together;
She was as jolly as a jay in feather,
Having well wet her whistle from the ladle.
And by her bed she planted down the cradle
To rock the baby or to give it sup.
   When what was in the crock had been drunk up,
To bed went daughter too, and thereupon
To bed went Alan and to bed went John.
That was the lot; no sleeping-draught was needed.
The miller had taken so much booze unheeded,
He snorted like a cart-horse in his sleep
And vented other noises, loud and deep.
His wife joined in the chorus hot and strong;
Two furlongs off you might have heard their song.
The wench was snoring too, for company.
   Alan the clerk in all this melody
Gave John a poke and said, 'Are ye awake?
Did ye ever hear sich sang for guidness sake?
There's family prayers for ye among they noddies!
Wild fire come doon and burn them up, the bodies!
Who ever heard a canny thing like that?

74

The devil take their souls for what they're at!
All this lang neet I shall na get nie rest.
    'But never ye mind, all shall be for the best;
I tell ye, John, as sure as I'm a man,
I'm going to have that wench there, if I can!
The law grants easement when things gang amiss,
For, John, there is a law that gans like this:
"If in one point a person be aggrieved,
Then in another he shall be relieved."
    'Wor corn is stolen, nivvor doubt of that;
Ill-luck has followed us in all we're at,
And since no compensation has been offered
Against wor loss, I'll take the easement proffered.
God's soul, it shall be so indeed, none other!'
    John whispered back to him, 'Be careful, brother,
The miller is a torble man for slaughter;
If he should wake and find ye with his daughter
He might do injury to you and me.'
'Injury? Him! I coont him nat a flea!'
    Alan rose up; towards the wench he crept.
The wench lay flat upon her back and slept,
And ere she saw him, he had drawn so nigh
It was too late for her to give a cry.
To put it briefly, they were soon at one.
Now, Alan, play! For I will speak of John.
    John lay there still for quite a little while,
Complaining and lamenting in this style:
'A bloody joke . . . Lord, what a chance to miss!
I shall be made a monkey of for this!
My meät has got some comfort for his harms,
He has the miller's daughter in his arms;
He took his chance and now his needs are sped,
I'm but a sack of rubbish here in bed.
And when this jape is told in times to come
They'll say I was a softie and a bum!
I'll get up too and take what chance I may,
For God helps those that help theirsels, they say.'
    He rises, steals towards the cradle, lifts it,
And stepping softly back again, he shifts it
And lays it by his bed upon the floor.
    The miller's wife soon after ceased to snore,
Began to wake, rose up, and left the room

And coming back she groped about in gloom,
Missing the cradle, John had snatched away.
'Lord, Lord,' she said, 'I nearly went astray
And got into the student's bed. . . . How dreadful!
There would have been foul doings. What a bed-ful!'
At last she gropes to where the cradle stands,
And so by fumbling upwards with her hands
She found the bed and thinking nought but good,
Since she was certain where the cradle stood,
Yet knew not where she was, for it was dark,
She well and fairly crept in with the clerk,
Then lay quite still and tried to go to sleep.
John waited for a while, then gave a leap
And thrust himself upon this worthy wife.
It was the merriest fit in all her life,
For John went deep and thrust away like mad.
It was a jolly life for either lad
Till the third morning cock began to sing.

    Alan grew tired as dawn began to spring;
He had been hard at work the long, long night.
'Bye-bye,' he said, 'sweet Molly . . . Are ye a'right?
The day has come, I cannot linger here,
But ever mair in life and death, my dear,
I am your own true clerk, or strike me deid!'
'Good-bye, my sweet,' she whispered, 'take good heed . . .
But first I'll tell you something, that I will!
When you are riding homewards past the mill
By the main entrance-door, a bit behind it,
There's the half-bushel cake – you're sure to find it –
And it was made out of the very meal
You brought to grind and I helped father steal. . . .
And, dearest heart, God have you in his keeping!'
And with that word she almost burst out weeping.

    Alan got up and thought, 'Dawn's coming on,
Better get back and creep in beside John.'
But there he found the cradle in his way.
'By God,' he thought, 'I nearly went astray!
My heed is tottering with my work to-neet,
That'll be why I cannot gan areet!
This cradle tells me I have lost my tether;
Yon must be miller and his wife together.'

    And back he went, groping his weary way

And reached the bed in which the miller lay,
And thinking it was John upon the bed
He slid in by the miller's side instead,
Grabbing his neck, and with no more ado
Said, 'Shake yourself, wake up, you pig's-head, you!
For Christ's soul, listen! O such noble games
As I have had! I tell you, by St James,
Three times the neet, from midnight into morn,
The miller's daughter helped me grind my corn
While you've been lying in your cowardly way . . .'
'You scoundrel!' said the miller. 'What d'you say?
You beast! You treacherous blackguard! Filthy rat!
God's dignity! I'll murder you for that!
How dare you be so bold as to fling mud
Upon my daughter, come of noble blood?'
  He grabbed at Alan by his Adam's apple,
And Alan grabbed him back in furious grapple
And clenched his fist and bashed him on the nose.
Down miller's breast a bloody river flows
Onto the floor, his nose and mouth all broke;
They wallowed like two porkers in a poke,
And up and down and up again they go
Until the miller tripped and stubbed his toe,
Spun round and fell down backwards on his wife.
  She had heard nothing of this foolish strife,
For she had fallen asleep with John the clerk,
Weary from all their labours in the dark.
The miller's fall started her out of sleep.
'Help!' she screamed. 'Holy cross of Bromeholme keep
Us! Lord! Into thy hands! To Thee I call!
Simon, wake up! The devil's among us all!
My heart is bursting, help! I'm nearly dead,
One's on my stomach, another's on my head.
  Help, Simpkin, help! These nasty clerks are fighting!'
  Up started John he needed no inciting,
And groped about the chamber to and fro
To find a stick; she too was on the go
And, knowing the corners better than them all,
Was first to find one leaning by the wall;
And by a little shaft of shimmering light
That shone in through a hole – the moon was bright –
Although the room was almost black as pitch

She saw them fight, not knowing which was which;
But there was something white that caught her eye
On seeing which she peered and gave a cry,
Thinking it was the night-cap of the clerk.

    Raising her stick, she crept up in the dark
And, hoping to hit Alan, it was her fate
To smite the miller on his shining pate,
And down he went, shouting, 'O God, I'm dying!'

    The clerks then beat him well and left him lying
And throwing on their clothes they took their horse
And their ground meal and off they went, of course,
And as they passed the mill they took the cake
Made of their meal the girl was told to bake.

    And thus the bumptious miller was well beaten
And done out of the supper they had eaten,
And done out of the money that was due
For grinding Alan's corn, who beat him too.
His wife was plumbed, so was his daughter. Look!
That comes of being a miller and a crook!

    I heard this proverb when I was a kid,
'Do evil and be done by as you did.'
Tricksters will get a tricking, so say I;
And God that sits in majesty on high
Bring all his company, great and small, to Glory!
Thus I've paid out the Miller with my story!

From Chaucer's THE CANTERBURY TALES, *translated into modern English by Nevill Coghill*

WINSTON S. CHURCHILL

How I Escaped from the Boers

In 1899 Winston Churchill became a prisoner-of-war of the Boers in the State Model Schools at Pretoria. This is his account of how he made his night escape:

'The State Model Schools stood in the midst of a quadrangle, and were surrounded on two sides by an iron grille and on two by a corrugated-iron fence about ten feet high. These boundaries offered little obstacle to anyone who possessed the activity of youth, but the fact that they were guarded on the inside by sentries, fifty yards apart, armed with rifle and revolver, made them a well-nigh insuperable barrier. No walls are so hard to pierce as living walls.

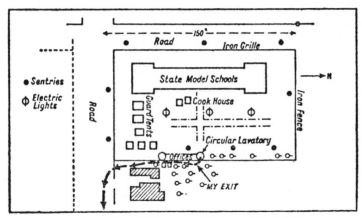

PLAN OF STATE MODEL SCHOOLS

'After anxious reflexion and continual watching, it was discovered by several of the prisoners that when the sentries along the eastern side walked about on their beats they were at certain moments unable to see the top of a few yards of the wall near the small circular lavatory office which can be seen on the plan. The electric lights in the middle of the quadrangle brilliantly lighted the whole place, but the eastern wall was in shadow. The first thing was therefore to pass the first two sentries near the office. It was necessary to hit off the exact moment when both their backs should be turned together. After the wall was scaled we should be in the garden of the villa next door. There the plan came to an end. Everything after this was vague and uncertain. How to get out of the garden, how to pass unnoticed through the streets, how to evade the patrols that surrounded the town, and above all how to cover the two hundred and eighty miles to the Portuguese frontier, were questions which would arise at a later stage.

'Together with Captain Haldane and Lieutenant Brockie I made an abortive attempt, not pushed with any decision, on 11th December. There was no difficulty in getting into the circular office. But to climb out of it over the wall was a hazard of the sharpest character. Anyone doing so must at the moment he was on the top of the wall be plainly visible to the sentries fifteen yards away, if they were in the right place and happened to look! Whether the sentries would challenge or fire depended entirely upon their individual dispositions, and no one could tell what they would do. Nevertheless I was determined that nothing should stop my taking the plunge the next day. As the 12th wore away my fears crystallised more and more into desperation. In the evening, after my two friends had made an attempt, but had not found the moment propitious, I strolled across the quadrangle and secreted myself in the circular office. Through an aperture in the metal casing of which it was built I watched the sentries. For some time they remained stolid and obstructive. Then all of a sudden one turned and walked up to his comrade, and they began to talk. Their backs were turned.

'Now or never! I stood on the ledge, seized the top of the wall with my hands, and drew myself up. Twice I let myself down again in sickly hesitation, and then with a third resolve scrambled up and over. My waistcoat got entangled with the ornamental metal-work on the top. I had to pause for an appreciable moment to extricate myself. In this posture I had one parting glimpse of the sentries still talking with their backs turned fifteen yards away. One of them was lighting his cigarette, and I remember the glow on the inside of his hands as a distinct impression which my mind recorded. Then I lowered myself lightly down into the adjoining garden and crouched among the shrubs. I was free! The first step had been taken, and it was irrevocable. It now remained to await the arrival of my comrades. The bushes in the garden gave a good deal of cover, and in the moonlight their shadows fell dark on the ground. I lay here for an hour in great impatience and anxiety. People were continually moving about in the garden, and once a man came and apparently looked straight at me only a few yards away. Where were the others? Why did they not make the attempt?

'Suddenly I heard a voice from within the quadrangle say, quite loud, "All up." I crawled back to the wall. Two officers were walking up and down inside, jabbering Latin words, laughing and talking all manner of nonsense – amid which I caught my name. I risked a cough. One of the officers immediately began to chatter alone. The other said, slowly and clearly, "They cannot get out. The sentry suspects. It's all up. Can you get back again?" But now all my fears fell from me at once. To go back was impossible. I could not hope to climb the wall unnoticed. There was no helpful ledge on the outside. Fate pointed onwards. Besides, I said to myself, "Of course, I shall be recaptured, but I will at least have a run for my money." I said to the officers, "I shall go on alone."

'Now I was in the right mood for these undertakings – failure being almost certain, no odds against success affected me. All risks were less than the certainty. A glance at the plan will show that the gate which led into the road was only a few yards from another sentry. I said to myself, "*Toujours de l'audace*," put my hat on my head, strode into the middle of the garden, walked past the windows of the house without any attempt at concealment, and so went through the gate and turned to the left. I passed the sentry at less than five yards. Most of them knew me by sight. Whether he looked at me or not I do not know, for I never turned my head. I restrained with the utmost difficulty an impulse to run. But after walking a hundred yards and hearing no challenge, I knew that the second obstacle had been surmounted. I was at large in Pretoria.

'I walked on leisurely through the night, humming a tune and choosing the middle of the road. The streets were full of burghers, but they paid no attention to me. Gradually I reached the suburbs, and on a little bridge I sat down to reflect and consider. I was in the heart of the enemy's country. I knew no one to whom I could apply for succour. Nearly three hundred miles stretched between me and Delagoa Bay. My escape must be known at dawn. Pursuit would be immediate. Yet all exits were barred. The town was picketed, the country was patrolled, the trains were searched, the line was guarded. I wore a civilian brown flannel suit. I had seventy-five pounds in my pocket and four slabs of chocolate, but the compass and the map which might have guided me, the opium tablets and meat lozenges which should have sustained me, were in my friends' pockets in the State Model Schools. Worst of all, I could not speak a word of Dutch or Kaffir, and how was I to get food or direction?

'But when hope had departed, fear had gone as well. I formed a plan. I would find the Delagoa Bay Railway. Without map or compass, I must follow that in spite of the pickets. I looked at the stars. Orion shone brightly. Scarcely a year before he had guided me when lost in the desert to the banks of the Nile. He had given me water. Now he should lead to freedom. I could not endure the want of either.

'After walking south for half a mile I struck the railway. Was it the line to Delagoa Bay or the Pietersburg branch? If it were the former, it should run east. But, so far as I could see, this line ran northwards. Still, it might be only winding its way out among the hills. I resolved to follow it. The night was delicious. A cool breeze fanned my face, and a wild feeling of exhilaration took hold of me. At any rate, I was free, if only for an hour. That was something. The fascination of the adventure grew. Unless the stars in their courses fought for me, I could not escape. Where, then, was the need of caution? I marched briskly along the line. Here and there the lights of a picket fire gleamed. Every bridge had its watchers. But I passed them all, making very short *detours* at the dangerous places, and really taking scarcely any precautions. Perhaps that was the reason I succeeded.

'As I walked I extended my plan. I could not march three hundred miles to the frontier. I would board a train in motion and hide under the seats, on the roof, on the couplings – anywhere. I thought of Paul Bultitude's escape from school in *Vice Versa*. I saw myself emerging from under the seat, and bribing or persuading some fat first-class passenger to help me. What train should I take? The first, of course. After walking for two hours I perceived the signal lights of a station. I left the line, and circling round it, hid in the ditch by the track about two hundred yards beyond the platform. I argued that the train would stop at the station and that it would not have got up too much speed by the time it reached me. An hour passed. I began to grow impatient. Suddenly I heard the whistle and the approaching rattle. Then the great yellow head-lights of the engine flashed into view. The train waited five minutes at the station, and started again with much noise and steaming. I crouched by the track. I rehearsed the act in my mind. I must wait until the engine had passed, otherwise I should be seen. Then I must make a dash for the carriages.

'The train started slowly, but gathered speed sooner than I had expected. The flaring lights drew swiftly near. The rattle became a roar. The dark mass hung for a second above me. The engine-driver silhouetted against his furnace glow, the black profile of the engine, the clouds of steam rushed past. Then I hurled myself on the trucks, clutching at something, missed, clutched again, missed again, grasped some sort of hand-hold, was swung off my feet – my toes bumping on the line, and with a struggle seated myself on the couplings of the fifth truck from the front of the train. It was a goods train, and the trucks were full of sacks, soft sacks covered with coal-dust. They were in fact bags filled with empty coal-bags going back to their colliery. I crawled on top and burrowed in among them. In five minutes I was completely buried. The sacks were warm and comfortable. Perhaps the engine-driver had seen me rush up to the train and would give the alarm at the next station; on the other hand, perhaps not. Where was the train going to? Where would it be unloaded? Would it be searched? Was it on the Delagoa Bay line? What should I do in the morning? Ah, never mind that. Sufficient for the night was the luck thereof. Fresh plans for fresh contingencies. I resolved to sleep, nor can I imagine a more pleasing lullaby than the clatter of the train that carries an escaping prisoner at twenty miles an hour away from the enemy's capital.

'How long I slept I do not know, but I woke up suddenly with all feelings of ex-hilaration gone, and only the consciousness of oppressive difficulties heavy on me. I must leave the train before daybreak, so that I could drink at a pool and find some hiding place while it was still dark. I would not run the risk of being unloaded with the coal-bags. Another night I would board another train. I crawled from my cosy hiding-place among the sacks and sat again on the couplings. The train was running at a fair speed, but I felt it was time to leave it. I took hold of the iron handle at the back of the truck, pulled strongly with my left hand, and sprang. My feet struck the ground in two gigantic strides, and the next instant I was sprawling in the ditch considerably shaken but unhurt. The train, my faithful ally of the night, hurried on its journey.

'It was still dark. I was in the middle of a wide valley, surrounded by low hills, and carpeted with high grass drenched in dew. I searched for water in the nearest gully, and soon found a clear pool. I was very thirsty, but long after I had quenched my thirst I continued to drink, that I might have sufficient for the whole day.

'Presently the dawn began to break, and the sky to the east grew yellow and red, slashed across with heavy black clouds. I saw with relief that the railway ran steadily towards the sunrise. I had taken the right line, after all.

'Having drunk my fill, I set out for the hills, among which I hoped to find some hiding-place, and as it became broad daylight I entered a small grove of trees which grew on the side of a deep ravine. Here I resolved to wait till dusk. I had one consolation: no one in the world knew where I was – I did not know myself. It was now four o'clock. Fourteen hours lay between me and the night. My impatience to proceed while I was still strong doubled their length. At first it was terribly cold, but by degrees the sun gained power, and by ten o'clock the heat was oppressive. My sole companion was a gigantic vulture, who manifested an extravagant interest in my condition, and made hideous and ominous gurglings from time to time. From my lofty position I commanded a view of the whole valley. A little tin-roofed town lay three miles to the westward. Scattered farmsteads, each with a clump of trees, relieved the monotony of the undulating ground. At the foot of the hill stood a Kaffir kraal, and the figures of its inhabitants dotted the patches of cultivation or surrounded the droves of goats and cows which fed on the pasture. . . . During the day I ate one slab of chocolate, which, with the heat produced a violent thirst. The pool was hardly half a mile away, but I dared not leave the shelter of the little wood, for I could see the figures of white men riding or walking occasionally across the valley, and once a Boer came and fired two shots at birds close to my hiding-place. But no one discovered me.

'The elation and the excitement of the previous night had burnt away, and a chilling reaction followed. I was very hungry, for I had had no dinner before starting, and chocolate, though it sustains, does not satisfy. I had scarcely slept, but yet my heart beat so fiercely and I was so nervous and perplexed about the future that I could not rest. I thought of all the chances that lay against me; I dreaded and detested more than words can express the prospect of being caught and dragged back to Pretoria. I found no comfort in any of the philosophical ideas which some men parade in their hours of ease and strength and safety. They seemed only fair-weather friends. I realised with awful force that no exercise of my own feeble wit and strength could save me from my enemies, and that without the assistance of that High Power which interferes in the eternal sequence of causes and effects more often than we are always prone to admit, I could never succeed. I prayed long and earnestly for help and guidance. My prayer, as it seems to me, was swiftly and wonderfully answered.'

I wrote these lines many years ago while the impression of the adventure was strong upon me. Then I could tell no more. To have done so would have compromised the liberty and perhaps the lives of those who had helped me. For many years these reasons have disappeared. The time has come when I can relate the events which followed, and which changed my nearly hopeless position into one of superior advantage.

During the day I had watched the railway with attention. I saw two or three trains pass along it each way. I argued that the same number would pass at night. I resolved to board one of these. I thought I could improve on my procedure of the previous evening. I had observed how slowly the trains, particularly long goods-trains, climbed some of the steep gradients. Sometimes they were hardly going at a foot's pace. It would probably be easy to choose a point where the line was not only on an up grade but also on a curve. Thus I could board some truck on the convex side of the train when both the engine and the guard's van were bent away, and when consequently neither the engine-driver nor the guard would see me. This plan seemed to me in every respect sound. I saw myself leaving the train again before dawn, having been carried forward another sixty or seventy miles during the night. That would be scarcely one hundred and fifty miles from the frontier. And why should not the process be repeated? Where was the flaw? I could not see it. With three long bounds on three successive nights I could be in Portuguese territory. Meanwhile I still had two or three slabs of chocolate and a pocketful of crumbled biscuit – enough, that is to say, to keep body and soul together at a pinch without taking the awful risk of recapture entailed by accosting a single human being. In this mood I watched with increasing impatience the arrival of darkness.

The long day reached its close at last. The western clouds flushed into fire; the shadows of the hills stretched out across the valley; a ponderous Boer wagon with its long team crawled slowly along the track towards the township, the Kaffirs collected their herds and drew them round their kraal; the daylight died, and soon it was quite dark. Then, and not until then, I set forth. I hurried to the railway line, scrambling along through the boulders and high grass and pausing on my way to drink at a stream of sweet cold water. I made my way to the place where I had seen the trains crawling so slowly up the slope, and soon found a point where the curve of the track fulfilled all the conditions of my plan. Here, behind a little bush, I sat down and waited hopefully. An hour passed; two hours passed; three hours – and yet no train. Six hours had now elapsed since the last, whose time I had carefully noted, had gone by. Surely one was due. Another hour slipped away. Still no train! My plan began to crumble and my hopes to ooze out of me. After all, was it not quite possible that no trains ran on this part of the line during the dark hours? This was in fact the case, and I might well have continued to wait in vain till daylight. However, between twelve and one in the morning I lost patience and started along the track resolved to cover at any rate ten or fifteen miles of my journey. I did not make much progress. Every bridge was guarded by armed men; every few miles were huts. At intervals there were stations with tin-roofed villages clustering around them. All the veldt was bathed in the bright rays of the full moon, and to avoid these dangerous places I had to make wide circuits and even to creep along the ground. Leaving the railroad I fell into bogs and swamps, brushed through high grass dripping with dew, and waded across the streams over which the bridges carried the railway. I was soon drenched to the waist. I had been able to take very little exercise during my month's imprisonment, and I was quickly tired with walking and with want of food and sleep. Presently I approached a station. It was a mere platform in the veldt, with two or three buildings and huts around it. But laid up on the sidings, obviously for the night, were three long goods-trains. Evidently the flow of traffic over the railway was uneven. These three trains, motionless in the moonlight, confirmed my fears that traffic was not maintained by night on this part of the line. Where, then, was my plan which in the afternoon had looked so fine and sure?

It now occurred to me that I might board one of these stationary trains immediately, and hiding amid its freight be carried forward during the next day – and night too if all were well. On the other hand, where were they going to? Where would they stop? Where would they be unloaded? Once I entered a wagon my lot would be cast. I might find myself ignominiously unloaded and recaptured at Witbank or Middelburg, or at any station in the long two hundred miles which separated me from the frontier. It was necessary at all costs before taking such a step to find out where these trains were going. To do this I must penetrate the station, examine the labels on the trucks or on the merchandise, and see if I could extract any certain guidance from them. I crept up to the platform and got between two of the long trains on the siding. I was proceeding to examine the markings on the trucks when loud voices rapidly approaching on the outside of the trains filled me with fear. Several Kaffirs were laughing and shouting in their unmodulated tones, and I heard, as I thought, a European voice arguing or ordering. At any rate, it was enough for me. I retreated between the two trains to the extreme end of the siding, and slipped stealthily but rapidly into the grass of the illimitable plain.

There was nothing for it but to plod on – but in an increasingly purposeless and hopeless manner. I felt very miserable when I looked around and saw here and there the lights of houses and thought of the warmth and comfort within them, but knew that they meant only danger to me. Far off on the moonlit horizon there presently began to shine the row of six or eight big lights which marked either Witbank or Middelburg station. Out of the darkness to my left gleamed two or three fires. I was sure they were not the lights of houses, but how far off they were or what they were I could not be certain. The idea formed in my mind that they were the fires of a Kaffir kraal. Then I began to think that the best use I could make of my remaining strength would be to go to these Kaffirs. I had heard that they hated the Boers and were friendly to the British. At any rate, they would probably not arrest me. They might give me food and a dry corner to sleep in. Although I could not speak a word of their language, yet I thought perhaps they might understand the value of a British banknote. They might even be induced to help me. A guide, a pony – but, above all, rest, warmth, and food – such were the promptings which dominated my mind. So I set out towards the fires.

I must have walked a mile or so in this resolve before a realisation of its weakness and imprudence took possession of me. Then I turned back again to the railway line and retraced my steps perhaps half the distance. Then I stopped and sat down, completely baffled, destitute of any idea what to do or where to turn. Suddenly without the slightest reason all my doubts disappeared. It was certainly by no process of logic that they were dispelled. I just felt quite clear that I would go to the Kaffir kraal. I had sometimes in former years held a 'Planchette' pencil and written while others had touched my wrist or hand. I acted in exactly the same unconscious or subconscious manner now.

I walked on rapidly towards the fires, which I had in the first instance thought were not more than a couple of miles from the railway line. I soon found they were much farther away than that. After about an hour or an hour and a half they still seemed almost as far off as ever. But I persevered, and presently between two and three o'clock in the morning I perceived they were not the fires of a Kaffir kraal. The angular outline of buildings began to draw out against them, and soon I saw that I was approaching a group of houses around the mouth of a coal-mine. The wheel which worked the winding gear was plainly visible, and I could see that the fires which had led me so far were from the furnaces of the engines. Hard by, surrounded by one or two slighter structures, stood a small but substantial stone house two storeys high.

I halted in the wilderness to survey this scene and to resolve my action. It was still possible to turn back. But in that direction I saw nothing but the prospect of further futile wanderings terminated by hunger, fever, discovery, or surrender. On the other hand, here in front was a chance. I had heard it said before I escaped that in the mining district of Witband and Middelburg there were a certain number of English residents who had been suffered to remain in the country in order to keep the mines working. Had I been led to one of these? What did this house which frowned dark and inscrutable upon me contain? A Briton or a Boer; a friend of a foe? Nor did this exhaust the possibilities. I had my seventy-five pounds in English notes in my pocket. If I revealed my identity, I thought that I could give reasonable assurance of a thousand. I might find some indifferent neutral-minded person who out of good-nature or for a large sum of money would aid me in my bitter and desperate need. Certainly I would try to make what bargain I could now – now while I still had the strength to plead my cause and perhaps to extricate myself if the results were adverse. Still the odds were heavy against me, and it was with faltering and reluctant steps that I walked out of the shimmering gloom of the veldt into the light of the furnace fires, advanced towards the silent house, and struck with my fist upon the door.

There was a pause. Then I knocked again. And almost immediately a light sprang up above and an upper window opened.

'*Wer ist da?*' cried a man's voice.

I felt the shock of disappointment and consternation to my fingers.

'I want help; I have had an accident,' I replied.

Some muttering followed. Then I heard steps descending the stairs, the bolt of the door was drawn, the lock was turned. It was opened abruptly, and in the darkness of the passage a tall man hastily attired, with a pale face and dark moustache, stood before me.

'What do you want?' he said, this time in English.

I had now to think of something to say. I wanted above all to get into parley with this man, to get matters in such a state that instead of raising an alarm and summoning others he would discuss things quietly.

'I am a burgher,' I began. 'I have had an accident. I was going to join my commando at Komati Poort. I have fallen off the train. We were skylarking. I have been unconscious for hours. I think I have dislocated my shoulder.'

It is astonishing how one thinks of these things. This story leapt out as if I had learnt it by heart. Yet I had not the slightest idea what I was going to say or what the next sentence would be.

The stranger regarded me intently, and after some hesitation said at length, 'Well, come in.' He retreated a little into the darkness of the passage, threw open a door on one side of it, and pointed with his left hand into a dark room. I walked past him and entered, wondering if it was to be my prison. He followed, struck a light, lit a lamp, and set it on the table at the far side of which I stood. I was in a small room, evidently a dining-room and office in one. I noticed besides the large table, a roll desk, two or three chairs, and one of those machines for making soda-water, consisting of two glass globes set one above the other and encased in thin wire-netting. On his end of the table my host had laid a revolver, which he had hitherto presumably been holding in his right hand.

'I think I'd like to know a little more about this railway accident of yours,' he said, after a considerable pause.

'I think,' I replied, 'I had better tell you the truth.'

'I think you had,' he said, slowly.

So I took the plunge and threw all I had upon the board.

'I am Winston Churchill, war-correspondent of the *Morning Post*. I escaped last night from Pretoria. I am making my way to the frontier. (Making my way!) I have plenty of money. Will you help me?'

There was another long pause. My companion rose from the table slowly and locked the door. After this act, which struck me as unpromising, and was certainly ambiguous, he advanced upon me and suddenly held out his hand.

'Thank God you have come here! It is the only house for twenty miles where you would not have been handed over. But we are all British here, and we will see you through.'

It is easier to recall across the gulf of years the spasm of relief which swept over me, than it is to describe it. A moment before I had thought myself trapped; and now friends, food, resources, aid, were all at my disposal. I felt like a drowning man pulled out of the water and told he has won the Derby!

My host now introduced himself as Mr John Howard, manager of the Transvaal Collieries. He had become a naturalised burgher of the Transvaal some years before the war. But out of consideration for his British race and some inducements which he had offered to the local Field Cornet, he had not been called up to fight against the British. Instead he had been allowed to remain with one or two others on the mine, keeping it pumped out and in good order until coal-cutting could be resumed. He had with him at the mine-head, besides his secretary, who was British, an engine-man from Lancashire and two Scottish miners. All these four were British subjects and had been allowed to remain only upon giving their parole to observe strict neutrality. He himself as burgher of the Transvaal Republic would be guilty of treason in harbouring me, and liable to be shot if caught at the time or found out later on.

'Never mind,' he said, 'we will fix it up somehow.' And added, 'The Field Cornet was around here this afternoon asking about you. They have got the hue and cry out all along the line and all over the district.'

I said that I did not wish to compromise him.

Let him give me food, a pistol, a guide, and if possible a pony, and I would make my own way to the sea, marching by night across country far away from the railway line or any habitation.

He would not hear of it. He would fix up something. But he enjoined the utmost caution. Spies were everywhere. He had two Dutch servant-maids actually sleeping in the house. There were many Kaffirs employed about the mine premises and on the pumping-machinery of the mine. Surveying these dangers, he became very thoughtful.

Then: 'But you are famishing.'

I did not contradict him. In a moment he had bustled off into the kitchen, telling me meanwhile to help myself from a whisky bottle and the soda-water machine which I have already mentioned. He returned after an interval with the best part of a cold leg of mutton and various other delectable commodities, and, leaving me to do full justice to these, quitted the room and let himself out of the house by a back door.

Nearly an hour passed before Mr Howard returned. In this period my physical well-being had been brought into harmony with the improvement in my prospects. I felt confident of success and equal to anything.

'It's all right,' said Mr. Howard. 'I have seen the men, and they are all for it. We must put you down the pit to-night, and there you will have to stay till we can see how to get you out of the country. One difficulty,' he said, 'will be the *skoff* (food). The Dutch girl sees every mouthful I eat. The cook will want to know what has happened to her leg of mutton. I shall have to think it all out during the night. You must get down the pit at once. We'll make you comfortable enough.'

Accordingly, just as the dawn was breaking, I followed my host across a little yard into the enclosure in which stood the winding-wheel of the mine. Here a stout man, introduced as Mr Dewsnap, of Oldham, locked my hand in a grip of crushing vigour.

'They'll all vote for you next time,' he whispered.

A door was opened and I entered the cage. Down we shot into the bowels of the earth. At the bottom of the mine were the two Scottish miners with lanterns and a big bundle which afterwards proved to be a mattress and blankets. We walked for some time through the pitchy labrynth, with frequent turns, twists, and alterations of level, and finally stopped in a sort of chamber where the air was cool and fresh. Here my guide set down his bundle, and Mr Howard handed me a couple of candles, a bottle of whisky, and a box of cigars.

'There's no difficulty about these,' he said. 'I keep them under lock and key. Now we must plan how to feed you tomorrow.'

'Don't you move from here, whatever happens,' was the parting injunction. 'There will be Kaffirs about the mine after daylight, but we shall be on the look-out that none of them wanders this way. None of them has seen anything so far.'

My four friends trooped off with their lanterns, and I was left alone. Viewed from the velvety darkness of the pit, life seemed bathed in rosy light. After the perplexity and even despair through which I had passed I counted upon freedom as certain. Instead of a humiliating recapture and long months of monotonous imprisonment, probably in the common jail, I saw myself once more rejoining the Army with a real exploit to my credit, and in that full enjoyment of freedom and keen pursuit of adventure dear to the heart of youth. In this comfortable mood, and speeded by intense fatigue, I soon slept the sleep of the weary – but of the triumphant.

From MY EARLY LIFE, *by Sir Winston S. Churchill*

Night in the desert

THE SUN going down left us drowned in the drooping gloom, which was soon dark night. We held on our march in hope to meet with the Arab, and there fell always a little rain. Serpentine lightning flickered over the ground before us, without thunder; long crested lightnings shot athwart and seemed suspended, by moments, in the wide horizon; other long cross flashes darted downward in double chains of light. The shape of all those lightnings was as an hair of wool that is fallen on water. Only sometimes we heard a little, not loud, roaring of thunder. In the lull of the weather we beheld the new moon, two days old, at her going down. The first appearing of the virgin moon is always greeted with a religious emotion in the deserts of Arabia, and we saluted her, poor night-wanderers, devoutedly; the day by my reckoning should be the 23rd. of April. We held on ever watching for the Beduin fires, and heard about us the night shrieks of I know not what wild birds. At length Hàmid thought he had seen a watch-fire glimmer far in front. As we rode further we saw it sometimes, and otherwhiles it was hidden by the uneven ground of the wilderness. The night darkness was very thick, the *nâga*[1] stumbled, and we could not see the earth. Hàmid, whose wit ever failed a little short of the mark, began to be afraid we might fall from some cragged place: he would adventure no further. We had nothing to eat, and alighting with wet clothes we lay down in the rain beside our camel; but the wind blew softly, and we soon slept.

Charles Doughty, TRAVELS IN ARABIA DESERTA 1888

1. A cow camel.

MARK TWAIN

The Boy and the River

Huckleberry Finn and Jim are making their way down the Mississippi, laying up by day and drifting downriver on their raft by night . . .

. . .THIS SECOND NIGHT we run between seven and eight hours, with a current that was making over four mile an hour. We catched fish, and talked, and we took a swim now and then to keep off sleepiness. It was kind of solemn, drifting down the big still river, laying on our backs looking at up the stars, and we didn't ever feel like talking loud, and it warn't often that we laughed, only a little kind of low chuckle. We had mighty good weather, as a general thing, and nothing ever happened to us at all, that night, nor the next, nor the next.

Every night we passed towns, some of them away up on black hillsides, nothing but just a shiny bed of lights, not a house could you see. The fifth night we passed St. Louis, and it was like the whole world lit up. In St. Petersburg they used to say there was twenty or thirty thousand people in St. Louis, but I never believed it till I see that wonderful spread of lights at two o'clock that still night. There warn't a sound there; everybody was asleep . . .

. . . Two or three days and nights went by. I reckon I might say they swum by, they slid along so quiet and smooth and lovely. Here is the way we put in the time. It was a monstrous big river down there – sometimes a mile and a half wide; we run nights, and laid up and hid day-times; soon as night was most gone, we stopped navigating and tied up – nearly always in the dead water under a tow-head; and then cut young cotton-woods and willows and hid the raft with them. Then we set out the lines. Next we slid into the river and had a swim, so as to freshen up and cool off; then we set down on the sandy bottom where the water was about knee-deep, and watched the daylight come. Not a sound anywheres – perfectly still – just like the whole world was asleep, only sometimes the bull-frogs a-clattering, maybe. The first thing to see, looking away over the water, was a kind of dull line – that was the woods on t'other side – you couldn't make nothing else out; then a pale place in the sky; then more paleness, spreading around; then the river softened up, away off, and warn't black any more, but grey; you could see little dark spots drifting along, ever so far away – trading scows, and such things; and long black streaks – rafts; sometimes you could hear a sweep screaking; or jumbled up voices, it was so still, and sounds come so far; and by and by you could see a streak on the water which you know by the look of the streak that there's a snag there in a swift current which breaks on it and makes that streak look that way; and you see the mist curl up off of the water, and the east reddens up, and the river, and you make out a log cabin in the edge of the woods, away on the bank on t'other side of the river, being a wood-yard, likely, and piled by them cheats so you can throw a dog through it anywheres; then the nice breeze springs up, and comes fanning you from over there, so cool and fresh, and sweet to smell, on account of the woods and the flowers; but sometimes not that way, because they've left dead fish laying around, gars, and such, and they do get pretty rank; and next you've got the full day, and everything smiling in the sun, and the song-birds just going it!

... Sometimes we'd have that whole river all to ourselves for the longest time. Yonder was the banks and the islands, across the water; and maybe a spark – which was a candle in a cabin window – and sometimes on the water you could see a spark or two – on a raft or a scow, you know; and maybe you could hear a fiddle or a song coming over from one of them crafts. It's lovely to live on a raft. We had the sky, up there, all speckled with stars, and we used to lay on our backs and look up at them, and discuss about whether they was made, or only just happened – Jim he allowed they was made, but I allowed they happened; I judged it would have took too long to *make* so many. Jim said the moon could a *laid* them; well, that looked kind of reasonable, so I didn't say nothing against it, because I've seen a frog lay most as many, so of course it could be done. We used to watch the stars that fell, too, and see them streak down. Jim allowed they'd got spoiled and was hove out of the nest.

Once or twice of a night we would see a steamboat slipping along in the dark, and now and then she would belch a whole world of sparks up out of her chimbleys, and they would rain down in the river and look awful pretty; then she would turn a corner and her lights would wink out and her pow-wow shut off and leave the river still again; and by and by her waves would get to us, a long time after she was gone, and joggle the raft a bit, and after that you wouldn't hear nothing for you couldn't tell how long, except maybe frogs or something.

ADVENTURES OF HUCKLEBERRY FINN, *by Mark Twain*

Dickens at Sea

1842. About midnight we shipped a sea, which forced its way through the skylights, burst open the doors above, and came raging and roaring down into the ladies' cabin, to the unspeakable consternation of my wife and a little Scotch lady – who, by the way, had previously sent a message to the captain by the stewardess, requesting him, with her compliments, to have a steel conductor immediately attached to the top of every mast, and to the chimney, in order that the ship might not be struck by lightning. They and the handmaid before-mentioned, being in such ecstasies of fear that I scarcely knew what to do with them, I naturally bethought myself of some restorative or comfortable cordial; and nothing better occurring to me, at the moment, than hot brandy-and-water, I procured a tumbler-full without delay. It being impossible to stand or sit without holding on, they were all heaped together in one corner of a long sofa – where they clung to each other in momentary expectation of being drowned. When I approached this place with my specific, and was about to administer it with many consolatory expressions to the nearest sufferer, what was my dismay to see them all roll slowly down to the other end! And when I staggered to that end, and held out the glass once more, how immensely baffled were my good intentions by the ship giving another lurch, and their all rolling back again! I suppose I dodged them up and down this sofa for at least a quarter of an hour, without reaching them once; and by the time I did catch them, the brandy-and-water was diminished, by constant spilling, to a teaspoonful. To complete the group, it is necessary to recognise in this disconcerted dodger, an individual very pale from seasickness, who had shaved his beard and brushed his hair, last, at Liverpool: and whose only articles of dress (linen not included) were a pair of dreadnought trousers; a blue jacket, formerly admired upon the Thames at Richmond; no stockings; and one slipper.

AMERICAN NOTES, *by Charles Dickens*

TWO MORE FOR THE SKYLARK
by Donald McCullin

THE BURNING LONGSHIP during
Up-Helly-Aa, the midwinter
Viking festival in the Shetlands
by Patrick Ward

LIVING SPACE, Calcutta
by Thurston Hopkins

RADIO TELESCOPE, Jodrell Bank, *by Axel Poignar*

Monday Nights in Space

To the rest of us it was Monday, Monday night and Tuesday morning. To three Russians it was twenty-four hours spent travelling nearly half a million miles to go sixteen times around the Earth. On the morning of Monday, 12th October 1964, three cosmonauts took off in the spaceship 'Voskhod'. They were Vladimir Konarov, the captain of the ship, Basil Egorov, the doctor, and Constantin Feoktistov, the scientist. To them, night came swiftly, and was day again. This is part of their story . . .

. . . And now the protective cone on the head of the capsule becomes separated from the ship with a slight clink. Through the portholes we see the distant earth wrapped in a thin layer of cloud. It is so beautiful that instinctively our hands reach out towards our logbooks to jot down our first impressions. Very soon the active part of the flight is finished; all noise stops, as well as the over-stresses, and we feel ourselves in a state of weightlessness.

The Voskhod is in its orbit, and it is time to get to work.

The captain sent back his first report to earth. We undid the straps which held us in our seats and went about our tasks. Everything had to be done in the course of but one day.

In the Voskhod's cabin we had far easier conditions than our predecessors. They were rather hampered in their movements by their space suits, their helmets and their hermetically sealed gloves, by everything which journalists have correctly compared to a medieval knight's armour, whereas we were perfectly unrestricted in our movements.

Unlike our predecessors, we worked unfastened during the whole flight, except when we were sleeping; and this allowed us to move about freely in the cabin, to change our working positions, and to get close to the portholes to observe the earth and the cosmos. So it was that we were able to make a complete study of the influence of the state of weightlessness on the human organism. Many people imagine that the state of weightlessness is a sort of nirvana. It is totally untrue. The loss of weight is a burden which brings with it its own problems. Fortunately, when we rested, we went to sleep very quickly, lying in our usual positions, on the right or the left side: but then we had been trained to rest peacefully in weightless conditions, and we were strapped in.

One of the marked advantages of the Voskhod over previous cosmic vessels was its far greater visibility. During the course of the first revolution, as soon as it came into the earth's shadow, we were struck by an extraordinary phenomenon which no other cosmonaut had told us about. We were flabbergasted. Imagine, about the level of the horizon up to a height of some sixty miles, a luminous zone, yellow-white, through which the stars are shining. This layer is perfectly visible by the light of the moon.

Above this layer stars are also shining like handfuls of diamonds on the dark black background of the sky. More than once we saw those luminous layers, and sometimes they were stretched out in several layers above the earth. An unforgettable picture waiting for its painters and poets.

When we had just completed the third revolution and we were above the Antarctic Konarov, who was peering through a porthole, cried, 'Look, look!'

And we saw something that had certainly never been seen before. Perpendicular with the horizon and above the second luminous layer, hiding the earth and oscillating slightly, arose columns of deep yellow light to a height of perhaps a hundred miles. Like a fence of unequal height, these rays ran along the visible horizon for a length of more than a thousand miles.

'It's an aurora borealis,' said Feoktistov, and he seized his camera.

There was no comparison whatsoever with the aurora borealis which we see from earth. Everything seemed to be fixed in a cold silence which united the Antarctic ice to the diamond-like brilliance of the stars. The planet's golden crown shone before our wonder-struck gaze.

Yet we had other things to do than admire the scenery. This ever-changing beauty of the universe had to be studied and its meaning sought and every detail noted down in the logs. Feoktistov, for whom every second was precious, checked the possibility of steering the ship by the stars. He demonstrated that it was possible to determine on board the ship our position in the cosmos and to calculate our trajectory.

And the doctor had much to do, too; for example, taking blood pressures, blood samples, and noting the electrical waves through the brain as we made voluntary and involuntary movements. He also had to observe our co-ordination of movement while we were drawing patterns on a piece of paper and to collect information to establish the wrist muscles' capacity for work. It was his responsibility, too, to watch the air pressure, the humidity and temperature inside the cabin.

The doctor also kept himself informed about our appetites and saw to it that we were not suffering from thirst. Actually, no one felt thirsty. It was apparently the absence of abrupt movements and the relative absence of muscular fatigue which needed watching; he reminded us, after we had taken a rest, to do some exercises with the chest expander to loosen up the muscles before we went on watch again.

In orbit the ship was turning in every direction, continually modifying its position in space. But as we ourselves were in the state of weightlessness we felt no sense of rotation. The captain, however, could give the ship the direction which the situation called for; and whereas during previous flights this could be done only in daylight the Voskhod, which was fitted with a new steering system, was able to steer itself also when into the dark side of the planet.

After the first revolution the captain took hold of the plastic steering lever. 'First of all,' he said, 'let us make a landing trial.'

The ship quietly took up the required position. All that would have been necessary to do to come down out of orbit would have been to start the reverse rockets. This was the first test of the steering system, and it was made at a height of about 250 miles. It worked perfectly. During the flight Konarov changed the ship's direction several times in relation to the earth, the stars, the horizon and the sun.

The fact that the spaceship could be guided allowed the crew, more than once, to make longer observations in favourable conditions; when, for example, Feoktistov, sextant in hand, asked the captain to change the Voskhod's direction in such a way that some constellation or other stayed as long as possible in view from the porthole.

In the ship's cabin, under our eyes, a very ingenious instrument was at work: it was a little globe of the world by which at any given moment we were able to check our position. If 'Gobus' pointed out that we were above the Andes chain of mountains, we were able to distinguish them very far away through the portholes. A meter on the instrument also counted our revolutions of the earth.

How beautiful our planet is, with its continents, its oceans and its mighty rivers! At the height at which Voskhod was flying the eye could take in vast stretches. We saw Tierra del Fuego and Cape Horn tapering like the stern post of a ship. We remembered Magellan, who first circumnavigated the world and gave practical proof that the earth was round. He needed three years to carry out his great exploit; our Voskhod went round the planet in ninety minutes. And every time we flew over the green uplands of Africa, Basil Egorov looked for the white cap of Kilimanjaro, so admired by his favourite writer Hemingway.

It was when we were passing over this region at night that he noticed some strange orange-coloured rays. We were just about to eat fried chicken, but we forgot the food and leaned towards the portholes. Down below sinuous flashes were lighting up the interior of enormous masses of cloud, which were bathed in the moon's fantastic light. It was a storm.

Yet we were way above all the storms, all the hurricanes and all the typhoons. Voskhod flying along at nearly 20,000 m.p.h. was outdistancing the fastest winds.

From THREE MEN IN A SPACE SHIP, *by Konarov, Egorov and Feoktistov*

ANTOINE DE SAINT-EXUPÉRY

Lost among the Stars

Antoine de Saint-Exupéry was born in 1900. He began his flying career in 1921, serving first as a French Air Force pilot, then in North Africa as a member of the Air Mail Service. He was a pilot in the Second World War, escaped to America after the fall of France and in 1943 returned to North Africa with the American forces. In a reconnaissance flight he disappeared: it is thought he was shot down by a German fighter. Here is an extract from his book 'Wind, Sand and Stars', dedicated to the airline pilots of America and their dead.

I REMEMBER, for my part, another of those hours in which a pilot finds suddenly that he has slipped beyond the confines of this world. All that night the radio messages sent from the ports in the Sahara concerning our position had been inaccurate, and my radio operator, Néri, and I had been drawn out of our course. Suddenly, seeing the gleam of water at the bottom of a crevasse of fog, I tacked sharply in the direction of the coast; but it was by then impossible for us to say how long we had been flying towards the high seas. Nor were we certain of making the coast, for our fuel was probably low. And even so, once we had reached it we would still have to make port – after the moon had set.

We had no means of angular orientation, were already deafened, and were bit by bit growing blind. The moon like a pallid ember began to go out in the banks of fog. Overhead the sky was filling with clouds, and we flew thenceforth between cloud and fog in a world voided of all substance and all light. The ports that signalled us had given up trying to tell us where we were. 'No bearing, no bearings', was all their message, for our voices reached them from everywhere and nowhere. With sinking hearts Néri and I leaned out, he on his side and I on mine, to see if anything, anything at all was distinguishable in this void. Already our tired eyes were seeing things – errant signs, delusive flashes, phantoms.

And suddenly, when already we were in despair, low on the horizon a brilliant point was unveiled on our port bow. A wave of joy went through me. Néri leaned forward and I could hear him singing. It could not but be the beacon of an airport, for after dark the whole Sahara goes black and forms a great dead expanse. That light twinkled for a space – and then went out! We had been steering for a star which was visible for a few minutes only, just before setting on the horizon between the layer of fog and the clouds.

Then other stars took up the game, and with a sort of dogged hope we set our course for each of them in turn. Each time that a light lingered for a while, we performed the same crucial experiment. Néri would send his message to the airport at Cisneros: 'Beacon in view. Put out your light and flash three times.' And Cisneros would put out its beacon and flash three times while the hard light at which we gazed would not, incorruptible star, so much as wink. And despite our dwindling fuel we continued to nibble at the golden bait which each time seemed more surely the true light of a beacon, was each time a promise of a landing and of life – and we had each time to change our star.

And with that we knew ourselves to be lost in interplanetary space among a thousand inaccessible planets, we who sought the one veritable planet, our own, that planet on which alone we should find our familiar countryside, the houses of our friends, our treasures.

On which alone we should find . . . Let me draw the picture that took shape before my eyes. It will seem to you childish; but even in the midst of danger a man retains his human concerns. I was thirsty and I was hungry. If we did find Cisneros we should re-fuel and carry on to Casablanca, and there we should come down in the cool of daybreak, free to idle the hours away. Néri and I would go into town. We would go to a little pub already open despite the early hour. Safe and sound, Néri and I would sit down at table and laugh at the night of danger as we ate our warm rolls and drank our bowls of coffee and hot milk. We would receive this matutinal gift at the hands of life. Even as an old peasant woman recognises her God in a painted image, in a childish medal, in a chaplet, so life would speak to us in its humblest language in order that we understand. The joy of living, I say, was summed up for me in the remembered sensation of that first burning and aromatic swallow, that mixture of milk and coffee and bread by which men hold communion with tranquil pastures, exotic plantations, the golden harvests, communion with the earth. Amidst all these stars there was but one that could make itself significant for us by composing this aromatic bowl that was its daily gift at dawn. And from that earth of men, that earth docile to the reaping of grain and the harvesting of the grape, bearing its rivers asleep in their fields, its villages clinging to their hillsides, our ship was separated by astronomical distances. All the treasures of the world were summed up in a grain of dust now blown far out of our path by the very destiny itself of dust and of the orbs of night.

And Néri still prayed to the stars.

Suddenly he was pounding my shoulder. On the bit of paper he held forth impatiently to me I read: 'All well. Magnificent news.' I waited with beating heart while he scribbled the half-dozen words that were to save us. At last he put this grace of heaven into my hands.

It was dated from Casablanca, which we had left the night before. Delayed in transmission, it had suddenly found us more than a thousand miles away, suspended between cloud and fog, lost at sea. It was sent by the government representative at the airport. And it said: 'Monsieur de Saint-Exupéry, I am obliged to recommend that you be disciplined at Paris for having flown too close to the hangars on leaving Casablanca.'

It was true that I had done this. It was also true that this man was performing his duty with irritability. I should have been humiliated if this reproach had been addressed to me in an airport. But it reached me where it had no right to reach me. Among these too rare stars, on this bed of fog, in this menacing savour of the sea, it bursts like a detonation. Here we were with our fate in our hands, the fate of the mails and of the ship; we had trouble enough to try to keep alive; and this man was purging his petty rancour against us.

But Néri and I were far from nettled. What we felt was a vast and sudden jubilation. Here it was we who were masters, and this man was letting us know it. The impudent little corporal! not to have looked at our stripes and seen that we had been promoted captain! To intrude into our musings when we were solemnly taking our constitutional between Sagittarius and the Great Bear! When the only thing we could be concerned with, the only thing of our order of magnitude, was this appointment we were missing with the moon!

The immediate duty, the only duty of the planet whence this man's message came, was to furnish us accurate figures for our computations among the stars. And its figures had been false. This being so, the planet had only to hold its tongue. Néri scribbled: 'Instead of wasting their time with this nonsense they would do better to haul us back to Cisneros, if they can.' By 'they' he meant all the peoples of the globe, with their parliaments, their senates, their navies, their armies, their emperors. We re-read the message from that man mad enough to imagine that he had business with us, and tacked in the direction of Mercury.

It was by the purest chance that we were saved. I had given up all thought of making Cisneros and had set my course at right angles to the coast-line in the hope that thus we might avoid coming down at sea when our fuel ran out. Meanwhile, however, I was in the belly of a dense fog, so that even with land below it was not going to be easy to set the ship down. The situation was so clear that already I was shrugging my shoulders ruefully when Néri passed me a second message which, an hour earlier, would have been our salvation. 'Cisneros,' it said, 'has deigned to communicate with us. Cisneros says. "216 doubtful."' Well, that helped. Cisneros was no longer swallowed up in space, it was actually out there on our left, almost within reach. But how far away? Néri and I talked it over briefly, decided it was too late to try for it (since that might mean missing the coast), and Néri replied; 'Only one hour fuel left continuing on 93.'

But the airports one by one had been waking each other up. Into our dialogue broke the voices of Agadir, Casablanca, Dakar. The radio stations at each of these towns had warned the airports and the ports had flashed the news to our comrades. Bit by bit they were gathering round us as round a sick-bed. Vain warmth, but human warmth after all. Helpless concern, but affectionate at any rate.

And suddenly into this conclave burst Toulouse, the headquarters of the Line three thousand miles away, worried along with the rest. Toulouse broke in without a word of greeting, simply to say sharply: 'Your reserve tanks bigger than standard. You have two hours' fuel left. Proceed to Cisneros.'

THOR HEYERDAHL

The Kon-Tiki's First Nights at Sea

ABOUT MIDNIGHT a ship's light passed in a northerly direction. At three another passed, on the same course. We waved our little paraffin lamp and called them up with flashes from an electric torch, but they did not see us, and the lights passed slowly northwards into the darkness and disappeared. Little did those on board guess that a real live Inca raft lay close to them tumbling among the waves. And just as little did we on board the raft guess that this was our last ship and the last trace of men we should see till we had reached the other side of the ocean.

We clung like flies, two and two, to the steering oar in the darkness, and felt the fresh sea water pouring off the oar hit us till we were tender both behind and before, and our hands grew stiff with the exertion of hanging on. We had a good schooling those first days and nights; it turned land-lubbers into seamen. For the first twenty-four hours every man, in unbroken succession, had two hours at the helm and three hours' rest. We arranged that every hour a fresh man should relieve the one of the two helmsmen who had been at the helm for two hours. Every single muscle in the body was strained to the uttermost throughout the watch to cope with the steering. When we were tired out with pushing the oar we went over to the other side and pulled, and when arms and chest were sore with pressing, we turned our backs, while the oar kneaded us green and blue in front and behind. When at last the relief came, we crept half dazed into the bamboo cabin, tied a rope round our legs, and fell asleep with our salty clothes on before we could get into our sleeping bags. Almost at the same moment there came a brutal tug at the rope; three hours had passed, and one had to go out again and relieve one of the two men at the steering oar.

The next night was still worse; the seas grew higher instead of going down. Two hours on end of struggling with the steering oar was too long; a man was not much use in the second half of his watch, and the seas got the better of us and hurled us round and sideways, while the water poured on board. Then we changed over to one hour at the helm and an hour and a half's rest. So the first sixty hours passed, in one continuous struggle against a chaos of waves that rushed upon us, one after another, without cessation. High waves and low waves, pointed waves and round waves, slanting waves and waves on top of other waves. The one of us who suffered most was Knut. He was let off steering watch, but to compensate for this he had to sacrifice to Neptune and suffered silent agonies in a corner of the cabin. The parrot sat sulkily in its cage and hung on with its beak and flapped its wings every time the raft gave an unexpected pitch and the sea splashed against the wall from astern. The *Kon-Tiki* did not roll so excessively. She took the seas more steadily than any boat of the same dimensions, but it was impossible to predict which way the deck would lean next time, and we never learned the art of moving about the raft easily, for she pitched as much as she rolled.

On the third night the sea went down a bit, although it was still blowing hard. About four o'clock an unexpected pursuer came foaming through the darkness and knocked the raft right round before the steersman realised what was happening. The sail thrashed against the bamboo cabin and threatened to tear both the cabin and itself to pieces. All hands had to go on deck to secure the cargo and haul on sheets and stays in the hope of getting the raft on her right course again, so that the sail might fill and curve forward peacefully. But the raft would not right herself. She would go astern foremost, and that was all. The only result of all our hauling and pushing and rowing was that two men nearly went overboard in a sea when the sail caught them in the dark. The sea had clearly become calmer. Stiff and sore, with skinned palms and sleepy eyes, we were not worth many rows of beans. Better to save our strength in case the weather should call us out to a worse passage of arms. One could never know. So we furled the sail and rolled it round the bamboo yard. The *Kon-Tiki* lay sideways on to the seas and took them like a cork. Everything on board was lashed fast, and all six of us crawled into the little bamboo cabin, huddled together, and slept like mummies in a sardine tin.

From THE KON-TIKI EXPEDITION, *by Thor Heyerdahl*

Noises in the Night

Apr. 27, 1802: To sleep in London, however, is an art which a foreigner must acquire by time and habit. Here was the watchman, whose business it is, not merely to guard the streets and take charge of the public security, but to inform the good people of London every half hour of the state of the weather. For the first three hours I was told it was a moonlight night, then it became cloudy, and at half past three o'clock was a rainy morning; so that I was as well acquainted with every variation of the atmosphere as if I had been looking from the window all night long.

. . . The clatter of the night coaches had scarcely ceased, before that of the morning carts began. The dustman with his bell, and his chaunt of dust-ho! succeeded to the watchman; then came the porter-house boy for the pewter-pots which had been sent out for supper the preceding night; the milkman next, and so on, a succession of cries, each in a different tune, so numerous, that I could no longer follow them in my inquiries.

From LETTERS FROM ENGLAND, *by Robert Southey*

Night Song

AND WHERE the evening mist clothes the riverside with poetry, as with a veil, and the poor buildings lose themselves in the dim sky, and the tall chimneys become campanili, and the warehouses are palaces in the night, and the whole city hangs in the heavens, and fairy-land is before us – then the wayfarer hastens home; the working man and the cultured one, the wise man and the one of pleasure, cease to understand, as they have ceased to see, and Nature, who, for once, has sung in tune, sings her exquisite song to the artist alone, her son and her master – her son in that he loves her; her master in that he knows her.

From THE GENTLE ART OF MAKING ENEMIES, 1890, *by James McNeill Whistler*

The Ant-heap

WANDERING lonely about London, through its stony lanes and through its stifling passages, sometimes not seeing a step before me for the thick, opaline fog, and running against flying shadows – I lived through a great deal.

In the evening when my son had gone to bed, I usually went out for a walk; I scarcely ever went to see anyone; I read the newspapers and stared in taverns at the alien race, and stood on the bridges across the Thames.

On the one hand, the stalactites of the Houses of Parliament would loom through the darkness ready to vanish again, on the other, the inverted bowl of Saint Paul's . . . and street-lamps . . . street-lamps without end in both directions. One city, fell-fed, lay sleeping, while the other, hungry, was not yet awake – the streets were empty, nothing could be heard but the even tread of the policeman with his lantern. I used to sit and look, and my soul would grow quieter and more peaceful. And so through all this I came to love this dreadful ant-heap, where every night a hundred thousand men know not where they will lay their heads, and the police often find women and children dead of hunger beside hotels where one cannot dine for less than two pounds.

Memoirs, ALEXANDER HERZEN

Child Stripping

THIS is generally done by females, old debauched drunken hags who watch their opportunity to accost children in the streets, tidily dressed with good boots and clothes. They entice them away to a low or quiet neighbourhood for the purpose, as they say, of buying them sweets, or with some other pretext. When they get into a convenient place, they give them a halfpenny or some sweets, and take off the articles of dress, and tell them to remain till they return, when they go away with the booty.

This is done most frequently in mews in the West End, and at Clerkenwell, Westminster, the Borough, and other similar localities. These heartless debased women sometimes commit these felonies in the disreputable neighbourhoods where they live, but more frequently in distant places, where they are not known and cannot be easily traced . . . In most cases, it is done at dusk in the winter evenings, from 7 to 10 o'clock.

From LONDON LABOUR AND THE LONDON POOR, *by Henry Mayhew*

London Magic

I HAVE passed all my days in London, until I have formed as many and intense local attachments as any of you mountaineers can have done with dead nature. The lighted shops of the Strand and Fleet Street, the innumerable trades, tradesmen and customers, coaches, waggons, playhouses, all the bustle and wickedness round about Covent Garden, the very women of the Town, the watchmen, drunken scenes, rattles – life awake, if you awake, at all hours of the night, the impossibility of being dull in Fleet street, the crowds, the very dirt and mud, and sun shining upon houses and pavements, the print shops, the old book-stalls, parsons cheap'ning books, coffee houses, steams of soups from kitchens, the pantomimes, London itself a pantomime and masquerade, – all these things work themselves into my mind and feed me, without a power of satiating me. The wonder of these sights impells me into night-walks about her crowded streets, and I often shed tears in the Motley Strand from fulness of joy at so much life.

Charles Lamb in a letter to William Wordsworth

Impression de Nuit

LONDON

See what a mass of gems the city wears
   Upon her broad live bosom! row on row
   Rubies and emeralds and amethysts glow.
See! that huge circle, like a necklace stares
With thousands of bold eyes to heaven, and dares
   The golden stars to dim the lamps below
   And in the mirror of the mire I know
The moon has left her image unawares.

That's the great town at night: I see her breasts,
   Prick'd out with lamps they stand like huge black towers,
   I think they move! I hear her panting breath.
And that's her head where the tiara rests.
   And in her brain, through lanes as dark as death,
   Men creep like thoughts . . . The lamps are like pale flowers.

Lord Alfred Douglas (1870–1945)

Journey to Westminster

AND IN the evening, a little after sunset, you may enjoy what I judge to be the most lovely experience in London – the journey through the dusk from Wapping to Westminster. There are not many lights in the Pool; the warehouses are dark, become dignified and mysterious; palaces, fortresses, or temples. The starboard light of a steamer coming up on the flood round the bend astern of you is a brilliant emerald, the eye of some pursuing monster; she sends her final hoot of warning to the Tower Bridge, the thrilling announcement that another ship has come home; the Tower Bridge is a colourless outline, a children's toy, against the faint rose of the western sky, and St Paul's dome, beyond, is only the ghost of a dome. Lighted buses are congregated on the bridge, waiting reverently for the ship to pass, and suddenly the road divides, the great arms of the bridge rise up and pronounce a blessing on you while your impudent craft scuttles through ahead of the steamer, as if the bascules had been lifted for you.

There are more lights now: London Bridge wears a moving frieze of light, and we have come back to the roar of traffic. The bridges come thick and fast – Cannon Street and Southwark, and St Paul's and Blackfriars. It is dark and alarming under the cavernous arches where the tide rushes fiercely round the piers, gleaming like swift snakes in the dim light. But in all the dark arches are framed a wide space of shining water ahead and the increasing lights of London. And you come out through Blackfriars Bridge at last into a fairyland of light and shadow, water tumbling and sparkling, water ebony and smooth. Round the great curve go the lamps and the lighted trees and the lighted, lumbering trams; and at the end the calm clock of Westminster hangs in the sky.

From NO BOATS IN THE RIVER, *by Sir Alan Herbert*

LIFE GUARDS AT DUSK, *by John Cowan*

BARROW BOY, *by Donald McCull.*

LONDON FOG, *by Thurston Hopkins*

Overleaf: OWL OF WESTMINSTER, *by Barnet Saidman*

MENTAL HOSPITAL
NIGHT SISTER
by Erich Auerbach

← Overleaf

PICCADILLY CIRCUS
by Frank Herrmann

CHARLES DICKENS

Night Thoughts on Bedlam

*In 'The Uncommercial Traveller' Charles Dickens described his wanderings
in the streets of London during those nights when he could not sleep . . .*

. . . I CHOSE next to wander by Bethlehem Hospital[1]; partly, because it lay on my road
round to Westminster; partly, because I had a night fancy in my head which could
be best pursued within sight of its walls and dome. And the fancy was this: Are not
the sane and the insane equal at night as the sane lie a-dreaming? Are not all of us outside
this hospital, who dream, more or less in the condition of those inside it, every night of
our lives? Are we not nightly persuaded, as they daily are, that we associate preposter-
ously with kings and queens, emperors and empresses, and notabilities of all sorts? Do
we not nightly jumble events and personages and times and places, as these do daily?
Are we not sometimes troubled by our own sleeping inconsistencies, and do we not
vexedly try to account for them or excuse them, just as these do sometimes in respect
of their waking delusions? Said an afflicted man to me, when I was last in a hospital like
this, 'Sir, I can frequently fly.' I was half ashamed to reflect that so could I – by night.
Said a woman to me on the same occasion, 'Queen Victoria frequently comes to dine
with me, and Her Majesty and I dine off peaches and maccaroni in our night-gowns, and
His Royal Highness the Prince Consort does us the honour to make a third on horseback
in a Field-Marshal's uniform.' Could I refrain from reddening with consciousness when
I remembered the amazing royal parties I myself had given (at night), the unaccountable
viands I had put on table, and my extraordinary manner of conducting myself on those
distinguished occasions? I wonder that the great master who knew everything, when
he called Sleep the death of each day's life, did not call Dreams the insanity of each
day's sanity.

1. Bethlehem Hospital: the infamous 'Bedlam', house of the mad. The building now houses the Imperial War
Museum.

Stow's London at Night

THE FALL OF GRIFFITH OF WALES

IN THE YEARE 1244. *Griffith* the eldest sonne of *Leoline*, prince of *Wales*, being kept prisoner in the Tower, deuised meanes of escape, and hauing in the night made of the hangings, sheetes, &c. a long line, he put himselfe downe from the toppe of the Tower, but in the sliding, the weight of his body, being a very bigge and fatte man, brake the rope, and he fell and brake his necke withall.

SLEEPIE DRINKE

IN THE YEARE 1321. The *Mortimers* yeelding themselues to the King, he sent them Prisoners to the Tower, where they remayned long, and were adiudged to be drawne and hanged. But at length *Roger Mortimer* of Wigmore, by giuing to his Keepers a sleepie drinke, escaped out of the Tower, and his unkle *Roger* being still kept there, dyed about fiue yeares after.

THE LONG SLEEP

IN THE YEARE 1546. the 27 of Aprill, being Tuesday in Easter weeke, *William Foxley*, Potmaker for the Mint in the tower of London, fell asleepe, and so continued sleeping, and could not be wakened, with pricking, cramping, or otherwise burning whatsoeuer, till the first day of the tearme, which was full xiiii. dayes, and xv nights, or more, for that Easter tearme beginneth not afore xvii. dayes after Easter. The cause of his thus sleeping could not be knowne, though the same were diligently searched after by the kings Phisitians, and other learned men: yea the king himselfe examining the said *William Foxley*, who was in all poynts found at his waking to be as if hee had slept but one night. And he lived more then fortie yeares after in the sayde Tower, to wit, vntil the yeare of Christ, 1587, and then deceased on Wednesday in Easterweeke.

A SHEW BY TORCHLIGHT,
being a Mommery of more then 100 horses

ONE OTHER shew in the yeare 1377, made by the Citizens for disport of the yong prince *Richard*, son of the blacke prince, in the feast of Christmas in this manner. On the

Sonday before Candlemas in the night, one hundred and thirty Cittizens disguised, and well horsed in a mummerie with sound of Trumpets, Shackbuts, Cornets, Shalmes, and other Minstrels, and innumerable torch lights of Waxe, rode from Newgate through Cheape ouer the bridge, through Southwarke, and so to Kennington besides Lambhith, where the young Prince remayned with his mother and the Duke of Lancaster his vncle, the Earles of Cambridge, Hertford, Warwicke and Suffolke, with diuers other Lordes. In the first ranke did ride 28. in the likenes and habite of Esquires, two and two together, cloathed in redde coates and gownes of Say or Sindall, with comely visors on their faces: after them came riding 48. knightes in the same liuery, of colour and stuffe: Then followed one richly arrayed like an Emperour, and after him some distance, one stately tyred like a Pope, whom followed 24. Cardinals, and after them eight or tenne with black visors not amiable, as if they had beene Legates from some forrain Princes. These maskers after they had entered the Mannor of Kennington, alighted from their horses, and entred the hall on foot, which done, the Prince, his mother, and the Lordes came out of the Chamber into the hall, whome the saide mummers did salute; shewing by a paire of dice vpon the table their desire to play with the Prince, which they so handled, that the Prince did alwayes winne when hee cast them. Then the mummers set to the Prince three jewels, one after another, which were a boule of gold, a cup of gold, and a ring of gold, which the Prince wanne at three casts. Then they set to the Princes mother, the Duke, the Earles, and other Lordes, to euery one a ring of gold, which they did also win: After which they were feasted, and the musicke sounded, the prince and Lords daunced on the one part with the mummers, which did also daunce: which iolitie being ended, they were againe made to drinke, and then departed in order as they came.

OF WATCHES IN THIS CITIE,
and other matters commanded, and the cause why

William Conqueror commaunded, that in euerie towne and village, a Bell should be nightly rung at eight of the clocke, and that all people should then put out their fire, and candle, and take their rest: which order was obserued through this Realme during his raigne, and the raigne of *William Rufus*: but *Henrie* the first, restoring to his subiects the vse of fire and lights, as afore: it followeth by reason of warres within the realme, that many men also gaue themselues to robberie and murders in the night, for example whereof in this Citie, *Roger Houeden* writeth thus: In the yeare 1175. a Councell was kept at Notingham: In time of which Councell, a brother of the Earle Ferrers being in the night priuily slaine at London, and throwne out of his Inne, into the durtie street, when ye king vnderstood therof, he sware that he would be auenged on the Citizens. For it was then (saith mine Authour) a common practise in the Citie, that an hundred or more in a company, yong and old, would make nightly invasions vpon houses of the wealthie, to the intent to rob them, and if they found any man stirring in the Citie within the night, that were not of their crew, they would presently murder him: insomuch, that when night was come, no man durst aduenture to walke in the streetes. When this had continued long, it fortuned that, as a crew of yong and wealthie Citizens, assembling togither in the night, assaulted a stone house of a certaine rich man, & breaking through the wall, the good man of that house, hauing prepared himselfe with other in a corner, when hee perceyued one of the theeues named *Andrew Bucquint* to leade the way, with a burning brand in the one hand, and a pot of coales in the other, which hee assaied to kindle with the brand, he flew vpon him, and smote off his right hand, and then with a loude voyce cried theeues: at the hearing whereof the theeues tooke their flight, all sauing hee that had lost his hande, whom the good man in the next morning deliuered to *Richard de Lucie* the kings Iustice. This theefe, vpon warrant of his life, appeached his confederates, of whom many were taken, and many were fled. Among the rest that were apprehended, a certaine Citizen of great countenance, credit, and wealth, named *Iohn Senex*, who for as much as hee could not acquit himselfe by the waterdome, (as that law was then,) he offered to the king fiue hundred pounds of siluer for his life: but forasmuch as he was condemned by iudgement of the water, the king would not take the offer, but commaunded him to bee hanged on the Gallowes, which was done, and then the Citie became quiet for a long time after.

BONEFIERS AND BANQUETING IN THE STREETES

IN THE MONETHS of Iune, and Iuly, on the Vigiles of festiuall dayes, and on the same festiuall dayes in the Euenings after the Sunne setting, there were vsually made Bonefiers in the streetes, euery man bestowing wood or labour towards them: the wealthier sort also before their doores neare to the said Bonefiers, would set out Tables on the Vigiles, furnished with sweete breade, and good drinke, and on the Featiuall dayes with meates and drinks plentifully, whereunto they would inuite their neighbours and passengers also to sit, and bee merrie with them in great familiaritie, praysing God for his benefites bestowed on them. These were called Bonefiers aswell of good amitie amongest neighbours that, being before at controuersie, were there by the labour of others, reconciled, and made of bitter enemies, louing friendes, as also for the vertue that a great fire hath to purge the infection of the ayre.

PIRATES IN THE THAMES

. . . I reade that in the yeare 1440. in the lent season, certaine persons with 6. ships brought from beyond the seas fish to victuaile the city of London, which fish when they had deliuered, and were returning homeward, a number of sea theeues, in a barge, in the night came vpon them, when they were a sleep in their vessels, riding at anker on the riuer Thames, and slew them, cut their throates, cast them ouer boord, tooke their money, and drowned their ships for that no man should espie or accuse them. Two of these theeues were after taken, and hanged in chaynes vpon a gallowes set vpon a raysed hill, for that purpose made, in the field beyond East Smithfield, so that they might be seene farre into the riuer Thames.

THE STEWE ON THE BANKSIDE

NEXT ON this banke was sometime the Bordello or stewes, a place so called, of certaine stew houses priuiledged there, for the repaire of incontinent men to the like women, of the which priuiledge I haue read thus.

In a Parliament holden at Westminster the 8. of *Henry* the second, it was ordayned by the commons and confirmed by the king and Lords, that diuers constitutions for euer should bee kept within that Lordship or franchise, according to the olde customes that had been there vsed time out of mind. Amongest the which these following were some, vz.

That no stewholder or his wife should let or staye any single Woman to goe and come freely at all times when they listed.

No stewholder to keepe any woman to borde, but she to borde abroad at her pleasure.

To take no more for the womans chamber for the weeke then foureteene pence.

Not to keep open his dores vpon the holydayes.

Not to keepe any single woman in his house on the holy dayes, but the Bayliffe to see them voyded out of the Lordship.

No single woman to be kept against her will that would leaue her sinne.

No stewholder to receiue any Woman of religion, or any mans wife.

No single woman to take money to lie with any man, but shee lie with him all night till the morrow.

No man to be drawn or inticed into any stewhouse.

The Constables, Balife, and others euery weeke to search euery stewhouse.

No stewholder to keepe any woman that hath the perilous infirmitie of burning, nor to sell bread, ale, flesh, fish, wood, coale, or any victuals, &c.

A SURVEY OF LONDON *(from the Text of 1603), by John Stow*

HEAVY PRICE

ON THE xxvj day of September, in anno 1564, beynge Tweseday, ware arraynyd at ye Gyldhalle of London iiij personas and there caste, for ye stelynge and receyvynge of ye queens lypott,[1] combe, and lokynge glasse, with a bodkyn of gold to brayd hir heare, and suche othar small ware out of hir chambar in her progresse. And on Thursday next

1. Chamberpot.

afftar, beynge Myhilmas even, and ye xxviij day of September, ij of them whiche had
bene servantis in Chepesyd, one of them with Master Bakehowse, dwellying agaynst
ye Standard, beyng a sylke man, were bothe hangyd before ye Cowrte gatte, upon ye
gallows that stode on Haye Hyll, whiche was for that tyme removyd for that purpose
to Saynt James, before ye wall, beynge at that tyme ye queens cowrte.

MEMORANDA, *John Stow*

The Great Fire

1666, 2nd Sept. – This fatal night, about ten, began that deplorable fire near Fish Street,
in London.

3rd – The fire continuing, after dinner I took coach with my wife and son, and went
to the Bank-side in Southwark, where we beheld that dismal spectacle, the whole city
in dreadful flames near the water-side; all the houses from the bridge, all Thames Street,
and upwards towards Cheapside, down to the Three Cranes, were now consumed.

The fire having continued all this night, (if I may call that night which was as light
as day for ten miles round about, after a dreadful manner), when conspiring with a
fierce eastern wind in a very dry season; I went on foot to the same place, and saw the
whole south part of the city burning from Cheapside to the Thames, and all along
Cornhill, (for it kindled back against the wind as well as forward,) Tower Street,
Fenchurch Street, Gracechurch Street, and so along to Bainard's Castle, and now taking
hold of St Paul's Church, to which the scaffolds contributed exceedingly. The conflagration was so universal, and the people so astonished, that from the beginning, I
know not by what despondency or fate, they hardly stirred to quench it; so that there
was nothing heard or seen but crying out and lamentation, running about like distracted
creatures, without at all attempting to save even their goods; such a strange consternation
there was upon them so as it burned both in breadth and length, the churches, public
halls, exchange, hospitals, monuments, and ornaments, leaping after a prodigious
manner from house to house, and street to street, at great distances one from the other;
for the heat, with a long set of fair and warm weather, had even ignited the air and
prepared the materials to conceive the fire, which devoured after an incredible manner,
houses, furniture and everything. Here we saw the Thames covered with goods floating,
all the barges and boats laden with what some had time and courage to save, as, on the
other, the carts, etc., carrying out to the fields, which for many miles were strewed
with movables of all sorts, and tents erecting to shelter both people and what goods
they could get away. Oh, the miserable and calamitous spectacle! such as haply the

world had not seen the like since the foundation of it, nor be outdone till the universal conflagration. All the sky was of a fiery aspect, like the top of a burning oven, the light seen above forty miles round about for many nights. God grant my eyes will never behold the like, now seeing above 10,000 houses all in one flame: the noise, and cracking, and thunder of the impetuous flames, the shrieking of women and children, the hurry of people, the fall of towers, houses, and churches was like an hideous storm, and the air all about so hot and inflamed, that at last one was not able to approach it; so that they were forced to stand still and let the flames burn on, which they did for near two miles in length and one in breadth. The clouds of smoke were dismal, and reached, upon computation, near fifty miles in length. Thus I left it this after noon burning, a resemblance of Sodom, or the last day. It forcibly called to my mind that passage – *non enim hic habemus stabilem civitatem*. London was, and is no more!

THE DIARY *of John Evelyn*

COLIN MACINNES

Night in Soho

Now, you can think what you like about the art of jazz – quite frankly, I don't really care *what* you think, because jazz is a thing so wonderful that if anybody doesn't rave about it, all you can feel for them is pity: not that I'm making out I really understand it *all* – I mean, certain LPs leave me speechless. But the great thing about the jazz world, and all the kids that enter into it, is that no one, not a soul, cares what your class is, or what your race is or what your income, or if you're a boy, or girl, or bent, or versatile, or what you are – so long as you dig the scene and can behave yourself, and have left all that crap behind you, too, when you come in the jazz club door. The result of all this is that, in the jazz world, you meet all kinds of cats, on absolutely equal terms, who can clue you up in all kinds of directions – in social directions, in culture directions, in sexual directions, and in racial directions . . . in fact, almost anywhere, really, you want to go to learn. So that's why, when the teenage thing began to seem to me to fall into the hands of exhibitionists and moneylenders, I cut out gradually from the kiddo water-holes, and made it for the bars, and clubs, and concerts where the older members of the jazz world gathered.

But this particular evening, I had to call at a teenage hut inside Soho, in order to contact two of my models, by names Dean Swift and the Misery Kid. Now, about Soho, there's this, that although so much crap's written about the area, of all London quarters, I think it's still one of the most authentic. I mean, Mayfair is just top spivs stepping into the slippers of the former gentry, and Belgravia, like I've said, is all flats in houses built as palaces, and Chelsea – well! Just take a look yourself, next time you're there. But in Soho, all the things they say happen, do: I mean, the vice of every kink, and speakeasies and spielers and friends who carve each other up, and, on the other hand, dear old Italians and sweet old Viennese who've run their honest, unbent little businesses there since the days of George six, and five, and backward far beyond. And what's more, although the pavement's thick with tearaways, provided you don't meddle, it's really a much safer area than the respectable suburban fringe. It's not in Soho a sex maniac leaps out of a hedge on to your back and violates you. It's in the dormitory sections.

The coffee spot where I hoped I'd find my two duets was of the kind that's now the chic-set thing to date among the juniors – namely, the pig-sty variety, the adolescent bum's delight. I don't exaggerate, as you'll see. What you do is, rent premises that are just as dear as any other, rip up the linos and tear out the nice fittings if there happen to be any, put in thick wood floors and tables, and take special care not to wipe the cups properly, or sweep the butts and crusts and spittle off the floor. Candles are a help or, at a pinch, non-pearl 40-watt blue bulbs. And a juke-box just for decoration, as it's considered rather naïve to *use* one in these places.

This example was called Chez Nobody, and sure enough, sitting far apart from each other at distant tables, were the Dean and the Misery Kid. Though both are friends of mine, and, in a way, even friends of each other, these two don't mix in public, on account of the Dean being a sharp modern jazz creation, and the Kid just a skiffle survival, with horrible leanings to the trad. thing. That is to say, the Kid admires the groups that play what is supposed to be the authentic music of old New Orleans, i.e., combos of booking-office clerks and quantity-surveyors' assistants who've handed in their cards, and dedicated themselves to blowing what they believe to be the same notes as the wonderful Creoles who invented the whole thing, when it all long ago began . . .

. . . So I went out to catch the summer evening breeze. The night was glorious, out there. The air was sweet as a cool bath, the stars were peeping nosily beyond the neons, and the citizens of the Queendom, in their jeans and separates, were floating down the Shaftesbury avenue canals, like gondolas. Everyone had loot to spend, everyone a bath with verbena salts behind them, and nobody had broken hearts, because they all were all ripe for the easy summer evening. The rubber-plants in the espressos had been dusted, and the smooth white lights of the new-style Chinese restaurants – not the old Mah Jongg categories, but the latest thing with broad glass fronts, and dacron curtainings, and a beige carpet over the interiors – were shining a dazzle, like some monster telly screens. Even those horrible old anglo-saxon public-houses – all potato crisps and flat, stale ale, and puddles on the counter bar, and spittle – looked quite alluring, provided you didn't push those two-ton doors that pinch your arse, and wander in. In fact, the capital was a night-horse dream. And I thought, 'My lord, one thing is certain, and that's that they'll make musicals one day about the glamour-studded 1950s'. . . .

From ABSOLUTE BEGINNERS, *by Colin MacInnes*

GAY TALESE

Nocturne, New York

NEW YORK is a city of things unnoticed. It is a city with cats sleeping under parked cars, two stone armadillos crawling up St Patrick's Cathedral, and thousands of ants creeping on top of the Empire State Building. The ants probably were carried up there by wind or birds, but nobody is sure; nobody in New York knows any more about the ants than they do about the panhandler who takes taxis to the Bowery; or the dapper man who picks trash out of Sixth Avenue trash cans; or the medium in the West Seventies who claims, 'I am clairvoyant, clairaudient and clairsensuous.'

New York is a city for eccentrics and a centre for odd bits of information. New Yorkers blink twenty-eight times a minute, but forty when tense. . . . A Park Avenue doorman has parts of three bullets in his head – there since World War I. Several young gypsy daughters, influenced by television and literacy, are running away from home because they don't want to grow up and become fortune-tellers. Each month a hundred pounds of hair is delivered to Louis Feder on 545 Fifth Avenue, where blonde hairpieces are made from German women's hair; brunette hairpieces from Italian women's hair; but no hairpieces from American women's hair which, says Mr Feder, is weak from too-frequent rinses and permanents. . . .

On Broadway each evening a big, dark, 1948 Rolls-Royce pulls into Forty-Sixth Street – and out hop two little ladies armed with Bibles and signs reading, 'The Damned Shall Perish'. These ladies proceed to stand on the corner screaming at the multitudes of Broadway sinners, sometimes until 3 a.m., when their chauffeur in the Rolls picks them up, and drives them back to Westchester.

By this time Fifth Avenue is deserted by all but a few strolling insomniacs, some cruising cab drivers, and a group of sophisticated females who stand in store windows all night and day wearing cold, perfect smiles. Like sentries they line Fifth Avenue – these window mannequins who gaze onto the quiet street with tilted heads and pointed toes and long rubber fingers reaching for cigarettes that aren't there.

At 5 a.m. Manhattan is a town of tired trumpet players and homeward-bound bartenders. Pigeons control Park Avenue and strut unchallenged in the middle of the street. This is Manhattan's mellowest hour. Most *night* people are out of sight – but the *day* people have not yet appeared. Truck drivers and cabs are alert, yet they do not disturb the mood. They do not disturb the abandoned Rockefeller Centre, or the motionless night watchmen in the Fulton Fish Market, or the gas-station attendant sleeping next to Sloppy Louie's with the radio on.

At 5 a.m. the Broadway regulars either have gone home or to all-night coffee shops where, under the glaring light, you see their whiskers and wear. And on Fifty-First Street a radio press car is parked at the kerb with a photographer who has nothing to do. So he just sits there for a few nights, looks through the windshield, and soon becomes a keen observer of life after midnight.

'At 1 a.m.,' he says, 'Broadway is filled with wise guys and with kids coming out of the Astor Hotel in white dinner jackets – kids who drive to dances in their fathers' cars. You also see cleaning ladies going home, always wearing kerchiefs. By 2 a.m. some of the drinkers are getting out of hand, and this is the hour for bar fights. At 3 a.m. the last show is over in the night clubs, and most of the tourists and out-of-town buyers are back in hotels. And small-time comedians are criticising big-time comedians in Hanson's Drugstore. At 4 a.m. after the bars close, you see the drunks come out – and also the pimps and prostitutes who take advantage of drunks. At 5 a.m., though, it is mostly quiet. New York is an entirely different city at 5 a.m.'

At 6 a.m. the early workers begin to push up from the subways. The traffic begins to move down Broadway like a river. And Mrs Mary Woody jumps out of bed, dashes to her office and phones dozens of sleepy New Yorkers to say in a cheerful voice, rarely appreciated: 'Good morning. Time to get up.' For twenty years, as an operator of Western Union's Wake-Up Service, Mrs Woody has gotten millions out of bed.

By 7 a.m. a floridly robust little man, looking very Parisian in a blue beret and turtle-neck sweater, moves in a hurried step along Park Avenue visiting his wealthy lady friends – making certain that each is given a brisk, before-breakfast rubdown. The uniformed doormen greet him warmly and call him either 'Biz' or 'Mac' because he is Biz Mackey, a ladies' masseur *extraordinaire*. He never reveals the names of his customers but most of them are middle-aged and rich. He visits each of them in their apartments, and has special keys to their bedrooms; he is often the first man they see in the morning, and they lie in bed waiting for him. . . .

Shortly after 7.30 each morning hundreds of people are lined along Forty-Second Street waiting for the 8 a.m. opening of the ten movie houses that stand almost shoulder-to-shoulder between Times Square and Eighth Avenue. Who are these people who go to the movies at 8 a.m? They are the city's insomniacs, night watchmen, and people who can't go home, do not want to go home, or have no home. They are derelicts, homosexuals, cops, hacks, truck drivers, cleaning ladies and restaurant men who have worked all night. They are also alcoholics who are waiting at 8 a.m. to pay forty cents for a soft seat and to sleep in the dark, smoky theatre. . . .

New York is a city of 38,000 cab drivers, 10,000 bus drivers but only one chauffeur who has a chauffeur. The wealthy chauffeur can be seen driving up Fifth Avenue each morning, and his name is Roosevelt Zanders. He earns $100,000 a year, is a gentleman of impeccable taste and, although he owns a $23,000 Rolls-Royce, does not scorn his friends who own Bentleys. For $150 a day Mr Zanders will drive anyone anywhere in his big, silver Rolls. Diplomats patronise him, models pose next to him, and each day he receives cables from around the world urging that he be waiting at Idlewild, or the docks, or outside the Plaza Hotel. Sometimes at night, however, he is too tired to drive any more. So Bob Clarke, his chauffeur, takes over, and Mr Zanders relaxes in the back. . . .

In New York there are 500 mediums, ranging from semi-trance to trance to deep-trance types. Most of them live in New York's West Seventies and Eighties, and on Sundays some of these blocks are communicating with the dead, vibrating to trumpets, and solving all problems. . . .

In New York from dawn to dusk to dawn, day after day, you can hear the steady rumble of tyres against the concrete span of George Washington Bridge. The bridge is never completely still. It trembles with traffic. It moves in the wind. Its great veins of steel swell when hot and contract when cold; its span often is ten feet closer to the Hudson River in summer than in winter. It is an almost restless structure of graceful beauty which, like an irresistible seductress, withholds secrets from the romantics who gaze upon it, the escapists who jump off it, the chubby girl who lumbers across its 3,500-foot span trying to reduce, and the 100,000 motorists who each day cross it, smash into it, short-change it, get jammed up on it.

When traffic dwindles and most people are sleeping in New York, some neighbourhoods begin to crawl with cats. They move quickly through the shadows of buildings; night watchmen, policemen, garbage collectors and other nocturnal wanderers see them – but never for very long. There are 200,000 stray cats in New York. A majority of them hang around the fish market, or in Greenwich Village, and in the East and West Side neighbourhoods where garbage cans abound. No part of the city is without its strays, however, and all-night garage attendants in such busy neighbourhoods as Fifty-Fourth Street have counted as many as twenty of them around the Ziegfeld Theatre early in the morning. Troops of cats patrol the water-front piers at night searching for rats. Subway trackwalkers have discovered cats living in the darkness. They seem never to get hit by trains, though some are occasionally liquidated by the third rail. About twenty-five cats live seventy-five feet below the west end of Grand Central Terminal, are fed by the underground workers, and never wander up into the daylight.

New York is a city in which large, cliff-dwelling hawks cling to skyscrapers and occasionally zoom to snatch a pigeon over Central Park, or Wall Street, or the Hudson River. Bird-watchers have seen these peregrine falcons circling lazily over the city. They have seen them perched atop tall buildings, even around Times Square. About twelve of these hawks patrol the city, sometimes with a wingspan of thirty-five inches. They have buzzed women on the roof of the St Regis Hotel, have attacked repairmen on smoke-stacks, and, in August, 1947, two hawks jumped women residents in the recreation yard of the Home of the New York Guild for the Jewish Blind. Maintenance men at the Riverside Church have seen hawks dining off pigeons in the bell tower. The hawks remain there for only a little while. And then they fly out to the river, leaving pigeons' heads for the Riverside maintenance men to clean up. When the hawks return, they fly in quietly – *unnoticed*, like the cats, the ants, the ladies' masseur, the doorman with three bullets in his head, and most of the other offbeat wonders in this town without time.

From NEW YORK, *by Gay Talese, reprinted by permission from 'Esquire Magazine'*

NEW YORK: PROP OF LOVE, *by Bruce Davidson*

Overleaf: NEW YORK: CENTRAL PARK, *by Bruce Davidson*

EDMUND SPENSER

From *Epithalamion*

. . . Now welcome, night! thou night so long expected,
That long daies labour doest at last defray,
And all my cares, which cruell Love collected
Hast sumd in ine, and cancellèd for aye:
Spread thy broad wing over my love and me,
That no man may us see;
And in thy sable mantle us enwrap,
From feare of perrill and foule horror free.
Let no false treason seeke us to entrap,
Nor any dread disquiet once annoy
The safety of our joy;
But let the night be calme, and quietsome,
Without tempestuous storms or sad afray:
Lyke as when Jove with fayre Alcmena lay,
When he begot the great Tirynthian groome:
Or lyke as when he with thy selfe did lie
And begot Majesty.
And let the mayds and yong men cease to sing;
Ne let the woods them answer nor theyr eccho ring.

Let no lamenting cryes, nor dolefull teares,
Be heard all night within, nor yet without:
Ne let false whispers, breeding hidden feares,
Breake gentle sleepe with misconceivèd dout.
Let no deluding dreames, nor dreadfull sights,
Make sudden sad affrights;
Ne let house-fyres, nor lightnings helpelesse harmes,
Ne let the Pouke, nor other evill sprights,
Ne let mischivous witches with theyr charmes,
Ne let hob Goblins, names whose sence we see not,
Fray us with things that be not:
Let not the shriech Oule nor the Storke be heard,
Nor the night Raven, that still deadly yels;
Nor damnèd ghosts, cald up with mighty spels,

THE LADY OF THE CAMELLIAS': Susan Strasberg, *by John Timbers*

Nor griesly vultures, make us once affeard:
Ne let th'unpleasant Quyre of Frogs still croking
Make us to wish theyr choking.
Let none of these theyr drery accents sing;
Ne let the woods them answer, nor theyr eccho ring.

But let stil Silence trew night-watches keepe,
That sacred Peace may in assurance rayne,
And tymely Sleep, when it is tyme to sleepe,
May pore his limbs forth on your pleasant playne;
The whiles and hundred little wingèd loves,
Like divers-fethered doves,
Shall fly and flutter round about your bed,
And in the secret darke, that none reproves,
Their prety stealthes shal worke, and snares shal spread
To filch away sweet snatches of delight,
Conceald through covert night.
Ye sonnes of Venus, play your sports at will!
For greedy pleasure, carelesse of your toyes,
Thinks more upon her paradise of joyes,
Then what ye do, albe good or ill.
All night therefore attend your merry play,
For it will soone be day:
Now none doth hinder you, that say or sing;
Ne will the woods now answer, nor your Eccho ring.

Who is the same, which at my window peepes?
Or whose is that faire face that shines so bright?
Is it not Cinthia, she that never sleepes,
But walkes about high heaven al the night?
O! fayrest goddesse, do thou not envy
My love with me to spy:
For thou likewise didst love, though now unthought,
And for a fleece of wooll, which privily
The Latmian shepherd once unto thee brought,
His pleasures with thee wrought.
Therefore to us be favourable now;
And sith of wemens labours thou hath charge,
And generation goodly dost enlarge,
Encline thy will t'effect our wishfull vow,
And the chast wombe informe with timely seed
That may our comfort breed:

Till which we cease our hopefull hap to sing;
Ne let the woods us answere, nor our Eccho ring.

And thou, great Juno! which with awful might
The lawes of wedlock still dost patronize;
And the religion of the faith first plight
With sacred rites hast taught to solemnize;
And eeke for comfort often callèd art
Of women in their smart;
Eternally blind thou this lovely band,
And all thy blessings unto us impart.
And thou, glad Genius! in whose gentle hand
The bridale bowre and geniall bed remaine,
Without blemish or staine;
And the sweet pleasures of theyr loves delight
With secret ayde doest succour and supply,
Till they bring forth the fruitfull progeny;
Send us the timely fruit of this same night.
And thou, fayre Hebe! and thou, Hymen free!
Grant that it may so be.
Til which we cease your further prayse to sing;
Ne any woods shall answer, nor your Eccho ring . . .

From EPITHALAMION, *by Edmund Spenser* (1552–1599)

Such harmony

How sweet the moonlight sleeps upon this bank!
Here will we sit, and let the sounds of music
Creep in our ears – soft stillness and the night
Become the touches of sweet harmony.
Sit, Jessica. Look how the floor of heaven
Is thick inlaid with patens of bright gold,
There's not the smallest orb which thou behold'st
But in his motion like an angel sings,
Still quiring to the young-eyed cherubims;
Such harmony is in immortal souls! . . .

THE MERCHANT OF VENICE, *William Shakespeare*

Sleep, angry beauty

Sleep, angry beauty, sleep and fear not me!
    For who a sleeping lion dares provoke?
It shall suffice me here to sit and see
    Those lips shut up that never kindly spoke:
What sight can more content a lover's mind
Than beauty seeming harmless, if not kind?

My words have charmed her, for secure she sleeps,
    Though guilty much of wrong done to my love;
And in her slumber, see! she close-eyed weeps:
    Dreams often more than waking passions move.
Plead, Sleep, my cause, and make her soft like thee,
That she in peace may wake and pity me.

Thomas Campion (1567?–1619)

And is it night?

And is it night? are they thine eyes that shine?
    Are we alone, and here? and here, alone?
May I come near, may I but touch thy shrine?
    Is jealousy asleep, and is he gone?
O Gods, no more! silence my lips with thine!
Lips, kisses, joys, hap, – blessings most divine!

Oh, come, my dear! our griefs are turned to night,
    And night to joys; night blinds pale envy's eyes;
Silence and sleep prepare us our delight;
    Oh, cease we then our woes, our griefs, our cries:
Oh, vanish words! words do but passions move;
O dearest life! joy's sweet! O sweetest love!

Anon.
(*R. Jones:* A MUSICAL DREAM, 1609)

Bridal Song

Now, Sleep, bind fast the flood of air,
    Strike all things dumb and deaf;
And, to disturb our nuptial pair,
    Let stir no aspen leaf.
Send flocks of golden dreams
    That all true joys presage,
Bring, in thy oily streams,
    The milk and honey age.
        Now close the world-round sphere of bliss,
        And fill it with a heavenly kiss.

George Chapman (1559–1634)

Bridal Song

Hold back thy hours, old Night, till we have done;
    The day will come too soon;
Young maids will curse thee, if thou steal'st away
And leav'st their losses open to the day:
    Stay, stay, and hide
The blushes of the bride.

Stay, gentle Night, and with thy darkness cover
    The kisses of her lover;
Stay, and confound her tears and her loud cryings,
Her weak denials, vows, and often-dyings;
    Stay, and hide all:
But help not, though she call.

Francis Beaumont? (1584–1616)

The Night-piece: To Julia

Her eyes the glow-worm lend thee,
The shooting stars attend thee;
   And the elves also,
   Whose little eyes glow
Like the sparks of fire, befriend thee.

No Will-o'-the-wisp mislight thee,
Nor snake or slow-worm bite thee;
   But on, on thy way
   Not making a stay,
Since ghost there's none to affright thee.

Let not the dark thee cumber:
What though the moon does slumber?
   The stars of the night
   Will lend thee their light
Like tapers clear without number.

Then, Julia, let me woo thee,
Thus, thus to come unto me;
   And when I shall meet
   Thy silv'ry feet,
My soul I'll pour into thee.

Robert Herrick (1591–1674)

Come, gentle night

Gallop apace, you fiery-footed steeds,
Towards Phoebus' lodging: such a waggoner
As Phaethon would whip you to the west,
And bring in cloudy night immediately.
Spread thy close curtain, love-performing night,
That runaways' eyes may wink, and Romeo
Leap to these arms, untalk'd of and unseen.
Lovers can see to do their amorous rites
By their own beauties; or, if love be blind,
It best agrees with night. Come, civil night,
Thou sober-suited matron, all in black,
And learn me how to lose a winning match,
Play'd for a pair of stainless maidenhoods:
Hood my unmann'd blood, bating in my cheeks,
With the black mantle; till strange love, grown bold,
Think true love acted simple modesty.
Come, night; come, Romeo; come, thou day in night;
For thou wilt lie upon the wings of night
Whiter than new snow on a raven's back.
Come, gentle night, come, loving, black-brow'd night,
Give me my Romeo; and, when he shall die,
Take him and cut him out in little stars,
And he will make the face of heaven so fine
That all the world will be in love with night
And pay no worship to the garish sun.
O, I have bought the mansion of a love,
But not possess'd it, and, though I am sold,
Not yet enjoy'd: so tedious is this day
As is the night before some festival
To an impatient child that hath new robes
And may not wear them.

Juliet in ROMEO AND JULIET, *William Shakespeare*

Meeting at Night

The gray sea and the long black land;
And the yellow half-moon large and low;
And the startled little waves that leap
In fiery ringlets from their sleep,
As I gain the cove with pushing prow,
And quench its speed i' the slushy sand.

Then a mile of warm sea-scented beach;
Three fields to cross till a farm appears;
A tap at the pane, the quick sharp scratch
And blue spurt of a lighted match,
And a voice less loud, thro' its joys and fears,
Than the two hearts beating each to each!

Robert Browning (1812–1889)

Last Sonnet

Bright Star, would I were steadfast as thou art –
Not in lone splendour hung aloft the night,
And watching, with eternal lids apart,
Like Nature's patient sleepless Eremite,
The moving waters at their priest-like task
Of pure ablution round earth's human shores,
Or gazing on the new soft-fallen mask
Of snow upon the mountains and the moors –
No – yet still steadfast, still unchangeable,
Pillow'd upon my fair love's ripening breast,
To feel for ever its soft fall and swell,
Awake for ever in a sweet unrest,
    Still, still to hear her tender-taken breath,
    And so live ever – or else swoon to death.

John Keats (1795–1821)

But One

The morning now was on the point of breaking,
   A turn of time at which I would advise
Ladies who have been dancing, or partaking
   In any other kind of exercise,
To make their preparations for forsaking
   The ball-room ere the sun begins to rise,
Because when once the lamps and candles fail,
His blushes make them look a little pale.

I've seen some balls and revels in my time,
   And stay'd them over for some silly reason,
And then I look'd (I hope it was no crime)
   To see what lady best stood out the season,
And though I've seen some thousands in their prime,
   Lovely and pleasing, and who may still please on,
I never saw but one (the stars withdrawn)
Whose bloom could after dancing dare the dawn.

The name of this Aurora I'll not mention,
   Although I might, for she was nought to me
More than that patent work of God's invention,
   A charming woman, whom we like to see;
But writing names would merit reprehension,
   Yet if you like to find out this fair *she*,
At the next London or Parisian ball
You still may mark her cheek out-blooming all.

From BEPPO, *by Lord Byron* (1788–1824)

— fainted into his out stretched arms

A Proposale

THEY ARRIVED at Windsor very hot from the jorney and Bernard at once hired a boat to row his beloved up the river. Ethel could not row but she much enjoyed seeing the tough sunburnt arms of Bernard tugging at the oars as she lay among the rich cushons of the dainty boat. She had a rarther lazy nature but Bernard did not know of this. However he soon got dog tired and sugested lunch by the mossy bank.

Oh yes said Ethel quickly opening the sparkling champaigne.

Dont spill any said Bernard as he carved some chicken.

They eat and drank deeply of the charming viands ending up with merangs and choclates.

Let us now bask under the spreading trees said Bernard in a passiunate tone.

Oh yes lets said Ethel and she opened her tiny parasole and sank down upon the long green grass. She closed her eyes but she was far from sleep. Bernard sat beside her in profound silence gazing at her pink face and long wavy eye lashes. He puffed at his pipe for some moments while the larks gaily caroled in the blue sky. Then he edged a trifle closer to Ethels form.

Ethel he murmered in a trembly voice.

Oh what is it said Ethel hastily sitting up.

Words fail me said Bernard horsly my passion for you is intense he added fervently. It has grown day and night since I first beheld you.

Oh said Ethel in surprise I am not prepared for this and she lent back against the trunk of a tree.

Bernard placed one arm tightly round her. When will you marry me Ethel he uttered you must be my wife it has come to that I love you so intensly that if you say no I shall perforce dash my body to the brink of yon muddy river he panted wildly.

Oh dont do that implored Ethel breathing rarther hard.

Then say you love me he cried.

Oh Bernard she sighed fervently I certinly love you madly you are to me like a Heathen god she cried looking at his manly form and handsome flashing face I will indeed marry you.

How soon gasped Bernard gazing at her intensly.

As soon as possible said Ethel gently closing her eyes.

My Darling whispered Bernard and he seiezed her in his arms we will be marrid next week.

Oh Bernard muttered Ethel this is so sudden.

No no cried Bernard and taking the bull by both horns he kissed her violently on her dainty face. My bride to be he murmered several times.

Ethel trembled with joy as she heard the mistick words.

Oh Bernard she said little did I ever dream of such as this and she suddenly fainted into his out stretched arms.

Oh I say gasped Bernard and laying the dainty burden on the grass he dashed to the waters edge and got a cup full of the fragrant river to pour on his true loves pallid brow.

She soon came to and looked up with a sickly smile Take me back to the Gaierty hotel she whispered faintly.

With plesure my darling said Bernard I will just pack up our viands ere I unloose the boat.

Ethel felt better after a few drops of champagne and began to tidy her hair while Bernard packed the remains of the food. Then arm in arm they tottered to the boat.

I trust you have not got an illness my darling murmered Bernard as he helped her in.

Oh no I am very strong said Ethel I fainted from joy she added to explain matters.

Oh I see said Bernard handing her a cushon well some people do he added kindly and so saying they rowed down the dark stream now flowing silently beneath a golden moon. All was silent as the lovers glided home with joy in their hearts and radiunce on their faces only the sound of the mystearious water lapping against the frail vessel broke the monotony of the night.

So I will end my chapter.

From THE YOUNG VISITERS, *by nine-year-old Daisy Ashford,*
illustrated by Heather Corlass

—they rowed down the dark stream

i like my body when it is with your
body. It is so quite new a thing.
Muscles better and nerves more.
i like your body. i like what it does,
i like its hows. i like to feel the spine
of your body and its bones, and the trembling
-firm-smooth ness and which i will
again and again and again
kiss, i like kissing this and that of you,
i like,slowly stroking the,shocking fuzz
of your electric fur,and what-is-it comes
over parting flesh . . . . And eyes big love-crumbs,

and possibly i like the thrill

of under me you so quite new

e.e.cummings

Body, remember . . .

Body, remember not only how much you were loved,
not only the beds on which you lay,
but also these desires for you
that glowed plainly in the eyes,
and trembled in the voice – and some
chance obstacle made futile.
Now that all of them belong to the past,
it almost seems as if you had yielded
to those desires – how they glowed,
remember, in the eyes gazing at you;
how they trembled in the voice, for you, remember, body.

From THE COMPLETE POEMS OF C. P. CAVAFY, *translated by Rae Dalven*

THE BODY, *by Otto Karminski*

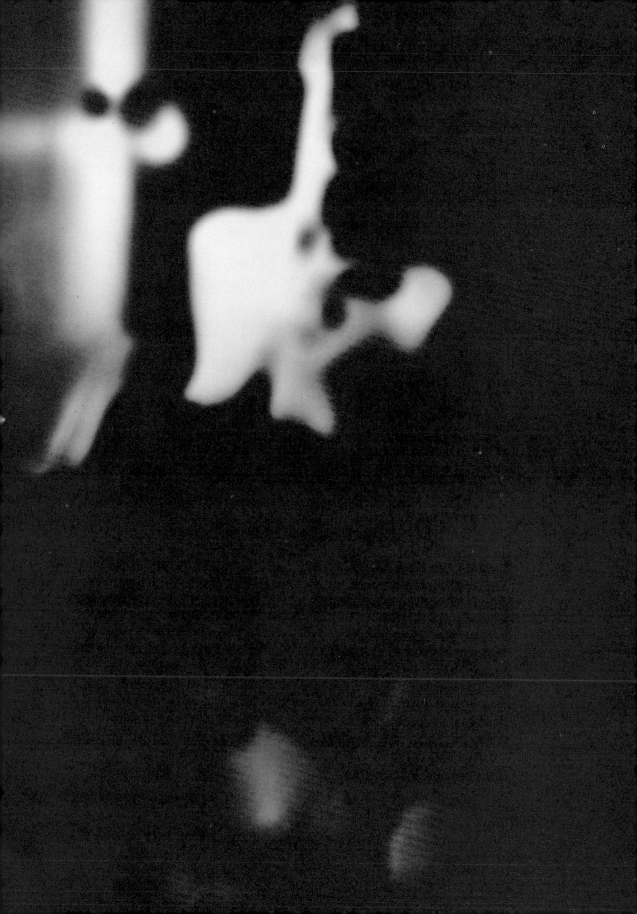

LOVE IN A CORRIDOR, *by John Hopkin.*

Now winter nights enlarge

Now winter nights enlarge
The number of their hours,
And clouds their storms discharge
Upon the airy towers.
Let now the chimneys blaze,
And cups o'erflow with wine;
Let well-tuned words amaze
With harmony divine.
Now yellow waxen lights
Shall wait on honey love,
While youthful revels, masques,
   and courtly sights
Sleep's leaden spells remove.

This time doth well dispense
With lovers' long discourse;
Much speech hath some defence,
Though beauty no remorse.
All do not all things well;
Some measures comely tread,
Some knotted riddles tell,
Some poems smoothly read.
The summer hath his joys
And winter his delights;
Though love and all his pleasures
   are but toys,
They shorten tedious nights.

Thomas Campion (1567?–1619)

146

DAWN AT THE HUNT BALL, *by Erich Auerba*

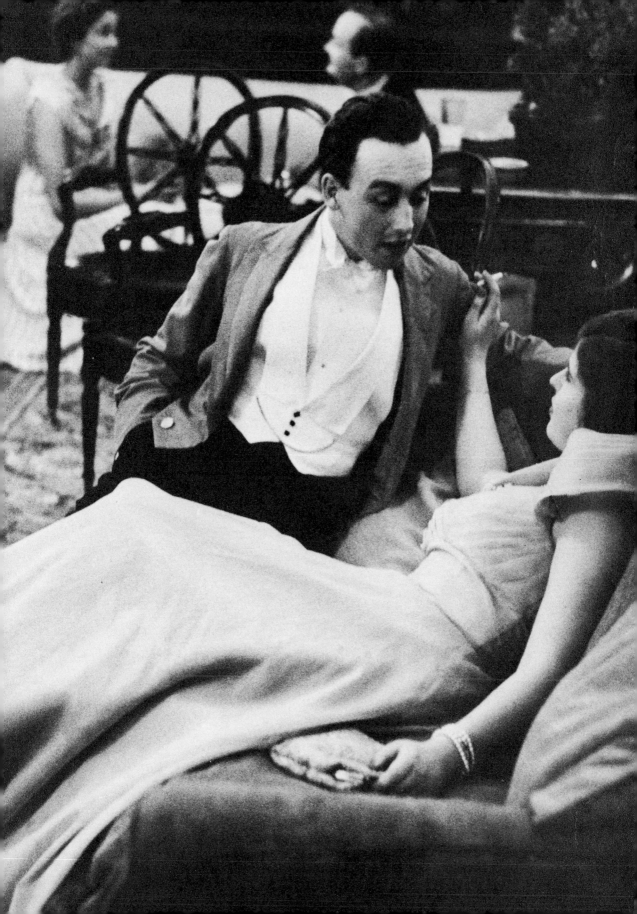

THE WAITER, *by Dennis Stock*

The Boy and the Owls

Many a time
At evening, when the earliest stars began
To move along the edges of the hills,
Rising or setting, would he stand alone,
Beneath the trees, or by the glimmering lake;
And there, with fingers interwoven, both hands
Pressed closely palm to palm and to his mouth
Uplifted, he, as though an instrument,
Blew mimic hootings to the silent owls,
That they might answer him. And they would shout
Across the watery vale, and shout again,
Responsive to his call, – with quivering peals,
And long halloos, and screams, and echoes loud
Redoubled and redoubled; concourse wild
Of mirth and jocund din! And, when there came a pause
Of silence such as baffled his best skill,
Then, sometimes, in that silence, while he hung
Listening, a gentle shock of mild surprise
Has carried far into his heart the voice
Of mountain torrents.

William Wordsworth

SHORT-EARED OWL, *by Eric Hosking*

There was a young lady in white,
Who looked out at the depths of the night;
But the birds of the air filled her heart with despair,
And oppressed that young lady in white.

EDWARD LEAR: *A Book of Nonsense*

Owls and Goblins

Selborne, July 8th 1773

WE HAVE had, ever since I can remember, a pair of white owls that constantly breed under the eaves of this church. As I have paid good attention to the manner of life of these birds during their season of breeding, which lasts the summer through, the following remarks may not perhaps be unacceptable:- About an hour before sunset (for then the mice begin to run) they sally forth in quest of prey, and hunt all round the hedges of meadows and small enclosures for them, which seem to be their only food. In this irregular country we can stand on an eminence and see them beat the fields over like a setting-dog, and often drop down in the grass or corn. I have minuted these birds with my watch for an hour together, and have found that they return to their nest, the one or the other of them, about once in five minutes; reflecting at the same time on the adroitness that every animal is possessed of as far as regards the well-being of itself and offspring. But a piece of address which they show when they return loaded should not, I think, be passed over in silence. – As they take their prey with their claws, so they carry it in their claws to their nest; but as the feet are necessary in their ascent under the tiles, they constantly perch first on the roof of the chancel, and shift the mouse from their claws to their bill, that their feet may be at liberty to take hold of the plate on the wall as they are rising under the eaves.

White owls seem not (but in this I am not positive) to hoot at all; all that clamorous hooting appears to me to come from the wood kinds. The white owl does indeed snore and hiss in a tremendous manner; and these menaces well answer the intention of intimidating; for I have known a whole village up in arms on such an occasion, imagining the churchyard to be full of goblins and spectres. White owls also often scream horribly as they fly along; from this screaming probably arose the common people's imaginary species of screech-owl, which they superstitiously think attends the windows of dying persons . . .

From THE NATURAL HISTORY OF SELBORNE, *by Gilbert White*

Sweet Suffolk Owl

Sweet Suffolk owl, so trimly dight
With feathers, like a lady bright,
Thou sing'st alone, sitting by night,
   Te whit, te whoo! Te whit, te whoo!

Thy note, that forth so freely rolls,
With shrill command the mouse controls;
And sings a dirge for dying souls,
   Te whit, te whoo! Te whit, te whoo!

Anon. 1619

Owl

is my favourite. Who flies
like a nothing through the night,
who-whoing. Is a feather
duster in leafy corners ring-a-rosy-ing
boles of mice. Twice

you hear him call. Who
is he looking for? You hear
him hoovering over the floor
of the wood. O would you be gold
rings in the driving skull

if you could? Hooded and
vulnerable by the winter suns
owl looks. Is the grain of bark
in the dark. Round beaks are at
work in the pellety nest,

resting. Owl is an eye
in the barn. For a hole
in the trunk owl's blood
is to blame. Black talons in the
petrified fur! Cold walnut hands

on the case of the brain! In the reign
of the chicken owl comes like
a god. Is a goad in
the rain to the pink eyes,
dripping. For a meal in the day

flew, killed, on the moor. Six
mouths are the seed of his
arc in the season. Torn meat
from the sky. Owl lives
by the claws of his brain. On the branch

in the sever of the hand's
twigs owl is a backward look.
Flown wind in the skin. Fine
rain in the bones. Owl breaks
like the day. Am an owl, am an owl.

From THE BROKEN PLACES (1963), *by George MacBeth*

Note *by the author:* Someone, perhaps a child, who is fascinated by owls creates a sort
of spell to bring an owl into being. By the end of the poem he has become the owl.

Nightingale

But the Nightingale, another of my airy creatures, breathes such sweet loud music out of her little instrumental throat, that it might make mankind to think miracles are not ceased. He that at midnight, when the very labourer sleeps securely, should hear, as I have very often, the clear airs, the sweet descants, the natural rising and falling, the doubling and redoubling of her voice, might well be lifted above earth, and say, 'Lord, what music has thou provided for the Saints in Heaven, when thou affordest bad men such music on earth!'

From THE COMPLEAT ANGLER, *by Izaak Walton* (1593–1683)

The Dramatist

ALTHOUGH the nightingale sings by day he needs the mystery of night for his song. He is a great dramatic singer, with more technical ability than any other species. His mysterious note, repeated on a crescendo, is both wonderful for its emotional effect and for masterly control of technique. The poise of that first suspended note has much of the mystery and remoteness of stars on a still summer night; from these heights the dramatist, with his intense vitality, brings the song back to earth by a contrasting brilliant display of dynamic rhythm; heard close, the effect being one of powerful mechanism. Forceful rhythmic phrases and bubbling trill crescendos are performed with amazing skill and driving power, the bird's vitality seeming inexhaustible. There is hardly a moment's pause between these phrases; then comes a longer pause, a pause that is part of the song, when the stillness and beauty of night are felt with growing intensity, then the wonderful note is heard and it seems sprung from the poetry of night.

From BIRDS AS INDIVIDUALS, *by Len Howard*

NIGHTINGALE, AGGRESSIVE, *by Eric Hosking*

THE VIOLA: Lionel Tertis plays for Vaughan Williams and his wife, *by Erich Auerbach*

ALDOUS HUXLEY

Music at Night

MOONLESS, this June night is all the more alive with stars. Its darkness is perfumed with faint gusts from the blossoming lime trees, with the smell of wetted earth and the invisible greenness of the vines. There is silence; but a silence that breathes with the soft breaking of the sea and, in the thin shrill noise of a cricket, insistently, incessantly harps on the fact of its own deep perfection. Far away, the passage of a train is like a long caress, moving gently, across the warm living body of the night.

Music, you say; it would be a good night for music. But I have music here in a box, shut up, like one of those bottled djinns in the *Arabian Nights*, and ready at a touch to break out of its prison. I make the necessary mechanical magic, and suddenly, by some miraculously appropriate coincidence (for I had selected the record in the dark, without knowing what music the machine would play), suddenly the introduction to the *Benedictus* in Beethoven's *Missa Solemnis* begins to trace its patterns on the moonless sky.

The *Benedictus*. Blessed and blessing, this music is in some sort the equivalent of the night, of the deep and living darkness, into which, now in a single jet, now in a fine interweaving of melodies, now in pulsing and almost solid clots of harmonious sound, it pours itself, stanchlessly pours itself, like time, like the rising and falling, falling trajectories of a life. It is the equivalent of the night in another mode of being, as an essence is the equivalent of the flowers, from which it is distilled.

There is, at least there sometimes seems to be, a certain blessedness lying at the heart of things, a mysterious blessedness, of whose existence occasional accidents or providences (for me, this night is one of them) make us obscurely, or it may be intensely, but always fleetingly, alas, always only for a few brief moments aware. In the *Benedictus* Beethoven gives expression to this awareness of blessedness. His music is the equivalent of this Mediterranean night, or rather of the blessedness at the heart of the night, of the blessedness as it would be if it could be sifted clear of irrelevance and accident, refined and separated out of its quintessential purity.

'*Benedictus, benedictus* . . .' One after another the voices take up the theme propounded by the orchestra and lovingly mediated through a long and exquisite solo (for the blessedness reveals itself most often to the solitary spirit) by a single violin. '*Benedictus, benedictus* . . .' And then, suddenly, the music dies; the flying djinn has been rebottled. With a stupid insect-like insistence, a steel point rasps and rasps into silence.

From MUSIC AT NIGHT, *by Aldous Huxley*

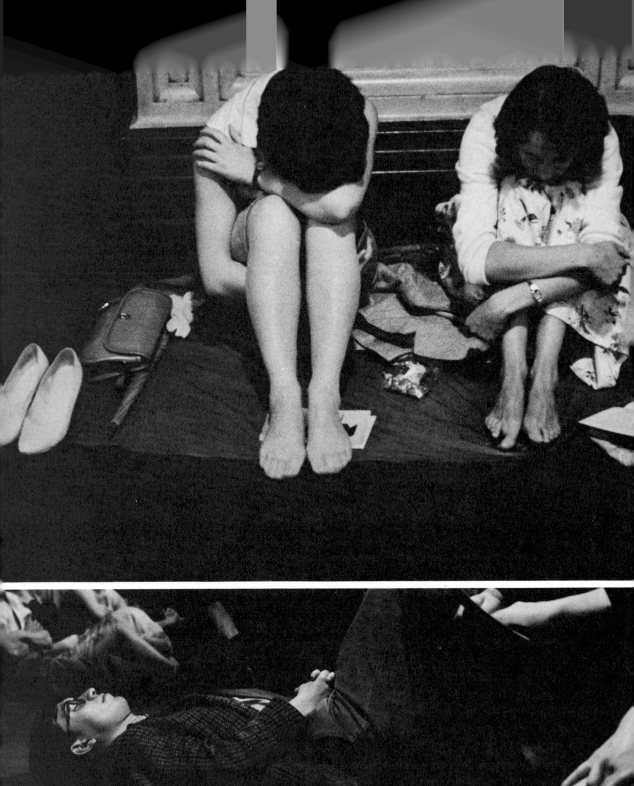

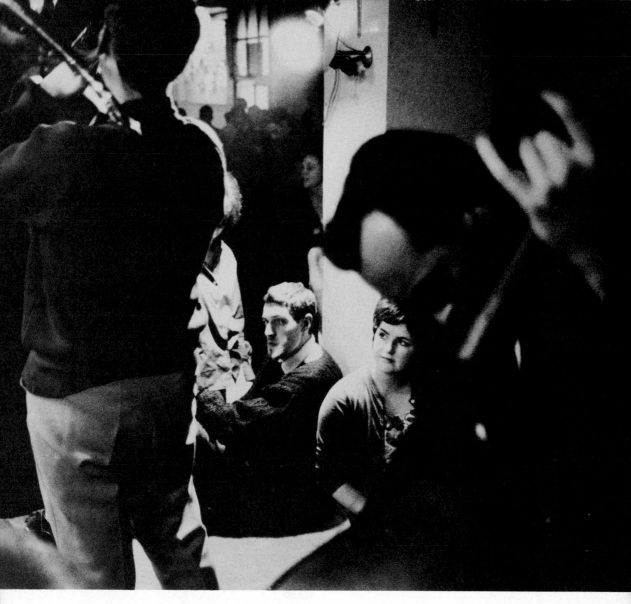

JAZZ CLUB, *by Frank Herrmann*

TREET MUSIC
y Godfrey MacDomnic
nd John Cowan

Overleaf:

ALL–NIGHT RAVE, *by John Hopkins*

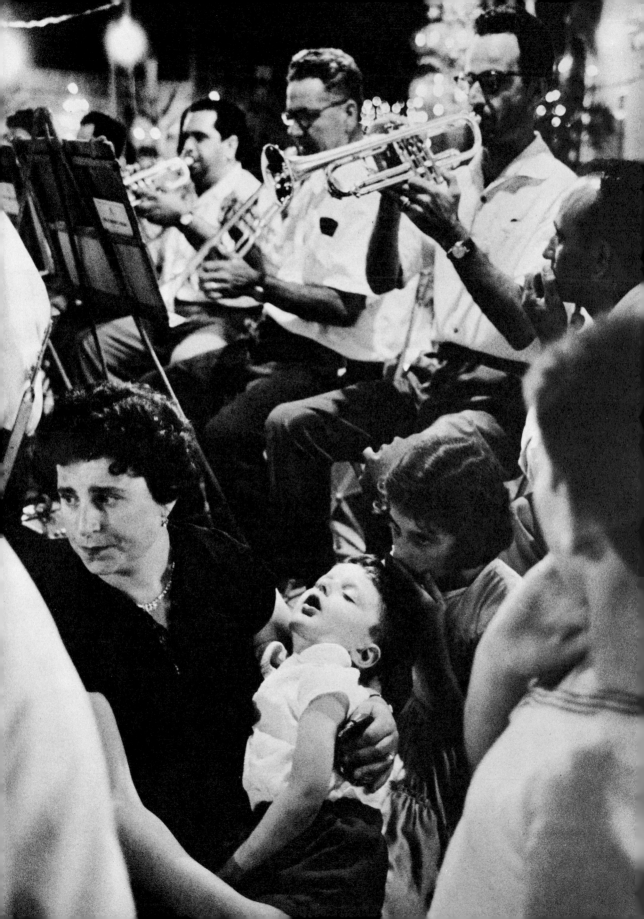

The Bed of Life

THE BED, my friend, is our whole life. It is there that we are born, it is there that we love, it is there that we die.

If I had the pen of M de Crébillon I would write the history of a bed, and what a record of adventures it would be – adventures thrilling and terrible, tender and gay. And what lessons could one not learn from such a record! And what morals could not be drawn for all mankind!

A young woman lies prostrated. From time to time she gasps, and then she groans, while the elders of the family stand round. And then there comes forth from her a little object, mewling like a cat, all shrivelled and lined. It is the beginning of a man!

Then there again are two lovers, flesh pressed to flesh for the first time in this tabernacle of life. They shudder but are transported with joy, and each feels the other's delicious nearness; then slowly their lips meet. They mingle in this divine kiss – this kiss which opens the gate to heaven on earth, this kiss which sings of human delights, promising all, and heralding the ecstasy to come. And their bed heaves as with the swell of the sea, whispers and sways, as if it were itself alive and joyful because it was seeing the consummation of the rapturous mystery of love.

And then again, my friend, think of death. For the bed is also the tomb of vanished hopes, the door that shuts out all, after once being the gateway to the world. What cries, what anguish, what suffering, what appalling despair, what groans of agony, what appeals to joy forever gone, has the bed not known? And what has it not seen of arms outstretched towards the past, of twisted bodies and hideous grins, of upturned eyeballs and contorted lips?

The bed is the symbol of life! The bed, indeed, is man!

From LE LIT, *by Guy de Maupassant. (From 'The Philosophy of the Bed', by Mary Eden and Richard Carrington)*

ᴵESTA WITH SLEEPING CHILD, *by Patrick Ward*

BYRON'S BEDROOM in Newstead Abbey, *by Bill Brand*

THE NIGHT THE BABY WAS BORN, *by Joseph McKeown*

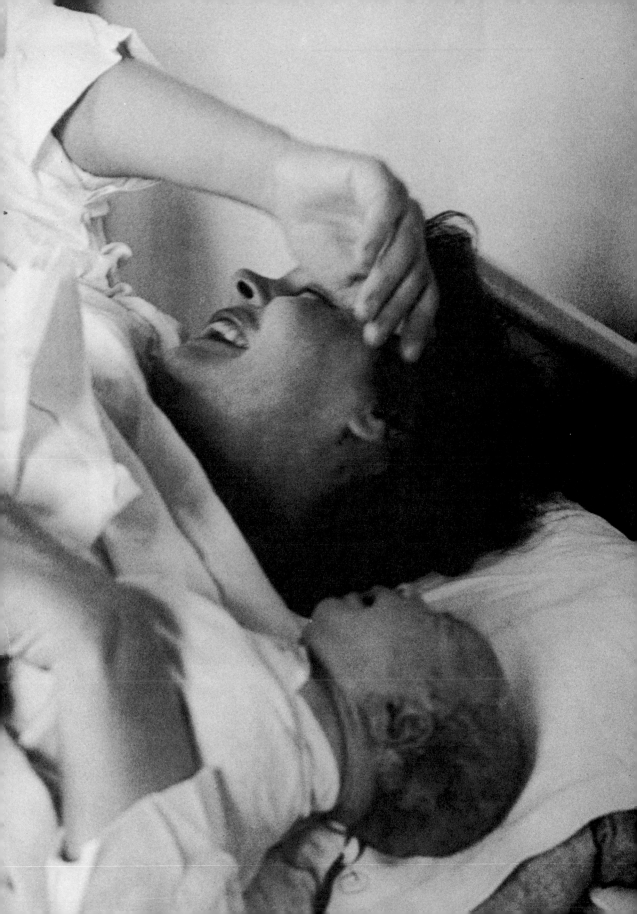

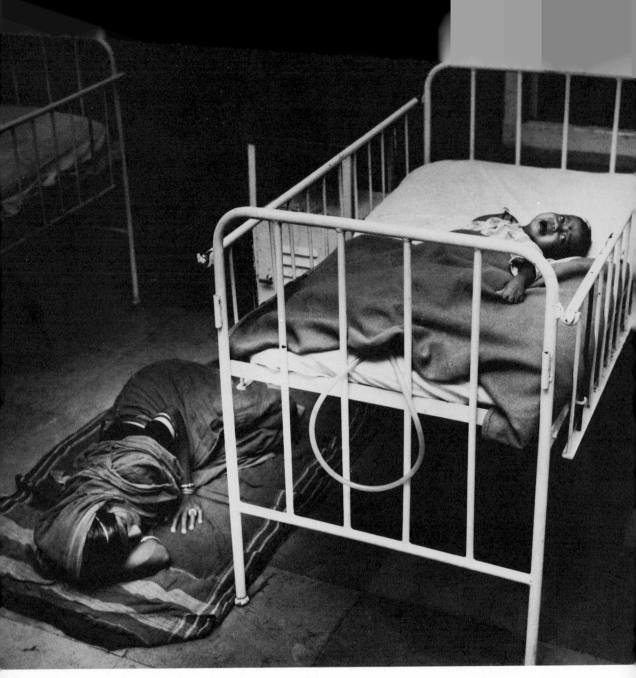

MOTHER AND CHILD, MADRAS, *by Barnet Saidman*

TIME TO GO TO BED, *by Michael Peto*

Overleaf:

TIME TO GET UP: Sir Roy Welensky,
by Kelvin Brodie

170

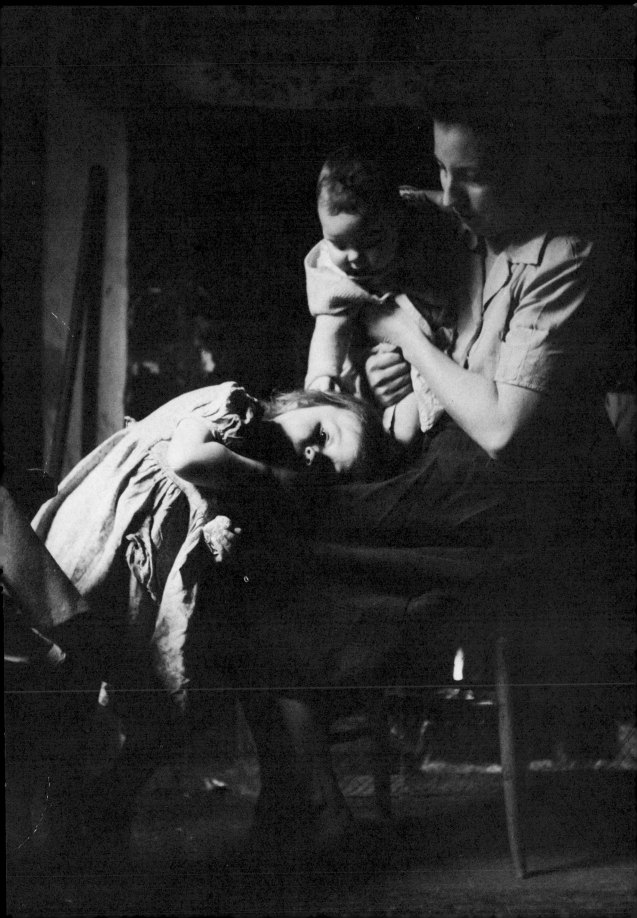

How to lie in bed

WHOLE men of what complexion soever they be of, shulde take theyr naturall rest and slepe in the nyght; and to eschewe merydall sleep. But and need shall compell a man to slepe after his meate: let hym make a pause, and than let hym stande & lene and slepe agaynst a cupborde, or els let hym sytte upryght in a chayre and slepe. Slepynge after a full stomacke doth ingendre dyvers infyrmyties, it doth hurt the splene, it relaxeth the synewes, it doth ingendre the dropses and the gowte, and doth make a man look evyll colored . . . to bedwarde be you mery, or have mery company aboute you, so that to bedwarde no angre, nor hevynes, sorowe, nor pensyfulnes, do trouble or disquyet you. To bedwarde, and also in the mornynge, use to have a fyre in your chambre, to wast and consume the evyl vapowres within the chambre, for the breath of man may putryfye the ayre within the chambre: I do advertyse you not to stande nor to sytte by the fyre, but stande or syt a good way of from the fyre, takynge the flavour of it, for fyre doth aryfie and doth drye up a mannes blode, and doth make sterke the synewes and joyntes of man. In the nyght let the wyndowes of your howse, specyallye of your chambre, be closed. When you be in your bedde, lye a lytle whyle on your lefte syde, and slepe on your ryght side. . . . To slepe grovellynge upon the stomacke and bely is not good, oneles the stomacke be slowe and tarde of dygestion; but better it is to laye your hande, or your bedfelowes hande, over your stomacke, than to lye grovellynge. To slepe on the backe upryght is utterly to be abhorred: whan that you do slepe, let not your necke, nother your sholders, nother your hands, nor feete, nor no other place of your bodye, lye bare undiscovered. Slepe not with an emptye stomacke, nor slepe not after that you have eaten meate one howre or two after. In your bed lye with your head somewhat hyghe, leaste that the meate whiche is in your stomacke, thorowe eructacions to some other cause, ascende to the oryfe of the stomacke. Let your nyght cap be of scarlet: and this I do advertyse you, to cause to be made a good thycke quylte of cotton, or els of pure flockes or of cleane wolle, and let the coverynge of it be of whyte fustyan, and laye it on the fetherbed that you do lye on; and in your bed lye not to hote nor to colde, but in a temporaunce. Old auncyent Doctors of physicke sayth viii howres of slepe in sommer, and ix in wynter, is suffycent for any man: but I do thynke that slepe oughte to be taken as the complexion of man is.

A COMPENDYOUS REGYMENT OR A DYETARY OF HELTHE (1542), *by Andrew Boorde*

The Honeymoon

February 13, 1840: . . . Her [Queen Victoria's] honeymoon seems to be a very curious affair, more strange than delicate; and even her best friends are shocked and hurt at her not conforming more than she is doing to English customs, and for not continuing for a short space in that retirement, which modesty and native delicacy generally prescribe and which few Englishwomen would be content to avoid. But She does not think any such restraint necessary. Married on Monday, she collected an immense party on Wednesday, and She sent off in a hurry for Clarence Paget to go down and assist at a ball or rather a dance, which she chose to have at the Castle last night. This is a proceeding quite unparalleled, and Lady Palmerston said to me last night that she was much vexed that She had nobody about her who could venture to tell her that this was not becoming and would appear indelicate; but She has nobody who dares tell her, or she will not endure to hear such truths. Normandy said to me the same thing. It is a pity Melbourne, when she desired him to go there on Wednesday, did not tell her she had better not have him nor anybody else except perhaps her own family. He probably did not think about it. It was much remarked too that She and P(rince) A(lbert) were up very early on Tuesday morning walking about, which is very contrary to her former habits. Strange that a bridal night should be so short; and I told Lady Palmerston that this was not the way to provide us with a Prince of Wales.

THE GREVILLE MEMOIRS

When His Majesty locked the doors

In June 1625 Charles I rode out from Canterbury to Dover to meet his newly arrived wife, Henrietta Maria of France, to whom he had been married by proxy the previous month. In two letters to Sir Martin Stuteville, both dated 17th June 1625, Joseph Mead describes the meeting:

SHE ARRIVED at Dover on Sunday about eight in the evening, lay there in the Castle that night; whither the King rode on Monday morning from Canterbury, came thither after 10 o'clock and she then being at meat, he stayed in the presence till she had done; which she, advertised of, made short work, rose, went unto him, kneeled down at his feet, took, and kissed his hand. The King took her up in his arms, kissed her, and talking with her, cast down his eyes towards her feet (she seeming higher than report was, reaching to his shoulders). Which she soon perceiving discovered [uncovered] and showed him her shoes, saying to this effect 'Sir, I stand upon mine own feet. I have no helps by art. Thus I am, and am neither higher nor lower.' She is nimble and quiet, black-eyed, brown-haired and in a word a brave Lady, though perhaps a little touched with a green sickness. . . .

174

At dinner (at Dover) being carved pheasant and venison by his Majesty (who had dined before) she ate heartily of both, notwithstanding that her confessor (who all this while stood by her) had forewarned her that it was the eve of St John Baptist, and was to be fasted, and that she should take heed how she gave ill example or a scandal at her first arrival.

. . . The same night, having supped at Canterbury, her Majesty went to bed; and, some space of time after, his Majesty followed her. And having entered his bedchamber, the first thing he did, he bolted all the doors round about (being seven), with his own hand, letting in but two of the bedchamber to undress him, which being done, he bolted them out also. The next morning he lay till seven of the clock, and was pleasant with the lords that he had beguiled them; and hath ever since been very jocund.

A Full Bed

December, 1795: At midnight we heard the arrival of a post from Madrid, who awoke the people of the house by cracking his whip. I cannot say he awoke me, for I, like Polonius, was at supper not where I eat, but where I was eaten. The ingenious gentleman who communicated his discovery to the public, in the Encyclopaedia, that ninety millions of mites' eggs amount exactly to the size of one pigeon's egg, may, if he please, calculate what quantity of blood was extracted from my body, in the course of seven hours; the bed being six feet two and a half, by four feet five, and as populous as possible in that given space.

LETTERS WRITTEN DURING A JOURNEY IN SPAIN AND
A SHORT RESIDENCE IN PORTUGAL, *by Robert Southey*

The Celestial Bed

... This bed, which is one of the most famous in history, was the property of Dr James Graham ... Graham was born in 1745 in Edinburgh and, although he claimed the degree of MD and studied at the University, it is improbable that he ever qualified; in any case his behaviour had all the hall-marks of the professional charlatan. After travelling in America and France he set up in practice in London, where his genius for publicity soon had patients swarming in hundreds to his consulting-rooms. This was the age when the therapeutic possibilities of electricity were first being investigated by physicians and, although orthodox members of the profession regarded such a mysterious novelty with suspicion, the less scrupulous were not so slow to exploit it for their own financial advantage. Among these was Graham, whose consulting-rooms were soon embellished with an electrical bath and a 'magnetic throne' to bring his patients the benefits of the new science. The physical advantage derived from treatment by these devices was of course non-existent, but the psychological effects were prodigious. The news spread rapidly through London's wealthier circles that the effects of this miraculous equipment were indeed electrifying in every sense of that word, and Graham's reputation soared. A man who combined charm of personality with such an enterprising use of the latest resources of science could not fail to become the most fashionable doctor in town.

Delighted by his success and the number of guineas that grateful dowagers left on his consulting-room table, Graham was encouraged to higher flights. In the autumn of 1779 he installed himself in a richly decorated house in the Royal Terrace, Adelphi, which he called 'The Temple of Health'. Two years later he moved to a new house in Pall Mall, known as 'The Temple of Health and Hymen', which he shared rather incongruously with the painter Thomas Gainsborough. Both premises were furnished in lavish style and equipped with a vast range of electrical apparatus.

Patients visited Graham from all parts of the country, and even from abroad, to listen to his lectures and enjoy the miraculous benefits of treatment on the various machines. The Temple was kept constantly open, and by the simple formality of paying six guineas at the door the most deserving cases could enter to inspect the wonders within; a personal consultation with the high priest himself was of course much more expensive, but few of the more wealthy could resist it once they found themselves inside. The high-spot of the day's visit came at a few minutes before 5 pm when the lights dimmed, soft music began to play, and the visitors gathered in a large room to hear a two-hour address from Graham on one or other of an astonishing variety of subjects. These ranged from 'the All-Cleansing, All-Healing, and All-Invigorating Qualities of the Simple Earth', and 'How to Live for many weeks, months, or years without Eating anything whatever', to 'a Paraphrase on Our Lord's Prayer, and a complete and infallible

Guide to everlasting Blessedness in Heaven'. On leaving the house after these addresses the visitors were deeply moved to see displayed in the hall the piles of crutches left by former patients who had been successfully electrified.

We now come to the *pièce de résistance* of this elaborate spectacle – the famous Celestial Bed. This structure, for it was no less, measured twelve feet long by nine feet wide, and was supported by 'forty pillars of brilliant glass, of great strength'. It stood in a room apart, known according to some accounts as the Great Apollo Chamber, and visitors were conducted there as to the innermost mystery of the Temple. A 'super-celestial dome' was raised above the bed, on top of which were placed, 'in the most loving attitudes', two exquisite figures, representing the marriage of Cupid and Psyche. The mattress was filled, not with common feathers or wool, but with rose leaves, lavender, and oriental spices; musical instruments incorporated in the supporting pillars breathed forth celestial sounds; and the sheets, of softest silk or satin were, 'suited to the complexion of the lady who is to repose on them'.

The reader will have gathered by now that the purpose of the bed was procreation, and indeed Dr Graham pronounced it to be an infallible cure for sterility. It was hired out at first for £50 a night, but the demand was so great that this was eventually raised to £500. The special attraction of the bed, apart from those already described, was of course its electrical and magnetic properties. Graham writes:

'The chief elastic principle of my celestial bed is produced by artificial load-stones. About fifteen hunded pounds weight of artificial and compound magnets, are so disposed and arranged, as to be continually pouring forth in an ever-flowing circle, inconceivable and irresistibly powerful tides of the magnetic effluvium, which every philosophical gentleman knows, has a very strong affinity with the electrical fire. These magnets too, being pressed give that charming springyness – that sweet undulating, tittulating, vibratory, soul-dissolving, marrow-melting motion; which on certain critical and important occasions, is at once so necessary and so pleasing.'

No wonder the bed could transform, in Graham's phrase, 'the *moment critique* into *l'heure critique*', and ensure that under 'the invigorating influences of music and magnets... strong, beautiful, brilliant, nay double-distilled children . . . must infallibly be begotten'.

As a postscript to this remarkable tale a word must be said about the erotic performances that accompanied Dr Graham's lectures, and which also doubtless gave further stimulus to users of the Celestial Bed. An outstanding member of this cast was Dr Graham's assistant, a kind of vestal virgin to the Temple, named Hebe Vestina, the Rosy Goddess of Health. This well-proportioned lady played a leading rôle in the display of the Celestial Meteors and of the Sacred Vital Fire, and was even exhibited in the nude on the Celestial Bed itself to enthusiastic representatives of the nobility and gentry.

The salacious quality of the performances at the Temple was sometimes too great even for an age which prided itself on its intellectual freedom and tolerant attitude towards sex. Thus one contemporary writer, quoted by Harvey Graham in *Eternal Eve*, denounced the whole elaborate ritual as 'an offensive absurdity and obscenity, thinly veiled by hocus-pocus, dim lights and soft music'. He took particular exception to 'the slow dances of half-naked wenches, notably one Emma Lyon, late a servant maid in the house of Dr Budd'. Here, however, few seemed to have agreed with him. The lady in question was destined to play an exceptionally important part in the later history of the bed, not least in the art of sharing it with the right people. She left Dr Graham's establishment about the beginning of 1780 and became the mistress of Sir Harry Fetherstonhaugh, a wealthy Sussex landowner, a man with more fortune than brain. When at last even he tired of her dissolute habits and threw her out, she accepted the somewhat dubious hospitality of the Honourable Charles Greville, a well-known sportsman and man-about-town. Due partly to that inexplicable spirit of generosity towards bookmakers which seems to characterise all racing men, and partly to Emma's own extravagant tastes, Greville was soon brought to the verge of bankruptcy. However, his uncle, Sir William Hamilton, kindly agreed to pay his debts on condition that the beautiful Miss Hart, as Emma was then calling herself, was ceded to him in exchange. This was, of course, an arrangement well suited to the interests of all concerned, but it was still not the end of the road for Emma. Having succeeded in becoming the wife of a famous diplomat and antiquary she was encouraged to raise her sights still higher. Thus Emma Lyon, alias Emma Hart, alias Emma Hamilton, erotic dancer and high priestess of electro-magnetical therapy, arrived at last, a little shop-soiled perhaps but still vigorous, in the bed of Horatio, Lord Nelson, to make a small but very special contribution to the winning of the Battle of Trafalgar. With these achievements to her credit it is not surprising that her legend has lasted for a hundred and fifty years.

From THE PHILOSOPHY OF THE BED, *by Mary Eden and Richard Carrington*

The Great Bed of Ware

LARGE beds have always been a source of fascination, and in England we are inclined to regard the Great Bed of Ware with special awe in this respect. Its name is taken from the town of Ware in Hertfordshire, where it formerly stood in an inn known as the Saracen's Head. It was moved from there to Hampton Court, among other places, and eventually arrived at the Victoria and Albert Museum, where it can still be seen to this day. The bed is a gigantic four-poster, measuring nearly twelve feet square and rising well over seven feet to the top of the canopy. Its age is unknown and some say that it dates from the fourteenth century. This is probably an exaggeration, however, for its style suggests that it is unlikely to have been made before the reign of Elizabeth I. That Shakespeare knew about it is proved by the passage in *Twelfth Night* where Sir Toby Belch is encouraging Sir Andrew Aguecheek to challenge Viola to a duel: 'Go, write in a martial hand . . . and as many lies as will lie in thy sheet of paper, although the sheet were big enough for the bed of Ware in England, set 'em down.'

There were numerous tales connected with the bed, of course, including a belief that it was haunted by the ghost of its maker, one Jonas Fosbrooke. The ghost did not usually manifest itself visibly, but its presence was made only too evident by the pinches and scratches with which it used to harry those who slept in the bed. In spite of such deterrents people came from far and wide to try it out, and the Saracen's Head did excellent business on the strength of the bed alone. The room in which it stood was sometimes let out to ten or twelve persons at a time who wished to test the bed's capacity; more usually, however, it bore the conventional complement of two. Seventeenth-century merchants were quite as ready to think up reasons for a business week-end away from their wives as are their counterparts today, and the Saracen's Head, with its great bed, was just the place for a spectacular seduction.

From THE PHILOSOPHY OF THE BED, *by Mary Eden and Richard Carrington*

The Lass that Made the Bed to Me

When Januar' wind was blawin cauld,
   As to the North I took my way,
The mirksome night did me enfauld,
   I knew na where to lodge till day.
But by guid luck a maid I met
   Just in the middle o' my care,
And kindly she did me invite
   To walk into a chamber fair.

I bow'd fu' low unto this maid,
   And thank'd her for her courtesie;
I bow'd fu' low unto this maid,
   An' bade her make a bed to me.
She made the bed baith large and wide,
   Wi' twa white hands she spread it down,
She put the cup to her rosy lips,
   And drank:— 'Young man, now sleep ye soun'.'

She snatch'd the candle in her hand,
   And frae my chamber went wi' speed,
But I call'd her quickly back again

To lay some mair below my head:
A cod she laid below my head,
   And servèd me with due respeck,
And, to salute her wi' a kiss,
   I put my arms about her neck.

'Haud aff your hands, young man,!' she said,
   'And dinna sae uncivil be;
Gif ye hae onie luve for me,
   O, wrang not my virginitie!'
Her hair was like the links o' gowd,
   Her teeth were like the ivorie,
Her cheeks like lilies dipt in wine,
   The lass that made the bed to me!

Her bosom was the driven snaw,
   Twa drifted heaps sae fair to see;
Her limbs the polish'd marble stane,
   The lass that made the bed to me!
I kiss'd her o'er and o'er again,
   And ay she wist na what to say.
I laid her 'tween me and the wa' –
   That lassie thocht na lang till day.

Upon the morrow, when we raise,
   I thank'd her for her courtesie;
But ay she blush'd and ay she sigh'd,
   And said:- 'Alas, ye've ruined me!'
I clasp'd her waist, and kiss'd her syne,
   While the tear stood twinkling in her e'e,
I said:- 'My lassie, dinna cry,
   For ye ay shall mak the bed to me.'

She took her mither's holland sheets,
   An' made them a' in sarks[1] to me,
Blythe and merry may she be,
   The lass that made the bed to me!
The bonie lass made the bed to me,
   The braw lass made the bed to me!
I'll ne'er forget till the day I die,
   The lass that made the bed to me.

Robert Burns

1. Sarks: Shirts.

Bedmate

Dr John Brown, in 'Horæ Subseivcæ', tells a story of Thomas Campbell the poet:

FROM TWEEDSMUIR we walked by the Bield, the old inn, where the Moffat carriers baited or slept . . . Campbell, the poet, in his young days, had walked out thus far, and had got snug into bed after his tumbler of toddy, when there was a knock at the door. 'Come in'; and behold, with a candle in her hand, stood the pretty maiden who had given him his supper – in her short-gown and petticoat. 'Please, sir, could ye tak' a neebor into yer bed?' 'With all my heart,' said the imaginative, susceptible poet, starting gaily up. 'Thank ye, sir, for the Moffat carrier's just come in a' wat, and there's no a single ither place.' Up came the huge and reeking man; exit the dainty little woman.

From A BOOK OF ANECDOTES, *by Daniel George*

JAMES THURBER

The Night the Bed Fell

I SUPPOSE that the high-water mark of my youth in Columbus, Ohio, was the night the bed fell on my father. It makes a better recitation (unless, as some friends of mine have said, one has heard it five or six times) than it does a piece of writing, for it is almost necessary to throw furniture around, shake doors, and bark like a dog, to lend the proper atmosphere and verisimilitude to what is admittedly a somewhat incredible tale. Still, it did take place.

It happened, then, that my father had decided to sleep in the attic one night, to be away where he could think. My mother opposed the notion strongly because, she said, the old wooden bed up there was unsafe; it was wobbly and the heavy headboard would crash down on father's head in case the bed fell, and kill him. There was no dissuading him, however, and at a quarter past ten he closed the attic door behind him and went up the narrow twisting stairs. We later heard ominous creakings as he crawled into bed. Grandfather, who usually slept in the attic bed when he was with us, had disappeared some days before. (On these occasions he was usually gone six or eight days and returned growling and out of temper, with the news that the federal Union was run by a passel of blockheads and that the Army of the Potomac didn't have any more chance than a fiddler's bitch.)

We had visiting us at the time a nervous first cousin of mine named Briggs Beall, who believed that he was likely to cease breathing while he was asleep. It was his feeling that if he were not awakened every hour during the night, he might die of suffocation.

He had been accustomed to setting an alarm clock to ring at intervals until morning, but I persuaded him to abandon this. He slept in my room and I told him that I was such a light sleeper that if anybody quit breathing in the same room with me, I would wake instantly. He tested me the first night – which I had suspected he would – by holding his breath after my regular breathing had convinced him I was asleep. I was not asleep, however, and called to him. This seemed to allay his fears a little, but he took the precaution of putting a glass of spirits of camphor on a little table at the head of his bed. In case I didn't arouse him until he was almost gone, he said, he would sniff at the camphor, a powerful reviver. Briggs was not the only member of his family who had his crotchets. Old Aunt Melissa Beall (who could whistle like a man, with two fingers in her mouth) suffered under the premonition that she was destined to die on South High Street, because she had been born on South High Street and married on South High Street. Then there was Aunt Sarah Shoaf, who never went to bed at night without the fear that a burglar was going to get in and blow chloroform under her door through a tube. To avert this calamity – for she was in greater dread of anesthetics than of losing her household goods – she always piled her money, silverware, and other valuables in a neat stack just outside her bedroom, with a note reading: 'This is all I have. Please take it and do not use your chloroform, as this is all I have.' Aunt Gracie Shoaf also had a burglar phobia, but she met it with more fortitude. She was confident that burglars had been getting into her house every night for forty years. The fact that she never missed anything was to her no proof to the contrary. She always claimed that she scared them off before they could take anything, by throwing shoes down the hallway. When she went to bed she piled, where she could get at them handily, all the shoes there were about her house. Five minutes after she had turned the light off she would sit up in bed and say 'Hark!' Her husband, who had learned to ignore the whole situation as long ago as 1903, would either be sound asleep or pretend to be sound asleep. In either case he would not respond to her tugging and pulling, so that presently she would arise, tiptoe to the door, open it slightly and heave a shoe down the hall in one direction, and its mate down the hall in the other direction. Some nights she threw them all, some nights only a couple of pair.

But I am straying from the remarkable incidents that took place during the night that the bed fell on father. By midnight we were all in bed. The layout of the rooms and the disposition of their occupants is important to an understanding of what later occurred. In the front room upstairs (just under father's attic bedroom) were my mother and my brother Herman, who sometimes sang in his sleep, usually 'Marching Through Georgia' or 'Onward, Christian Soldiers'. Briggs Beall and myself were in a room adjoining this one. My brother Roy was in a room across the hall from ours. Our bull terrier, Rex, slept in the hall.

My bed was an army cot, one of those affairs which are made wide enough to sleep on comfortably only by putting up, flat with the middle section, the two sides which ordinarily hang down like the side-boards of a drop-leaf table. When these sides are up, it is perilous to roll too far toward the edge, for then the cot is likely to tip completely over, bringing the whole bed down on top of one, with a tremendous banging crash. This, in fact, is precisely what happened, about two o'clock in the morning. (It was my mother who, in recalling the scene later, first referred to it as 'the night the bed fell on your father'.)

Always a deep sleeper, slow to arouse (I had lied to Briggs), I was at first unconscious of what had happened when the iron cot rolled me onto the floor and toppled over on

Some nights she threw them all

me. It left me still warmly bundled up and unhurt, for the bed rested above me like a canopy. Hence I did not wake up, only reached the edge of consciousness and went back. The racket, however, instantly awakened my mother, in the next room, who come to the immediate conclusion that her worst dread was realised: the big wooden bed upstairs had fallen on father. She therefore screamed, 'Let's go to your poor father!' It was this shout, rather than the noise of my cot falling, that awakened Herman, in the same room with her. He thought that mother had become, for no apparent reason, hysterical. 'You're all right, Mamma!' he shouted, trying to calm her. They exchanged shout for shout for perhaps ten seconds: 'Let's go to your poor father!' and 'You're all right!' That woke up Briggs. By this time I was conscious of what was going on, in a vague way, but did not yet realise that I was under my bed instead of on it. Briggs, awakening in the midst of loud shouts of fear and apprehension, came to the quick conclusion that he was suffocating and that we were all trying to 'bring him out'. With a low moan, he grasped the glass of camphor at the head of his bed and instead of sniffing it poured it over himself. The room reeked of camphor. 'Ugf, ahfg,' choked Briggs, like a drowning man, for he had almost succeeded in stopping his breath under the deluge of pungent spirits. He leaped out of bed and groped toward the open window, but he came up against one that was closed. With his hand, he beat out the glass, and I could hear it crash and tinkle on the alleyway below. It was at this juncture that I, in trying to

He came to the conclusion that he was suffocating

get up, had the uncanny sensation of feeling my bed above me! Foggy with sleep, I now suspected, in my turn, that the whole uproar was being made in a frantic endeavour to extricate me from what must be an unheard-of and perilous situation. 'Get me out of this!' I bawled. 'Get me out!' I think I had the nightmarish belief that I was entombed in a mine. 'Gugh,' gasped Briggs, floundering in his camphor.

By this time my mother, still shouting, pursued by Herman, still shouting, was trying to open the door of the attic, in order to go up and get my father's body out of the wreckage. The door was stuck, however, and wouldn't yield. Her frantic pulls on it only added to the general banging and confusion. Roy and the dog were now up, the one shouting questions, the other barking.

Father, farthest away and soundest sleeper of all, had by this time been awakened by the battering on the attic door. He decided that the house was on fire. 'I'm coming, I'm coming!' he wailed in a slow, sleepy voice – it took him many minutes to regain full consciousness. My mother, still believing he was caught under the bed, detected in his

'I'm coming!' the mournful, resigned note of one who is preparing to meet his Maker. 'He's dying!' she shouted.

'I'm all right!' Briggs yelled to reassure her. 'I'm all right!' He still believed that it was his own closeness to death that was worrying mother. I found at last the light switch in my room, unlocked the door, and Briggs and I joined the others at the attic door. The dog, who never did like Briggs, jumped for him – assuming that he was the culprit in whatever was going on – and Roy had to throw Rex to hold him. We could hear father crawling out of bed upstairs. Roy pulled the attic door open, with a mighty jerk, and father came down the stairs, sleepy and irritable but safe and sound. My mother began to weep when she saw him. Rex began to howl. 'What in the name of God is going on here?' asked father.

The situation was finally put together like a gigantic jig-saw puzzle. Father caught a cold from prowling around in his bare feet but there were no other bad results. 'I'm glad,' said mother, who always looked on the bright side of things, 'that your grandfather wasn't here.'

From THE THURBER CARNIVAL, *written and illustrated by James Thurber*

Ron had to throw Rex

WILKIE COLLINS

A Terribly Strange bed

*A young Englishman in Paris tells the story of how, one night, he visits a gambling house –
'as blackguard a place as you could possibly wish to see'. He plays Rouge et Noir, is incred-
ibly lucky – and breaks the bank. His coffee is drugged. Bewildered, he is persuaded to take
a bed in the house for the night. He continues his story . . .*

I HAD but two ideas left: – one, that I must never let go hold of my handkerchief full of
money; the other, that I must lie down somewhere immediately, and fall off into a
comfortable sleep. So I agreed to the proposal about the bed, and took the offered arm
of the old soldier, carrying my money with my disengaged hand. Preceded by the
croupier, we passed along some passages and up a flight of stairs into the bedroom which
I was to occupy. The ex-brave shook me warmly by the hand, proposed that we should
breakfast together, and then, followed by the croupier, left me for the night.

I ran to the wash-hand stand; drank some of the water in my jug; poured the rest
out, and plunged my face into it; then sat down in a chair and tried to compose myself.
I soon felt better. The change for my lungs, from the fetid atmosphere of the gambling-
room to the cool air of the apartment I now occupied; the almost equally refreshing
change for my eyes, from the glaring gas-lights of the 'Salon' to the dim, quiet flicker
of one bedroom candle, aided wonderfully the restorative effects of cold water. The
giddiness left me, and I began to feel a little like a reasonable being again. My first
thought was of the risk of sleeping all night in a gambling-house; my second, of the
still greater risk of trying to get out after the house was closed, and of going home
alone at night, through the streets of Paris, with a large sum of money about me. I had
slept in worse places than this on my travels; so I determined to lock, bolt and barricade
my door, and take my chance till the next morning.

Accordingly, I secured myself against all intrusion; looked under the bed, and into the
cupboard; tried the fastening of the window; and then, satisfied that I had taken every
proper precaution, pulled off my upper clothing, put my light, which was a dim one,
on the hearth among a feathery litter of wood ashes, and got into bed, with the handkerchief full of money under my pillow.

I soon felt not only that I could not go to sleep, but that I could not even close my
eyes. I was wide awake, and in a high fever. Every nerve in my body trembled – every
one of my senses seemed to be preternaturally sharpened. I tossed and rolled, and tried
every kind of position, and perseveringly sought out the cold corners of the bed, and
all to no purpose. Now, I thrust my arms over the clothes; now, I poked them under

186

the clothes; now, I violently shot my legs straight out down to the bottom of the bed; now, I convulsively coiled them up as near my chin as they would go; now, I shook out my crumpled pillow, changed it to the cool side patted it flat, and lay down quietly on my back; now, I fiercely doubled it in two, set it up on end, thrust it against the board of the bed, and tried a sitting posture. Every effort was in vain; I groaned with vexation, as I felt that I was in for a sleepless night.

What could I do? I had no book to read. And yet, unless I found out some method of diverting my mind, I felt certain that I was in the condition to imagine all sorts of horrors; to rack my brain with forebodings of every possible and impossible danger; in short, to pass the night in suffering all conceivable varieties of nervous terror.

I raised myself on my elbow, and looked about the room – which was brightened by a lovely moonlight pouring straight through the window – to see if it contained any pictures or ornaments that I could at all clearly distinguish. While my eyes wandered from wall to wall, a remembrance of Le Maistre's delightful little book, *Voyage autour de ma Chambre*, occurred to me. I resolved to imitate the French author, and find occupation and amusement enough to relieve the tedium of my wakefulness, by making a mental inventory of every article of furniture I could see, and by following up to their sources the multitude of associations which even a chair, a table, or a wash-hand stand may be made to call forth.

In the nervous unsettled state of my mind at that moment, I found it much easier to make my inventory than to make my reflections, and thereupon soon gave up all hope of thinking in Le Maistre's fanciful track – or, indeed, of thinking at all. I looked about the room at the different articles of furniture, and did nothing more.

There was, first, the bed I was lying in; a four-post bed, of all things in the world to meet with in Paris! – yes, a thorough clumsy British four-poster, with the regular top lined with chintz – the regular fringed valance all round – the regular stifling un-wholesome curtains, which I remembered having mechanically drawn back against the posts without particularly noticing the bed when I first got into the room. Then there was the marble-topped wash-hand stand, from which the water I had spilt, in my hurry to pour it out, was still dripping, slowly and more slowly, on to the brick floor. Then two small chairs, with my coat, waistcoat, and trousers flung on them. Then a large elbow-chair covered with dirty-white dimity, with my cravat and shirt-collar thrown over the back. Then a chest of drawers with two of the brass handles off, and a tawdry, broken china inkstand placed on it by way of ornament for the top. Then the dressing-table, adorned by a very small looking-glass, and a very large pincushion. Then the window – an unusually large window. Then a dark old picture, which the feeble candle dimly showed me. It was the picture of a fellow in a high Spanish hat, crowned with a plume of towering feathers. A swarthy sinister ruffian, looking upward, shading his eyes with his hand, and looking intently upward – it might be at some tall gallows at which he was going to be hanged. At any rate, he had the appearance of thoroughly deserving it.

This picture put a kind of constraint upon me to look upward too – at the top of the bed. It was a gloomy and not an interesting object, and I looked back at the picture. I counted the feathers in the man's hat – they stood out in relief – three white, two green. I observed the crown of his hat, which was of a conical shape, according to the fashion supposed to have been favoured by Guido Fawkes. I wondered what he was looking up at. It couldn't be at the stars; such a desperado was neither astrologer nor astronomer. It must be at the high gallows, and he was going to be hanged presently. Would the executioner come into possession of his conical-crowned hat and plume of feathers? I counted the feathers again – three white, two green.

While I still lingered over this very improving and intellectual employment, my thoughts insensibly began to wander. The moonlight shining into the room reminded me of a certain moonlight night in England – the night after a picnic party in a Welsh valley. Every incident of the drive homeward, through lovely scenery, which the moon-light made lovelier than ever, came back to my remembrance, though I had never given the picnic a thought for years; though if I had *tried* to recollect it, I could certainly have recalled little or nothing of that scene long past. Of all the wonderful faculties that help to tell us we are immortal, which speaks the sublime truth more eloquently than memory? Here was I, in a strange house of the most suspicious character, in a situation of uncertainty, and even of peril, which might seem to make the cool exercise of my recollection almost out of the question; nevertheless, remembering, quite involuntarily, places, people, conversations, minute circumstances of every kind, which I had thought forgotten for ever; which I could not possibly have recalled at will, even under the most favourable auspices. And what cause had produced in a moment the whole of this strange, complicated, mysterious effect? Nothing but some rays of moonlight shining in at my bedroom window.

I was still thinking of the picnic – of our merriment on the drive home – of the sentimental young lady who *would* quote *Childe Harold* because it was moonlight. I was absorbed by these past scenes and past amusements, when, in an instant, the thread on which my memories hung snapped asunder; my attention immediately came back to present things more vividly than ever and I found myself, I neither knew why nor wherefore, looking hard at the picture again.

Looking for what!

Good God! the man had pulled his hat down on his brows! – No! the hat itself was gone! Where was the conical crown! Where the feathers – three white, two green? Not there? In place of the hat and feathers, what dusky object was it that now hid his forehead, his eyes, his shading hand?

Was the bed moving?

I turned on my back and looked up. Was I mad? drunk? dreaming? giddy again? or was the top of the bed really moving down – sinking slowly, regularly, silently, horribly, right down throughout the whole of its length and breadth – right down upon me, as I lay underneath?

My blood seemed to stand still. A deadly paralysing coldness stole all over me, as I turned my head round on the pillow, and determined to test whether the bed-top was really moving or not, by keeping my eye on the man in the picture.

The next look in that direction was enough. The dull, black, frowsy outline of the valance above me was within an inch of being parallel with his waist. I still looked breathlessly. And steadily, and slowly – very slowly – I saw the figure, and the line of frame below the figure, vanish as the valance moved down before it.

I am, constitutionally, anything but timid. I have been on more than one occasion in peril of my life, and have not lost my self-possession for an instant; but when the conviction first settled on my mind that the bed-top was really moving, was steadily and continuously sinking down upon me, I looked up shuddering, helpless, panic-stricken, beneath the hideous machinery for murder, which was advancing closer and closer to suffocate me where I lay.

I looked up, motionless, speechless, breathless. The candle, fully spent, went out; but the moonlight still brightened the room. Down and down, without pausing and without sounding, came the bed-top, and still my panic-terror seemed to bind me faster and faster to the mattress on which I lay – down and down it sank, till the dusty odour from the lining of the canopy came stealing into my nostrils.

At that final moment the instinct of self-preservation startled me out of my trance, and I moved at last. There was just room for me to roll myself sideways off the bed. As I dropped noiselessly to the floor, the edge of the murderous canopy touched me on the shoulder.

Without stopping to draw my breath, without wiping the cold sweat from my face, I rose instantly on my knees to watch the bed-top. I was literally spell-bound by it. If I had heard footsteps behind me, I could not have turned round; if a means of escape had been miraculously provided for me, I could not have moved to take advantage of it. The whole life in me was, at that moment, concentrated in my eyes.

It descended – the whole canopy, with the fringe round it, came down – down – close down; so close that there was not room now to squeeze my finger between the bed-top and the bed. I felt at the sides, and discovered that what had appeared to me from beneath to be the ordinary light canopy of a four-post bed, was in reality a thick, broad mattress, the substance of which was concealed by the valance and its fringe. I looked up and saw the four posts rising hideously bare. In the middle of the bed-top was a huge wooden screw that had evidently worked it down through a hole in the ceiling, just as ordinary presses are worked down on the substance selected for compression. The frightful apparatus moved without making the faintest noise. There had been no creaking as it came down; there was now not the faintest sound from the room above. Amid a dead and awful silence I beheld before me – in the nineteenth century, and in the civilised capital of France – such a machine for secret murder by suffocation as might have existed in the worst days of the Inquisition, in the lonely inns among the Hartz Mountains, in the mysterious tribunals of Westphalia! Still, as I looked on it, I could not move, I could hardly breathe, but I began to recover the power of thinking, and in a moment I discovered the murderous conspiracy framed against me in all its horror.

My cup of coffee had been drugged, and drugged too strongly. I had been saved from being smothered by having taken an overdose of some narcotic. How I had chafed and fretted at the fever-fit which had preserved my life by keeping me awake! How recklessly I had confided myself to the two wretches who had led me into this room, determined, for the sake of my winnings, to kill me in my sleep by the surest and most horrible contrivance for secretly accomplishing my destruction! How many men, winners like me, had slept, as I had proposed to sleep, in that bed, and had never been seen or heard of more! I shuddered at the bare idea of it.

But ere long, all thought was again suspended by the sight of the murderous canopy moving once more. After it had remained on the bed – as nearly as I could guess – about ten minutes, it began to move up again. The villains who worked it from above evidently believed that their purpose was now accomplished. Slowly and silently, as it had descended, that horrible bed-top rose towards its former place. When it reached the upper extremities of the four posts, it reached the ceiling too. Neither hole nor screw could be seen; the bed became in appearance an ordinary bed again – the canopy an ordinary canopy – even to the most suspicious eyes.

Now, for the first time, I was able to move – to rise from my knees – to dress myself in my upper clothing – and to consider of how I could escape. If I betrayed, by the smallest noise, that the attempt to suffocate me had failed, I was certain to be murdered. Had I made any noise already? I listened intently, looking towards the door.

No! no footsteps in the passage outside – no sound of a tread, light or heavy, in the room above – absolute silence everywhere. Besides locking and bolting my door, I had moved an old wooden chest against it, which I had found under the bed. To remove this chest (my blood ran cold as I thought of what its contents *might* be! without making some disturbance was impossible; and, moreover, to think of escaping through the house, now barred up for the night, was sheer insanity. Only one chance was left me – the window. I stole to it on tiptoe.

My bedroom was on the first floor, above an *entresol*, and looked into the back street, which you have sketched in your view. I raised my hand to open the window, knowing that on that action hung, by the merest hair's-breadth, my chance of safety. They keep vigilant watch in a House of Murder. If any part of the frame cracked, if the hinge creaked, I was a lost man! It must have occupied me at least five minutes, reckoning by time – five *hours*, reckoning by suspense – to open that window. I succeeded in doing it silently – in doing it with all the dexterity of a housebreaker – and then looked down into the street. To leap the distance beneath me would be almost certain destruction! Next, I looked round at the sides of the house. Down the left side ran the thick water-pipe which you have drawn – it passed close by the outer edge of the window. The moment I saw the pipe, I knew I was saved. My breath came and went freely for the first time since I had seen the canopy of the bed moving down upon me! . . .

An extract from THE TRAVELLER'S STORY OF A TERRIBLY STRANGE BED,
by William Wilkie Collins (1824–1889)

From 'Rape of the Fair Country', Alexander Cordell's powerful novel on the lives of the Welsh iron-workers in the early 'nineties, comes this account of

A Bed with a History

As LONG as I live I will remember the coming of Iolo's iron bed.

Jethro saw it first and came in whooping like an Indian and pointing. Up the hill laboured Enid Donkey with the bed over her back and steadied either side by Iolo's Irish friends. And up to the door came Iolo, dressed in his Sunday best with the mock carnation he wore especially for women-killing and his white teeth flashing.

'Good afternoon, Mrs Mortymer,' said he. 'Here is a good strong bed fit to hold a fighter for the community,' and he swept off his cap into the gutter with a nobility and grace that would have brought joy to the Young Queen.

'God bless you, Iolo,' said Mam, all blushes.

'And the same to you, girl,' he replied. 'I am having a better welcome this time than last, remember? Flat down by here your man hit me, and I came with the same honourable intentions as now, mind.'

'But he was not himself that day, boy. Eh dear! There is a strong iron bed,' said she, patting it.

'Very comfortable the pair of you will be, Mrs Mortymer, for I have spent enjoyable hours on this feather mattress. And with a woman of your proportions a man would be a fool not to follow my example, no offence intended.'

'O, Iolo!' giggled Mam.

'In with it,' I said to him, 'no need for details,' for the neighbours were gathering and whispering. Giggles, too, for everybody knew that Iolo used his beds for anything but sleeping in.

'How now?' asked Iolo, when it was set up for examination.

'Wonderful,' said Mam, and everybody nodded, for the window was up and the door open and half the neighbours were in or coming.

'Then up with a broom to scatter the crowd,' shouted Iolo, 'for we need a bit of privacy. There is a history to this four-poster, Mrs Mortymer, and I am just in the mood to tell it.'

'Hush, you!' I said, elbowing him while the neighbours roared and my mother went scarlet.

'*Diawl!*' he cried. 'Here is an example of false modesty. With little Iestyn scarcely out of his woollens it is understandable, woman, but for the likes of you and me, girl, we could teach this old bed a thing or two, look you. *Dammo!* Do not look so grieved, Elianor. A very fine friend is a bed, with blankets over it in cold and nothing at all in hot, and every other page of the Good Book talking about courtings, deaths and births between four posts. And look you how soft!' Up with him then and down on it and bounced three feet. 'Now settle yourself here with me, Elianor, and we will christen the thing, for to lie full length with a milkman in the sight of neighbours is going half way to a fortune.'

'O, Iolo!' giggled Mam. 'Hell and damnation on you for such a suggestion, and me married!' And she peeped and wriggled like a maid. 'True, is it?'

'*Mam!*' I said.

'Whoo, there!' cried Iolo, getting ferocious. 'Here is a sixpence to clear the neighbours while I tell your mam the story of this very fine bed, Iestyn.'

'Good afternoon,' I said. 'We have had enough of you.'

'Enough? And with your little mam here just coming girlish? I would harm her, you think? In the same house as her man who has taken a flogging? Cleanse your mind, my boy. When the great call comes I will be there in the Upper Palace under the hand of St Peter while you brew tea in the coals of hell. Eh dear, Mrs Mortymer, forgive the rising generation who do turn a little harmless fun into an improper suggestion.'

'Do not heed him, Iolo,' she replied, keen now. 'What about the history of the bed?'

'It is a pleasant history in truth,' said Iolo, sighing. 'Megan and me were two years married and childless when this bed came to us – through the family, you understand, after knowing nothing but happy lovers and easy births. My grandfather from Carmarthen bought it in London from a travelling tinker who was in tears at parting with it, for his three wives had rested their fair limbs in it, cleaving in joy before dying in peace on it. Fifteen children had that tinker, all on this bed, mind, and two wives had my grandfather and each brought forth six. And since we are four now and Megan waiting for the fifth you cannot but respect an article that bore half the population of Carmarthen before coming to Monmouthshire to start all over again.'

'Wonderful!' everybody cried.

'Aye,' said Iolo, 'so you can have it with my blessing, for with Megan full again I would rather she slept on heather than this old mattress. Out with the old thing, Megan said, and take it down to Hywel Mortymer, who has less chance of being caught turning than me.'

Which put everybody double, of course.

'And proper, too,' said my mother, crimson again 'for some beds are suspicious things indeed, but my man will sleep soft upon it. A cup of tea before you go, Iolo?'

Inscription for an Old Bed

The wind's on the wold
And the night is a-cold,
And Thames runs chill
'Twixt mead and hill.
But kind and dear
Is the old house here
And my heart is warm
Midst winter's harm.
Rest then and rest,
And think of the best
'Twixt summer and spring,
When all birds sing
In the town of the tree,
And ye lie in me
And scarce dare move,
Lest the earth and its love
Should fade away
Ere the full of the day.
I am old and have seen
Many things that have been;
Both grief and peace
And wane and increase.
No tale I tell
Of ill or well,
But this I say:
Night treadeth on day,
And for worst or best
Right good is rest.

William Morris (1834–1896)

The Golden Chain

FOR DO but consider what an excellent thing sleep is; it is so inestimable a jewel, that, if a tyrant should give his crown for an hour's slumber, it cannot be bought: of so beautiful a shape is it, that, though a man lie with an empress, his heart cannot be at quiet till he leaves her embracements to be at rest with the other: yea, so greatly indebted are we to this kinsman of death, that we owe the better tributary half of our life to him; and there's good cause why we should do so, for sleep is that golden chain that ties health and our bodies together. Who complains of want, of wounds, of cares, of great men's oppressions, of captivity, whilst he sleepeth? Beggars in their beds take as much pleasure as kings. Can we therefore surfeit on this delicate ambrosia? Can we drink too much of that, whereof to taste too little tumbles us into a churchyard; and to use it but indifferently throws us into Bedlam? No, no! Look upon Endymion, the Moon's minion, who slept threescore and fifteen years; and was not a hair the worse for it.

THE GULL'S HORNBOOK, 1609, *by Thomas Dekker*

A Plea

Care-charmer Sleepe, sonne of the sable night,
Brother to death, in silent darkness borne:
Relieve my languish, and restore the light,
With darke forgetting of my cares returne.
   And let the day be time enough to morne
The shipwracke of my ill-adventred youth:
   Let waking eyes suffice to waile their scorne,
Without the torment of the nights untruth.
   Cease dreams, th'Images of day desires,
To modell foorth the passions of the morrow:
Never let rising Sunne approve you liers,
To adde more griefe to aggravate my sorrow.
   Still let me sleepe, imbracing clowdes in vaine;
   And never wake to feele the dayes disdayne.

Samuel Daniel (1562–1619)

EDWARD GIBBON

The Seven Sleepers

AMONG THE insipid legends of ecclesiastical history, I am tempted to distinguish the memorable fable of the Seven Sleepers; whose imaginary date corresponds with the reign of the younger Theodosius, and the conquest of Africa by the Vandals. When the emperor Decius persecuted the Christians, seven noble youths of Ephesus concealed themselves in a spacious cavern in the side of an adjacent mountain where they were doomed to perish by the tyrant, who gave orders that the entrance should be firmly secured with a pile of huge stones. They immediately fell into a deep slumber, which was miraculously prolonged, without injuring the powers of life, during a period of one hundred and eighty-seven years. At the end of that time, the slaves of Adolius, to whom the inheritance of the mountain had descended, removed the stones, to supply materials for some rustic edifice: the light of the sun darted into the cavern, and the Seven Sleepers were permitted to awake. After a slumber, as they thought of a few hours, they were pressed by the calls of hunger; and resolved that Jamblichus, one of their number, should secretly return to the city to purchase bread for the use of his companions. The youth (if we may still employ that appellation) could no longer recognise the once familiar aspect of his native country; and his surprise was increased by the appearance of a large cross, triumphantly erected over the principal gate of Ephesus. His singular dress and obsolete language confounded the baker, to whom he offered an ancient medal of Decius as the current coin of the empire; and Jamblichus, on the suspicion of a secret treasure, was dragged before the judge. Their mutual inquiries produced the amazing discovery that two centuries were almost elapsed since Jamblichus and his friends had escaped from the rage of the Pagan tyrant. The bishop of Ephesus, the clergy, the magistrates, the people, and, it is said, the emperor Theodosius himself, hastened to visit the cavern of the Seven Sleepers; who bestowed their benediction, related their story, and at the same instant peacably expired.

From THE DECLINE AND FALL OF THE ROMAN EMPIRE, *by Edward Gibbon* (1737–1794)

Michelangelo's 'Night'

A contemporary admirer wrote of Michelangelo's 'Night' that the figure, turned into stone by an angel, seemed to be only sleeping: 'if you believe not, wake it – it will speak'. Michelangelo replied with these lines:

THE SPEECH OF NIGHT

Sweet is my sleep, but more to be mere stone,
So long as ruin and dishonour reign;
To bear nought, to feel nought, is my great gain;
Then wake me not, speak in an undertone!

Detail of NIGHT, *from Ludwig Goldscheider's authoritative and beautiful book,* MICHELANGELO. (*The Phaidon Press*)

VISHNU SLEEPING ON THE SHESH SNAKE, Yamapuri Cave, Mahabalipuram, *by W. Suschitzky*

It was to this statue that Alexander Pope wrote these lines:

Nymph of the grot, these sacred springs I keep
And to the murmur of these waters sleep;
Ah! spare my slumbers, gently tread the cave
And drink in silence or in silence leave.

From Bill Brandt's book LITERARY BRITAIN

198

SLEEPING NYMPH in the gardens of Stourhead, Wiltshire, *by Bill Brandt*

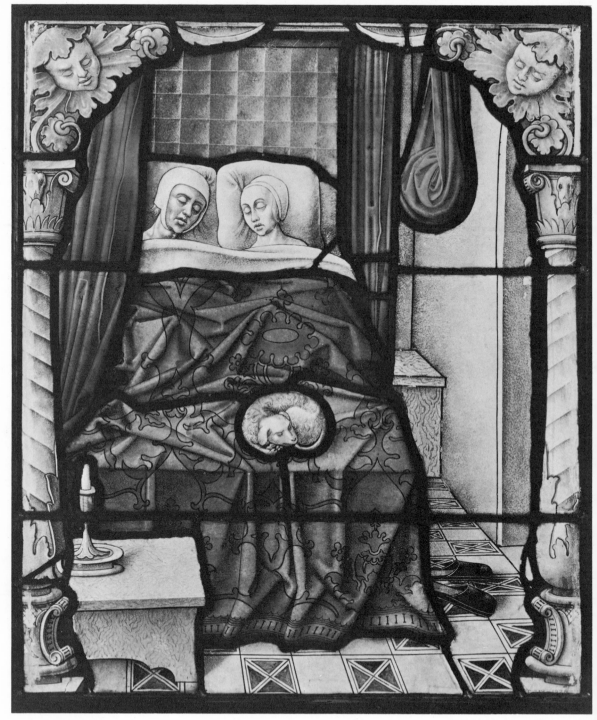

TOBIAS AND SARA: German stained glass panel, *c.* 1530

To Sleep

O soft embalmer of the still midnight!
Shutting with careful fingers and benign
Our gloom-pleased eyes, embower'd from the light,
   Enshaded in forgetfulness divine;
O soothest Sleep! if so it please thee, close,
   In midst of this thine hymn, my willing eyes,
Or wait the amen, ere thy poppy throws
   Around my bed its lulling charities;
   Then save me, or the passèd day will shine
Upon my pillow, breeding many woes;
Save me from curious conscience, that still lords
Its strength for darkness, burrowing like a mole
Turn the key deftly in the oilèd wards,
   And seal the hushèd casket of my soul.

John Keats (1795–1821)

Sleep

Others may praise thee, Sleep; so will not I.
   I loathe thee from the bottom of my heart.
Thou art a dull and ill-conceivèd lie,
   To turn quick nature into cunning art.

'The sleeping and the dead are pictures.' Yea,
   I love not pictures eyeless, soulless, still,
Mere portraits of the perishable clay,
   Bereft of reason, passion, strength, and will.

Others may woo thee, Sleep; so will not I.
   Dear is each minute of my conscious breath,
Hard fate, that ere the time be come to die,
   Myself, to live, must nightly mimic death.

Mary Coleridge (1861–1907)

Sleepers, by Greville

THE DUKE OF WELLINGTON

November 18, 1838, Wolbeding: . . . During the battles of the Pyrenees Cole proposed to the Duke and his staff to go and eat a very good dinner he had ordered for himself at his house in the village he occupied, as he could not leave his division. They went and dined, and then the Duke went into the next room threw, himself upon a bed without a mattress, on the boards of which he presently went to sleep with his despatch-box for a pillow. Fitzroy and the A.D.C. slept in chairs or on the floor scattered about. Presently arrived, in great haste and alarm, two officers of Artillery, Captain Cairne and another, who begged to see the Duke, the former saying that he had just brought up some Guns from the rear, and that he had suddenly found himself close to the Enemy and did not know what to do. They went and woke the Duke, who desired him to be brought in. The officer entered and told his story, when the Duke said, very composedly, 'Well, Sir, you are certainly in a very bad position, and you must get out of it in the best way you can,' turned around, and was asleep again in a moment . . .

GEORGE IV

March 19, 1829: . . . He [George IV] leads a most extraordinary life – never gets up till six in the afternoon. They come to him and open the window curtains at six or seven o'clock in the morning; he breakfasts in bed, does whatever business he can be brought to transact in bed too, he reads every newspaper quite through, dozes three or four hours, gets up in time for dinner, and goes to bed between ten and eleven. He sleeps very ill, and rings his bell forty times in the night; if he wants to know the hour, though a watch hangs close to him, he will have his *valet de chambre* down rather than turn his head to look at it. The same thing if he wants a glass of water; he won't stretch out his hand to get it. His valets are nearly destroyed, and at last Lady Conyngham prevailed on him to agree to an arrangement by which they wait on him on alternate days. The service is still most severe, as on days they are in waiting their labours are incessant, and they cannot take off their clothes at night, and hardly lie down . . .

LORD PALMERSTON

February 3, 1858: . . . He [Lord Palmerston] is always asleep both in the Cabinet and in the House of Commons, where he endeavours to conceal it by wearing his hat over his eyes. Clarendon made me laugh heartily the other day at his account of the Cabinet, where one half of them seem to be almost always asleep, the first to be off being Lansdowne, closely followed by Palmerston and Charles Wood. I remember his giving me a very droll account of Melbourne's Cabinet, and of the drowsiness which used to reign there, more particularly with Melbourne himself.

THE GREVILLE MEMOIRS

The Stuff that sleep is made of

IN A NUMBER of laboratories round the world, volunteers are now spending their nights in quiet cubicles, with wires attached to their heads.

The wires lead to gently humming amplifiers and delicate recording machines with which scientists are beginning to explore one of the most mysterious realms of human life – sleep and dreams.

One of the first, and most unexpected, results of this work is that we can suffer not only from sleep starvation but, apparently, from dream starvation. We all need sleep – although why we do is still not known. But the discovery that we also need to dream is a surprise, and has caused a flurry of interest among psychiatrists.

The experiments have disclosed that during a normal eight-hour sleep there are four to five periods when electrical brainwaves picked up by the wires show a change. At the same time, the eyeballs start to move.

If people are awakened during these periods, they recount vivid dreams – but if they are awakened during deep sleep periods they have nothing to report. Thus it has been concluded that the brainwave changes and eyeball movements reveal a dream in progress. Such experiments indicate that dreams get longer as the night proceeds.

Yesterday, psychiatrists at the University of California reported some of their latest experiments in *Nature*. Two volunteer subjects first slept for some nights in the laboratory so that the psychiatrists could record their normal sleep and dream pattern.

Then for six successive nights they were awakened every time their eyeballs started to move (i.e., as a dream was starting). Each night, they made more 'attempts to dream', and had to be awakened more often.

The subjects were next allowed two recovery nights, during which they spent about 30 per cent of the time dreaming compared to the normal 20 per cent. Then they submitted to a control experiment in which they were awakened an equal number of times during deep sleep, rather than in dreaming periods. This did not affect their dreaming at all.

This whole procedure was repeated later over ten nights, with the same two subjects, but using as an awakening cue electrical changes in face muscles which are found to precede eye movements. This reduced the time during which the subjects could snatch a quick bit of dream.

This seemed to result in an even higher number of 'attempts to dream'. One subject had to be awakened 51 times on the tenth night – and his dreaming time doubled on the first recovery night.

Earlier workers have suggested that such dream starvation might have dire psychic effects. During the day, however, these two subjects were given various psychological tests to see if dream deprivation was affecting their waking lives. But the test scores were unaffected by dream starvation.

However, when awakened using the muscle-change cue, both subjects reported vivid dreams, even though there was barely time to have any. One subject's dreams were bizarre and vivid, and he claimed they had lasted about a minute. The other subject reported briefer but still vivid dreams.

The California experimenters conclude that the subjects may have been able to 'speed up' their dreams to compensate for dream deprivation, thus snatching a considerable ration of dream during the brief periods before they could be awakened. These snatched dreams, the experimenters speculate, may be sufficient 'to prevent significant psychic changes'.

John Davy in 'The Observer', 1964

Parvenu

Where does Cinderella sleep?
By Heaven's jungle-river,
A secret place her burning Prince
Decks, while his heart-strings quiver.

Homesick for our cinder world,
Her low-born shoulders shiver;
She longs for sleep in cinders curled—
We, for the jungle-river.
Vachel Lindsay

The Middle of the Night

Open, box, for the child
Who lifts out, one by one,
Impudent and self-willed
Dolls from the living heap
– Their antics never done
Which took him from his sleep.

Lion and citizen,
Soldier in pose of fight,
A wicker stork, small men,
Small gods and animals . . .
The box is emptied out:
The floor is bright with dolls.

Year after year the same,
A town of perfect size.
Who calls it a mere game?
Round him, alive and shrunk
Each finished burgher lies,
Whose cargoes have been sunk.

He learns their histories –
Jerk, posture, giggle, prance,
And grows to recognise
In each doll, passive, faded,
Some man who is at once
Transfigured and degraded.

At length he writes it down,
Recording what befalls
Until the dark is gone.
Children who know by heart
The vices of their dolls
Will stay awake at night.

From MY SAD CAPTAINS AND OTHER POEMS, *by Thom Gunn*

Mystery of the Vanishing Shirts

*A strange instance of somnambulism is reported
in 'Ten Thousand Wonderful Things' (1860):*

SOME YEARS ago a Hampshire Baronet was nearly driven to distraction by the fact that, every night, he went to bed in a shirt, and every morning awoke naked, without the smallest trace of the missing garment being discovered.

Hundreds of shirts disappeared in this manner: and as there was no fire in his room, it was impossible to account for the mystery. The servants believed their master to be mad; and even he began to fancy himself bewitched. In this conjecture, he implored an intimate friend to sleep in the room with him; and ascertain by what manner of mysterious midnight visitant his garment was so strangely removed. The friend, accordingly, took up his station in the haunted chamber; and lo! as the clock struck one, the unfortunate Baronet, who had previously given audible intimation of being fast asleep, rose from his bed, rekindled with a match the candle which had been extinguished, deliberately opened the door, and quitted the room. His astonished friend followed; saw him open in succession a variety of doors, pass along several passages, traverse an open court, and eventually reach the stable-yard; where he divested himself of his shirt, and disposed of it in an old dung-heap, into which he thrust it by means of a pitchfork. Having finished this extraordinary operation, without taking the smallest heed of his friend who stood looking on, and plainly saw that he was walking in his sleep, reclosed the doors, re-extinguished the light, and returned to bed; where the following morning he awoke as usual, stripped of his shirt!

The astonished eye-witness of this extraordinary scene, instead of appraising the sleep-walker of what had occurred, insisted that the following night, a companion should sit up with him; choosing to have additional testimony to the truth of the statement he was about to make; and the same singular events were renewed, without the slightest change or deviation. The two witnesses, accordingly, divulged all they had seen to the Baronet; who, though at first incredulous, became of course convinced, when, on proceeding to the stable-yard, several dozens of shirts were discovered; though it was surmised that as many more had been previously removed by one of the helpers, who probably looked upon the hoard as stolen goods concealed by some thief.

From A BOOK OF ANECDOTES, *selected and edited by Daniel George*

Bed and Board

A LADY was awoke in the night with the disagreeable sense of not being alone in the room, and soon felt a thud upon her bed. There was no doubt that someone was moving to and fro in the room, and that hands were constantly moving over her bed. She was so dreadfully frightened, that at last she fainted. When she came to herself, it was broad daylight, and she found that the butler had walked in his sleep and had laid the table for fourteen upon her bed. *From* THE STORY OF MY LIFE (1896), *by Augustus Hare*

The Eye Awake

It is thy wil, thy Image should keepe open
My heavy eielids to the weary night?
Dost thou desire my slumbers should be broken,
While shadowes like to thee do mocke my sight?
Is it thy spirit that thou send'st from thee
So farre from home into my deeds to prye,
To find out shames and idle houres in me,
The skope and tenure of thy Jelousie?
O no, thy love though much, is not so great,
It is my love that keepes mine eie awake,
Mine owne true love that doth my rest defeat,
To plaie the watch-man ever for thy sake.
  For thee watch I, whilst thou dost wake elsewhere,
  From me farre off, with others all too neere.

William Shakespeare

Sonnet

Sleep, Silence' child, sweet father of soft rest,
Prince, whose approach peace to all mortals brings,
Indifferent host to shepherds and to kings,
Sole comforter of minds with grief oppressed;
Lo, by thy charming rod all breathing things
Lie slumb'ring with forgetfulness possessed,
And yet o'er me to spread thy drowsy wings
Thou spares, alas! who cannot be thy guest.
Since I am thine, oh, come, but with that face
To inward light which thou art wont to show,
Or if, deaf god, thou do deny that grace,
  Come as thou wilt, and what thou wilt bequeath,
  I long to kiss the image of my death.

POEMS, 1616: *William Drummond of Hawthornden* (1558–1649)

Sleepless

A flock of sheep that leisurely pass by,
One after one; the sound of rain, and bees
Murmuring; the fall of rivers, winds and seas,
Smooth fields, white sheets of water, and pure sky;
By turns have all been thought of; yet I lie
Sleepless, and soon the small birds' melodies
Must hear, first uttered from my orchard trees;
And the first cuckoo's melancholy cry.
Even thus last night, and two nights more, I lay,
And could not win thee, sleep! by any stealth;
So do not let me wear tonight away:
Without thee what is all the morning's wealth?
Come, blessed barrier betwixt day and day,
Dear mother of fresh thoughts and joyous health!

William Wordsworth

Watchyng or they that can nat slepe

The cause. This impediment doth come thorowe ydelnesse or wekenesse of ye brayne, or els thorowe sicknesse, anger or fastynge, or els thorowe solicitudnesse or replecion, or extreme heate, or extreme colde in the fete or suche lyke.

A remedy. Take of the oyle of violettes an ounce, of opium halfe an ounce, incorporate this togither with woman's milke and with a fyne lynnen cloth lay it to the temples, or els use to eat of letuce sedes, of white popy sedes, or mandragor sedes . . . of eche iii drams, but above all thynges myrthe is best to bedwarde.

BREVIARY OF HELTHE (1547), *by Andrew Boorde*

SHEEP ON THE WELSH HILLS, *by Otto Karminski*

Overleaf:
THE NIGHT WALKER, *by Thurston Hopkins*
STARLINGS, Victoria Embankment, *by Barnet Saidman*

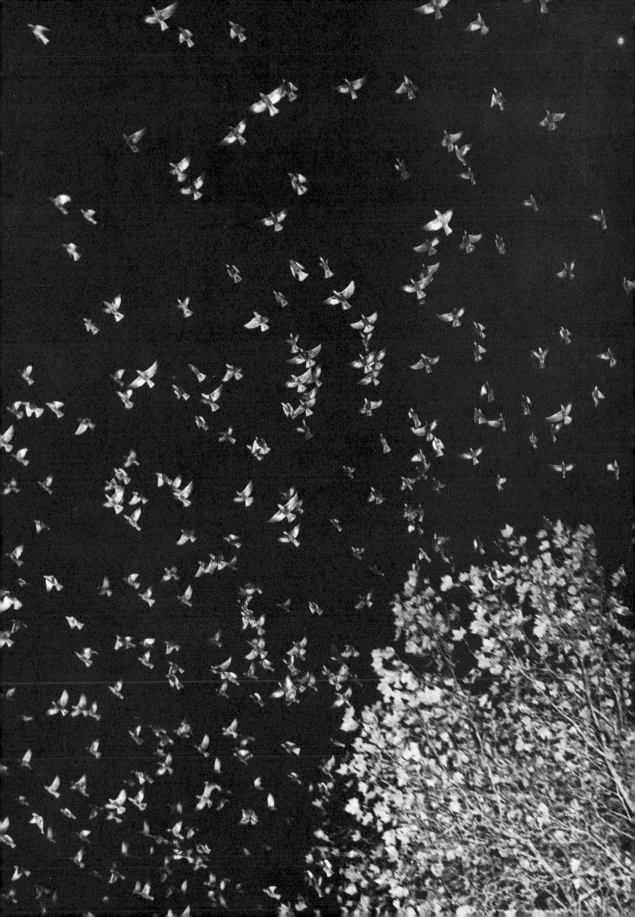

Dog Watch

I BEGAN my young marriage days in and near Philadelphia . . . In the middle of the burning hot month of July, I was greatly afraid of fatal consequences to my wife for want of sleep, she not having, after the great danger was over, had any sleep for more than forty-eight hours. All great cities, in hot countries, are, I believe, full of dogs; and they, in the very hot weather, keep up, during the night, a horrible barking and fighting and howling. Upon the particular occasion to which I am adverting, they made a noise so terrible and so unremitted, that it was next to impossible that even a person in full health and free from pain should obtain a minute's sleep. I was about nine in the evening sitting by the bed: 'I do think', she said, 'that I could go to sleep *now* if it were not *for the dogs.*' Down stairs I went, and out I sallied, in my shirt and trowsers, and without shoes and stockings; and, to a heap of stones lying beside the road, set to work upon the dogs, going backwards and forward, and keeping them at two or three hundred yards' distance from the house. I walked thus the whole night, barefooted, lest the noise of my shoes might possibly reach her ears; and I remember that the bricks of the causeway were, even in the night, so hot as to be disagreeable to my feet. My exertions produced the desired effect: a sleep of several hours was the consequence; and, at eight o'clock in the morning off went I to a day's business, which was to end at six in the evening.

ADVICE TO YOUNG MEN (1829), *by William Cobbett*

Gorillas in their Nest

The gorillas generally bedded down for the night at dusk and began to stir in the morning during the hour after sunrise, having slept some thirteen hours. They were silent at night, except for the rumbling of stomachs or breaking wind; I never heard them snore. When excited in some way, a male sometimes beat his chest during the night . . .

From THE YEAR OF THE GORILLA, *by George B. Schaller*

GUY, THE GORILLA OF THE LONDON ZOO, *by W. Suschitzky*

Pillows of Stone

MALEVOLE. I cannot sleepe, my eyes ill neighbouring lids
Will holde no fellowship: O thou pale sober night,
Thou that in sluggish fumes all sece doost steepe:
Thou that gives all the world full leave to play,
Unbendst the feebled veines of sweatie labour;
The gally-slave that, all the toilesome day,
Tugges at his oare against the stubburne wave,
Straining his rugged veines; snores fast:
The stooping sith-man that doth barbe the field,
Thou makest winke sure: in night all creatures sleepe,
Onely the Malecontent that gainst his fate,
Repines and quarrels, alas hee's goodman tell-clocke;
His sallow jaw-bones sinke with wasting mone,
Whilst others beds are downe, his pillowes stone.

From THE MALCONTENT, *by John Marston* (1575?–1634)

To his watch
when he could not sleep

Uncessant minutes, whilst you move you tell
   The time that tells our life, which though it run
Never so fast or far, your new-begun
   Short steps shall overtake; for though life well

May 'scape his own account, it shall not yours:
   You are Death's auditors, that both divide
And sum whate'er that life inspired endures
   Past a beginning, and through you we bide

The doom of Fate, whose unrecalled decree
   You date, bring, execute; making what's new
(Ill and good) old; for as we die in you,
   You die in Time, Time in Eternity.

Lord Herbert of Cherbury (1583–1648)

Uneasy Heads

Now many thousand of my poorest subjects
Are at this hour asleep! O sleep, O gentle sleep,
Nature's soft nurse, how have I frightened thee,
That thou no more wilt weigh my eyelids down,
And steep my senses in forgetfulness?
Why rather, sleep, liest thou in smoky cribs,
Upon uneasy pallets stretching thee,
And hush'd with buzzing night-flies to thy slumber,
Than in the perfumed chambers of the great,
Under the canopies of costly state,
And lull'd with sound of sweetest melody?
O thou dull god, why liest thou with the vile
In loathsome beds, and leavest the kingly couch
A watch-case or a common 'larum-bell?
Wilt thou upon the high and giddy mast
Seal up the ship-boy's eyes, and rock his brains
In cradle of the rude imperious surge,
And in the visitation of the winds,
Who take the ruffian billows by the top,
Curling their monstrous heads, and hanging them
With deafening clamour in the slippery clouds,
That, with the hurly, death itself awakes?
Canst thou, O partial sleep, give thy repose
To the wet sea-boy in an hour so rude;
And in the calmest and most stillest night,
With all appliances and means to boot,
Deny it to a king? Then happy low, lie down!
Uneasy lies the head that wears a crown.

The king in KING HENRY IV, PART II: *William Shakespeare*

'Tis not the balm, the sceptre and the ball,
The sword, the mace, the crown imperial,
The intertissued robe of gold and pearl,
The farced title running 'fore the king,
The throne he sits on, nor the tide of pomp
That beats upon the high shore of this world,

No, not all these, thrice-gorgeous ceremony,
Not all these, laid in bed majestical,
Can sleep so soundly as the wretched slave,
Who with a body fill'd and vacant mind
Gets him to rest, cramm'd with distressful bread;
Never sees horrid night, the child of hell,
But, like a lackey, from the rise to set
Sweats in the eye of Phoebus and all night
Sleeps in Elysium; next day after dawn
Doth rise and help Hyperion to his horse,
And follows so the ever-running year,
With profitable labour, to his grave:
Winding up days with toil and nights with sleep,
Had the fore-hand and vantage of a king.

The king in KING HENRY V, *William Shakespeare*

The Other World

'It's like those nights when I was a kid, lying awake thinking the darkness would go on for ever. And I couldn't go back to sleep because of the dream of the whatever it was in the cellar coming out of the corner. I'd lie in the hot, rumpled bed, hot burning hot, trying to shut myself away and know that there were three eternities before the dawn. Everything was the night world, the other world where everything but good could happen, the world of ghosts and robbers and horrors, of things harmless in the daytime coming to life, the wardrobe, the picture in the book, the story, coffins, corpses, vampires, and always squeezing, tormenting darkness, smoke thick. And I'd think of anything because if I didn't go on thinking I'd remember whatever it was in the cellar down there, and my mind would go walking away from my body and go down three stories defenceless, down the dark stairs past the tall, haunted clock, through the whining door, down the terrible steps to where the coffin ends were crushed in the walls of the cellar – and I'd be held helpless on the stone floor, trying to run back, run away, climb up –'

From PINCHER MARTIN, *by William Golding*

Jacob's Dream

And Jacob went out from Beer-sheba, and went toward Haran.

And he lighted upon a certain place, and tarried there all night, because the sun was set; and he took of the stones of that place, and put them for his pillows, and lay down in that place to sleep.

And he dreamed, and behold a ladder set up on the earth, and the top of it reached to heaven: and behold the angels of God ascending and descending on it.

And, behold, the Lord stood above it, and said, I am the Lord God of Abraham thy father, and the God of Isaac: the land whereon thou liest, to thee will I give it, and to thy seed;

And thy seed shall be as the dust of the earth, and thou shalt spread abroad to the west, and to the east, and to the north, and to the south: and in thee and in thy seed shall all the families of the earth be blessed.

And, behold, I am with thee, and will keep thee in all places whither thou goest, and will bring thee again into this land; for I will not leave thee, until I have done that which I have spoken to thee of.

And Jacob awakened out of his dream, and he said, Surely the Lord is in this place; and I knew it not.

And he was afraid, and said, How dreadful is this place! this is none other but the house of God, and this is the gate of heaven.

GENESIS

Be cheerful, sir:
Our revels now are ended. These our actors,
As I foretold you, were all spirits and
Are melted into air, into thin air:
And, like the baseless fabric of this vision,
The cloud-capp'd towers, the gorgeous palaces,
The solemn temples, the great globe itself,
Yea, all which it inherit, shall dissolve
And, like this insubstantial pageant faded,
Leave not a rack behind. We are such stuff
As dreams are made on, and our little life
Is rounded with a sleep.

From THE TEMPEST, *by William Shakespeare*

Plato on Dreams

. . . Certain of the unnecessary pleasures and appetites I conceive to be unlawful; every one appears to have them, but in some persons they are controlled by the laws and by reason, and the better desires prevail over them – either they are wholly banished or they become few and weak; while in the case of others they are stronger, and there are more of them.

Which appetites do you mean?

I mean those which are awake when the reasoning and human and ruling power is asleep; . . . and there is no conceivable folly or crime – not excepting incest or other unnatural union, or parricide, or the eating of forbidden food – which at such a time when he had parted company with all shame and sense, a man may not be ready to commit.

Most true, he said.

But when a man's pulse is healthy and temperate, and when before going to sleep he has awakened his rational powers, and fed them on noble thoughts and enquiries, collecting himself in meditation; after having first indulged his appetites neither too much nor too little, but just enough to lay them to sleep, and prevent them and their enjoyments and pains from interfering with the higher principle – which he leaves in the solitude of pure abstraction, free to contemplate and aspire to the knowledge of the unknown, whether in past, present or future: when again he has allayed the passionate element, if he has a quarrel against anyone – I say, when, after pacifying the two irrational principles, he rouses up the third, which is reason, before he takes his rest, then, as you know, he attains truth most nearly, and is least likely to be the sport of fantastic and lawless visions.

I quite agree.

In saying this I have been running into a digression; but the point which I desire to note is that in all of us, even in good men, there is a lawless wild-beast nature, which peers out in sleep. Pray, consider whether I am right, and you agree with me.

Yes, I agree.

From Plato's THE REPUBLIC, *translated into English by B. Jowett*

Last night I dreamed that I was a butterfly: and
now I do not know whether I am a man
dreaming that he was a butterfly or a butterfly
dreaming it is a man.

From the Chinese

218

The Dream

Dear love, for nothing less than thee
Would I have broke this happy dream;
   It was a theme
For reason, much too strong for phantasy:
Therefore thou wak'dst me wisely; yet
My dream thou brok'st not, but continued'st it,
Thou art so truth, that thoughts of thee suffice,
To make dreams truths, and fables histories;
Enter these arms, for since thou thoughtst it best
Not to dream all my dream, let's act the rest.

As lightning, or a taper's light,
Thine eyes, and not thy noise, waked me;
   Yet I thought thee
– For thou lov'st truth – an angel at first sight;
But when I saw thou saw'st my heart,
When thou knew'st what I dreamt, when thou knew'st when
Excess of joy would wake me, and cam'st then,
I must confess, it could not choose but be
Profane, to think thee any thing but thee.

Coming and staying show'd thee, thee,
But rising makes me doubt that now
   Thou art not thou.
That love is weak where fear's as strong as he;
'Tis not all spirit, pure and brave,
If mixture it of fear, shame, honour, have;
Perchance as torches, which must ready be,
Men light and put out, so thou deal'st with me;
Thou cam'st to kindle, go'st to come; then I
Will dream that hope again, but else would die.

John Donne (1571–1631)

Golden Dreams

It is as true as strange, else trial feigns,
That whosoever in the moonshine sleeps
Are hardly waked, the moon so rules the brains;
For she is sovereign of the brains and deeps:
So thou, fair Cynthia, with thy borrowed beams –
Borrowed of glory's Sun, great lord of light, –
Mak'st me still sleep in love, whose golden dreams
Give love right current – sith well-coined – delight.
I cannot wake while thou on me doth shine,
Thy shining so makes me so sweetly dream:
For still methinks I kiss those lips of thine,
And – nothing else, for I will not blaspheme:
    But thought is free, and dreams are dreams, and so
    I dream, and dream, and dream; but let that go.

John Davies of Hereford (1565?–1618)

The Terrors of the Night

WHEN Night in her rustie dungeon hath imprisoned our ey-sight, and that we are shut seperatly in our chambers from resort, the divell keepeth his audit in our sin-guilty consciences, no sense but surrenders to out memorie a true bill of parcels of his detestable impietis. The table of our hart is turned to an index of iniquities, and all our thoughts are nothing but texts to condemn us. The rest we take in our beds is such another kinde of rest as the weerie traveller taketh in the coole soft grasse in summer, who thinking there to lye at ease, and refresh his tyred limmes, layeth his fainting head unawares on a loathsome neast of snakes . . . Therefore are the terrors of the night more than of the day, because the sinnes of the night surmount the sinnes of the day.

Thomas Nashe, 1594

Dreams are but interludes which fancy makes
When monarch reason sleeps, this mimic wakes;
Compounds a medley of disjointed things,
A court of cobblers and a mob of kings.
Light fumes are merry, grosser fumes are sad –
Both are the reasonable soul run mad;
And many monstrous forms in sleep we see,
That neither were, nor are, nor e'er can be.

John Dryden

A KIND OF DREAMING, *by Donald McCul*

PORTER, VICTORIA STATION, *by Malcolm Aird*

Overleaf:

THE DREAM . . .
    by John Hedgecoe

. . . AND THE DREAMER,
    by Henri Cartier-Bresson

RL FROM CHINA, *by Zoë Dominic*

GIRL OF THE GORBALS, *by Bert Hardy*

From *Darkness*

I had a dream, which was not all a dream.
The bright sun was extinguish'd, and the stars
Did wander darkling in the eternal space,
Rayless, and pathless, and the icy earth
Swung blind and blackening in the moonless air;
Morn came and went – and came, and brought no day,
And men forgot their passions in the dread
Of this their desolation; and all hearts
Were chill'd into a selfish prayer for light . . .

Happy were those who dwelt within the eye
Of the volcanoes, and their mountain-torch:
A fearful hope was all the world contain'd;
Forests were set on fire – but hour by hour
They fell and faded – and the crackling trunks
Extinguish'd with a crash – and all was black . . .

And War, which for a moment was no more,
Did glut himself again: – a meal was bought
With blood, and each sate sullenly apart
Gorging himself in gloom: no love was left;
All earth was but one thought – and that was death
Immediate and inglorious . . .

               The world was void,
The populous and the powerful was a lump,
Seasonless, herbless, treeless, manless, lifeless,
A lump of death – a chaos of hard clay.
The rivers, lakes and ocean all stood still,
And nothing stirr'd within their silent depths:
Ships sailorless lay rotting on the sea,
And their masts fell to piecemeal: as they dropp'd
They slept on the abyss without a surge –
The waves were dead; the tides were in their grave,
The moon, their mistress, had expired before;
The winds were wither'd in the stagnant air,
And the clouds perish'd; Darkness had no need
Of aid from them – She was the Universe.

Lord Byron (1788–1824)

E MAN OUTSIDE, *by John Chillingworth*

Abraham Lincoln's Dream

LINCOLN was elected President of the United States in 1860. His presidency ended in 1865, with his assassination. Just after his election he is said to have seen in a mirror a double image of himself. One image was healthy and lifelike, the other ghastly and like a wraith, according to Ward Hill Lamon, his biographer. This appears to be an interesting example of the form of autocospy that the old Germans called *Doppelgänger*, or double, to see which presaged death. But the better authenticated and more relevant incident in Lincoln's life was the dream he had a few days before he was assassinated. The biographer declares that he made notes of Lincoln's conversation immediately after the President, in the company of his wife and two or three other persons, related a dream that was haunting him. Lincoln remarked upon the abundance of references to dreams in the Bible, but would not admit, in answer to his wife's question, that he 'believed in' dreams. Lincoln's recital is reported as follows:

'About ten days ago, I retired very late. I had been up waiting for important dispatches from the front. I could not have been long in bed when I fell into a slumber, for I was weary. I soon began to dream. There seemed to be a death-like stillness about me. Then I heard subdued sobs, as if a number of people were weeping. I thought I left my bed and wandered downstairs. There the silence was broken by the same pitiful sobbing, but the mourners were invisible. I went from room to room; no living person was in sight, but the same mournful sounds of distress met me as I passed along. It was light in all the rooms; every object was familiar to me; but where were all the people who were grieving as if their hearts would break? I was puzzled and alarmed. What could be the meaning of all this? Determined to find the cause of a state of things so mysterious and so shocking, I kept on until I arrived at the East Room, which I entered. There I met with a sickening surprise. Before me was a catafalque, on which rested a corpse wrapped in funeral vestments. Around it were stationed soldiers who were acting as guards; and there was a throng of people, some gazing mournfully upon the corpse, whose face was covered, others weeping pitifully. 'Who is dead in the White House?' I demanded of one of the soldiers. 'The President,' was his answer; 'he was killed by an assassin!' Then came a loud burst of grief from the crowd, which awoke me from my dream. I slept no more that night; and although it was only a dream, I have been strangely annoyed by it ever since.

' "This is horrid!" said Mrs Lincoln (according to the biographer). "I wish you had not told it. I am glad I do not believe in dreams, or I should be in terror from this time forth."

' "Well," responded Mr Lincoln, thoughtfully, "it is only a dream, Mary. Let us say no more about it, and try to forget it. . . ." '

From THE DREAM WORLD, *by R. L. Megroz*

ERNEST JONES

On the Nightmare

WE HAVE already commented on the interesting circumstance, so significant for our sexual theory of the Nightmare, that the scientific name for this condition in the Middle Ages also denoted a lewd demon who visits women at night, lies heavily on their chest and violates them against their will. These visitors of women were called Incubi; those of men were called Succubi. . . .

Up to the year 1400 Incubi were supposed to have had intercourse with human beings only against the will of the latter, but after this date the appearance of a race of lecherous witches led to people giving themselves voluntarily to the Incubi. It is apparent that, just when people were beginning to emancipate themselves from the belief in hallucinated beings in connection with erotic dreams and retaining the belief only in connection with Nightmares, a theological elaboration of the Incubus concept re-animated the ancient belief that the partner in a sexual dream was an actual being.

A neat description of this conflict, with more than a hint of dawning insight, may be quoted from an old play of the early seventeenth century. In it Ursula speaks: 'I have heard you say that dreames and visions were fabulous; and yet one time I dreamt fowle water ran through the floore, and the next day the house was on fire. You us'd to say hobgoblins, fairies, and the like, were nothing but our owne affrightments, and yet o' my troth, cuz, I once dream'd of a young batchelour, and was ridd with the night-mare. But come, so my conscience be cleere, I never care how fowle my dreames are.'

Even the bigoted royal author, King James I, at a still earlier date shows signs of a certain amount of insight:[1]

'*Philomates*: Is it not the thing which we call the *Mare*, which takes folkes sleeping in their beds, a kinde of these spirits, whereof ye are speaking?

'*Epistemon*: No, that is but a naturall sicknesse, which the Mediciners have given that name of *Incubus* unto, *ab incubando*, because it being a thick fleume, falling into our breast upon the heart, while we are sleeping, intercludes so our vitall spirits, and takes all power from us, as makes us think that there were some unnaturall burden or spirit, lying upon us, and holding us down.'

ON THE NIGHTMARE, *Ernest Jones*

King James I: *Daemonologie*.

The Hand

31st January 1938.

I had a dream which alarmed me. I thought I was in my own bed in my own room, and I saw a hand come round my closed door. It fumbled for the key and stealthily unlocked the door. I was terrified as I watched this hand with the fingers of a man moving slowly and carefully seeking the key, although I knew I had locked and shut the door. I saw no person, only the door slowly opening as the hand unfastened it. I awoke in horror, for I was alone in the house, both in dream and in reality. I put on the light, and of course all was safe, but it was some time before I could go to sleep again.

I happened to go to a film in the afternoon of the next day, an unusual event for me. In one of the films presented (not the one I went to see, but a subsidiary film), a hand appeared as in my dream, fumbling round the door with no view of the face of the assassin or thief. I recognised this at once with the sharp pang I had felt in the dream. In the film the door was pushed open a crack before the hand appeared, while in my dream it was a locked door round which the fingers came. The door opened in the same way, from left to right, and in both the hand was that of a man. I was relieved to see this end to the experience, but I had the same acute discomfort I had in dream as I watched it.

From THE STUFF OF DREAMS, *by Alison Uttley*

From this ignorance of how to distinguish Dreams and other strong fancies from Vision and Sense did arise the greater part of the religion of the Gentiles in times past that worshipped Satyres, Faunes, Nymphs, and the like; and nowadays the opinion that rude people have of Fayries, Ghosts, and Goblins, and of the power of Witches.

LEVIATHAN, 1651: *Hobbes*

Indigestion doesn't account for beautiful women in keyholes.

MYTHS AND MYTH-MAKERS, 1872, *J. Friske*

When a woman sleeps alone, the Devil sleeps with her.

Abyssinian proverb

THOMAS DE QUINCEY

The Dreams of the Opium Eater

. . . I NOW PASS to what is the main subject of these latter Confessions – to the history and journal of what took place in my dreams; for these were the immediate and proximate cause of shadowy terrors that settled and brooded over my whole waking life.

The first notice I had of any important change going on in this part of my physical economy, was from the re-awaking of a state of eye oftentimes incident to childhood. I know not whether my reader is aware that many children have a power of painting, as it were, upon the darkness all sorts of phantoms; in some that power is simply a mechanic affection of the eye; others have a voluntary or semi-voluntary power to dismiss or summon such phantoms; or, as a child once said to me, when I questioned him on this matter, 'I can tell them to go and they go; but sometimes they come when I don't tell them to come.' He had by one-half as unlimited a command over apparitions as a Roman centurion over his soldiers. In the middle of 1817 this faculty became increasingly distressing to me: at night, when I lay awake in bed, vast processions moved along continually in mournful pomp; friezes of never-ending stories, that to my feelings were as sad and solemn as stories drawn from times before Oedipus or Priam, before Tyre, before Memphis. And, concurrently with this, a corresponding change took place in my dreams; a theatre seems suddenly opened and lighted up within my brain, which presented nightly spectacles of more than earthly splendour. And the four following facts may be mentioned, as noticeable at this time:-

1. That, as the creative state of the eye increased, a sympathy seemed to arise between the waking and the dreaming states of the brain in one point – that whatsoever I happened to call up and to trace by a voluntary act upon the darkness was very apt to transfer itself to my dreams; and at length I feared to exercise this faculty; for, as Midas turned all things to gold that yet baffled his hopes and defrauded his human desires, so whatsoever things capable of being visually represented I did but think of in the darkness, immediately shaped themselves into phantoms for the eye; and, by a process apparently no less inevitable, when thus once traced in faint and visionary colours, like writings in sympathetic ink, they were drawn out by the fierce chemistry of my dreams, into insufferable splendour that fretted my heart.

2. This and all other changes in my dreams were accompanied by deep-seated anxiety and funereal melancholy, such as are wholly incommunicable by words. I seemed every night to descend – not metaphorically, but literally to descend – into chasms and sunless abysses, depths below depths, from which it seemed hopeless that I could ever re-ascend. Nor did I, by waking, feel that I *had* re-ascended. Why should I dwell upon this?

For indeed the state of gloom which attended these gorgeous spectacles, amounting at last to utter darkness, as of some suicidal despondency, cannot be approached by words.

3. The sense of space, and in the end the sense of time, were both powerfully affected. Buildings, landscapes, etc., were exhibited in proportions so vast as the bodily eye is not fitted to receive. Space swelled, and was amplified to an extent of unutterable and self-repeating affinity. This disturbed me very much less than the vast expansion of time. Sometimes I seemed to have lived for seventy or a hundred years in one night; nay, sometimes had feelings representative of a duration far beyond the limits of any human experience.

4. The minutest incidents of childhood, or forgotten scenes of later years, were often revived. I could not be said to recollect them; for, if I had been told of them when waking, I should not have been able to acknowledge them as parts of my past experience. But placed as they were before me, in dreams like intuitions, and clothed in all their evanescent circumstances and accompanying feelings, I *recognised* them instantaneously . . .

Many years ago, when I was looking over Piranesi's *Antiquities of Rome*, Coleridge, then standing by, described to me a set of plates from that artist, called his *Dreams*, and which record the scenery of his own visions during the delirium of a fever. Some of these (I describe only from memory of Coleridge's account) represented vast Gothic halls; on the floor of which stood mighty engines and machinery, wheels, cables, catapults, etc., expressive of enormous power put forth, or resistance overcome. Creeping along the sides of the walls, you perceived a staircase; and upon this, groping his way upwards, was Piranesi himself. Follow the stairs a little farther, and you perceive them reaching an abrupt termination, without any balustrade, and allowing no step onwards to him who should reach the extremity, except into the depths below. Whatever is to become of poor Piranesi, at least you suppose that his labours must now in some way terminate. But raise your eyes, and behold a second flight of stairs still higher, on which again Piranesi is perceived, by this time standing on the very brink of the abyss. Once again elevate your eye, and a still more aërial flight is descried; and there, again, is the delirious Piranesi, busy on his aspiring labours: and so on, until the unfinished stairs and the hopeless Piranesi both are lost in the upper gloom of the hall. With the same power of endless growth and self-reproduction did my architecture proceed in dreams. In the early stage of the malady, the splendours of my dreams were indeed chiefly architectural; and I beheld such pomp of cities and palaces as never yet was beheld by the waking eye, unless in the clouds. . . .

. . . Hitherto the human face had often mixed in my dreams, but not despotically, nor with any special power of tormenting. But now that affection, which I have called the tyranny of the human face, began to unfold itself. Perhaps some part of my London life (the searching for Ann amongst fluctuating crowds) might be answerable for this. Be that as it may, now it was that upon the rocking waters of the ocean the human face began to reveal itself; the sea appeared paved with innumerable faces, upturned to the heavens; faces, imploring, wrathful, despairing; faces that surged upwards by thousands, by myriads, by generations: infinite was my agitation; my mind tossed, as it seemed, upon the billowy ocean, and weltered upon the weltering waves.

May 1818. – The Malay has been a fearful enemy for months. Every night, through his means, I have been transported into Asiatic scenery. I know not whether others share in my feelings on this point; but I have often thought that if I were compelled to forego England, and to live in China, among Chinese manners and modes of life and scenery, I should go mad. The causes of my horror lie deep, and some of them must be common to others. Southern Asia, in general, is the seat of awful images and associations. As the cradle of the human race, if on no other ground, it would have a dim, reverential feeling connected with it. But there are others reasons. No man can pretend that the wild, barbarous, and capricious superstitions of Africa, or of savage tribes elsewhere, affect him in a way that he is affected by the ancient, monumental, cruel, and elaborate religions of Hindostan. The mere antiquity of Asiatic things, of their institutions, histories, above all, of their mythologies, &c., is so impressive, that to me the vast age of the race and name overpowers the sense of youth in the individual. A young Chinese seems to me an antediluvian man renewed. Even Englishmen, though not bred in any knowledge of such institutions, cannot but shudder at the mystic sublimity of *castes* that have flowed apart, and refused to mix, through such immemorial tracts of time; nor can any man fail to be awed by the sanctity of the Ganges, or by the very name of the Euphrates. It contributes much to these feelings that South-eastern Asia is, and has been for thousands of years, the part of the earth most swarming with human life, the great *officina gentium*. Man is a weed in those regions. The vast empires, also, into which the enormous population of Asia has always been cast give a further sublimity to the feelings associated with all oriental names or images. In China, over and above what it has in common with the rest of Southern Asia, I am terrified by the modes of life, by the manners, by the barrier of utter abhorrence placed between myself and *them*, by counter-sympathies deeper than I can analyse. I could sooner live with lunatics, with vermin, with crocodiles or snakes. All this, and much more than I can say, the reader must enter into before he can comprehend the unimaginable horror which these dreams of oriental imagery and mythological tortures impressed upon me. Under the connecting feeling of tropical heat and vertical sunlights, I brought together all creatures, birds, beasts, reptiles, all trees and plants, usages and appearances, that are found in all tropical regions, and assembled them together in China or Hindostan. From kindred feelings, I soon brought Egypt and her gods under the same law. I was stared at, hooted at, grinned at, chattered at, by monkeys, by paroquets, by cockatoos. I ran into pagodas, and was fixed for centuries at the summit, or in secret rooms; I was the idol; I was the priest; I was worshipped; I was sacrificed. I fled from the wrath of Brama through all the forests of Asia; Vishnu hated me; Seeva lay in wait for me. I came suddenly upon Isis and Osiris: I had done a deed, they said, which the ibis and the crocodile trembled at. Thousands of years I lived and was buried in stone coffins, with mummies and sphinxes, in narrow chambers at the heart of eternal pyramids. I was kissed, with cancerous kisses by crocodiles, and was laid, confounded with all unutterable abortions, amongst reeds and Nilotic mud.

Some slight abstraction I thus attempt of my oriental dreams, which filled me always with such amazement at the monstrous scenery, that horror seemed absorbed for a while in sheer astonishment. Sooner or later came a reflux of feeling that swallowed up the astonishment, and left me, not so much in terror, as in hatred and abomination of what I saw. Over every form, and every threat, and punishment, and dim sightless incarceration, brooded a killing sense of eternity and infinity. Into these dreams only it was, with one or two slight exceptions, that any circumstances of physical horror entered. But here the main agents were ugly birds, or snakes, or crocodiles, especially the last. The cursed crocodile became to me the object of more horror than all the rest. I was compelled to live with him; and (as was always the case in my dreams) for centuries. Sometimes I escaped, and found myself in Chinese houses. All the feet of the tables, sofas, &c., soon became instinct with life; the abominable head of the crocodile, and his leering eyes, looked out at me, multiplied into ten thousand repetitions; and I stood loathing and fascinated. So often did this hideous reptile haunt my dreams, that many times the very same dream was broken up in the very same way: I heard gentle voices speaking to me (I hear everything when I am sleeping), and instantly I awoke; it was broad noon, and my children were standing, hand in hand, at my bedside, come to show me their coloured shoes, or new frocks, or to let me see them dressed for going out. No experience was so awful to me, and at the same time so pathetic, as this abrupt translation from the darkness of the infinite to the gaudy summer air of highest noon, and from the unutterable abortions of miscreated gigantic vermin to the sight of infancy, and innocent *human* natures.

From CONFESSIONS OF AN ENGLISH OPIUM-EATER, *by Thomas De Quincey* (1785–1859)

'With the same power of endless growth and self-reproduction did my architecture proceed in dreams': One of the plates by Piranesi described by Coleridge to de Quincey. *From the Victoria and Albert Museum, London*

'I ran into pagodas, and was fixed for centuries at the summit':
PAGODA IN BURMA, *by Roloff Beny*

WET NIGHT, New Orleans, *by Thurston Hopkins*

THREE IN THE UNDERGROUND, *by Donald McCullin*

PRAYER-MEETING IN PADDINGTON, *by Malcolm Aird*

The Vision of the Cross

This poem is perhaps the finest example of Anglo-Saxon religious verse. Sombre and plangent, it has the elegaic quality of many poems of that period. It is the first English poem to employ the 'dream form', later used by other medieval authors, notably Langland and Chaucer. The date of composition of this work is uncertain. The version newly translated here by Graham C. Rees is taken from the Vercelli text, written between A.D. 950 and A.D. 1000 in the West Saxon dialect – the best surviving version. However, a runic inscription on the Ruthwell Cross in Dumfriesshire of an earlier date (circa A.D. 700) preserves passages of the poem in the Northumbrian dialect.

LISTEN! I will tell of a profound vision which came to me at midnight, when mankind was at rest. I thought I saw a marvellous cross rising aloft, a brilliant tree enfolded in light, a beacon overlaid with gold. Rare gems shone from the surface of the earth, and five more were set on the shoulder-span. The angels looked on, beautiful by ancient commandment. The holy spirits watched it, with men on earth and all creation. That cross had never been the gallows of a felon. That cross, the cross of victory, was splendid – I, stained with sin, disfigured with evil. But I saw it, the glorious tree clothed, adorned with gold, shining with joy; Christ's cross covered finely with precious stones. Yet through the gold I felt the former strife of wretched men, where it had first bled on the right-hand side. I was troubled with sorrows, made fearful by that terrible sight. I saw the bright beacon, its colour and clothing changed. For a moment it was wet, drenched with running blood, then again it was clothed with gold.

I lay there a long time watching, filled with sorrow, until suddenly I heard it speak,

'A long time ago I was cut down in the forest, parted from my roots: I remember it clearly. I was taken by powerful evil men who turned me into a spectacle, forcing me to carry their criminals. Men, wicked enough, bore me on their shoulders and set me on a hill.

'I saw the Son of Man hasten with much zeal for he would climb upon me. I saw the surface of the earth shake. I might have crushed all those evil-doers, but I stood firm. I did not dare bend or fall, against God's word. The young hero, strong and steadfast, who was the Almighty God, cast off his clothes. He mounted the high cross, brave in the sight of man, for he sought to redeem mankind. I trembled as the Prince clasped me, I did not dare bend earthward or fall to the ground. I was raised as a cross; I lifted the King of Heaven nor could I bend! They drove cruel nails through me, leaving gaping, malicious wounds which can be seen to this day. I dared not kill any of them, and they reviled us together. I was stained with blood which ran from his side, when he had sent his soul to Heaven.

'On that hill I have endured countless torments. I saw the Lord of Hosts harshly stretched out. His corpse, a shining splendour, was covered by sombre clouds; a shadow spread dark under the skies. Creation wept, lamenting the death of Christ on the cross.

From distant lands the devout came to the Prince. I saw everything even though I was tormented with grief. I bowed to their hands with the courage of humility. They carried away the Almighty God, raising him out of cruel torment. The warriors left me; I was blackened with blood and pierced with spikes.

'Christ was laid down weary of limb. Men stood at his head watching Heaven's Lord as he slept exhausted by his great agony. They began to carve a tomb in the bright rock as his slayer looked on. They laid the Victorious Prince within, sang a dirge, wretched in the evening. They departed wearily to their homes, they left the Mighty Lord with little company. We, the three crosses standing on that hill, mourned a long time after the voices of the troop had drifted away. The corpse, the beautiful body, grew cold. Men came and cut us to the ground, buried us deep in the earth – a dreadful fate, but the servants of God, his liegemen, heard of it. They robed me in gold and silver.

'Now you, beloved man, may also hear of the surging sorrow which I have suffered at the hands of evil men. Now the time has come that I am adored. All vast creation and men below pray at this cross. I shall reveal to you this vision, disclose the precious tree on which the Almighty God suffered for man's many sins, the ancient works of Adam. Here he tasted death but rose to uphold mankind with his great strength. On me the Son of God suffered for a while so now I am exalted, towering under Heaven. I can save any man who stands in awe of me – I who was made a cruel punishment, hateful to men until I showed them the Path of Life. The Father of Creation, the Guardian of Heaven has set me above every tree of the forest as he honoured his own mother, setting her above all womankind; Mary, whom all men adore. But he will come again on the Day of Doom to visit mankind, the Lord himself, with his angels to pass that judgement he alone can bestow. Each man will be paid in full that which he has earned in this fleeting life. No one will be unafraid at the words which the World's Lord shall utter. He will ask who would suffer the agonies of death in his name as Christ did on the cross. They will all be terrified and few will try to answer, but they that carry the sacred sign in their hearts need not be afraid, for by that cross every soul on earth who wishes to live with God shall find that Kingdom.'

Then I prayed cheerfully, with great zeal to the cross. I found myself alone again, but my spirit was eager to start that journey for which it had yearned in times of weariness. My hope in this life is now to seek out the cross of victory, to honour it more than any other man. Desire for it swells my heart, my protection rests in that cross. I have few friends to sustain me on earth. They have gone from here, departed the joys of this world, seeking the King of Heaven. They live now in Heaven with the Father, dwelling in bliss. I hope each day for the time when Christ's cross, which I saw before here on earth, will fetch me from this transient life, and bring me to that place where great joy, the joy of Heaven, exists; where the people of God are seated at a feast of perpetual joy. He will place me where I may dwell in joy with the saints, and partake of full bliss. God be my friend, he who here on earth suffered on the gallows for the sins of man. He freed us, giving life and shelter in Heaven. Hope was restored with blessings and joy to those tortured in the flames. The Son triumphed, sped on that voyage into darkness. The souls of many rose with him, the all-powerful Lord, to God's King-dom, and the bliss of angels, the joy of all the saints, already living in Heaven when the Almighty God returned to his home.

Ode on Melancholy

I

No, no, go not to Lethe, neither twist
   Wolf's-bane, tight-rooted, for its poisonous wine;
Nor suffer thy pale forehead to be kiss'd
   By nightshade, ruby grape of Proserpine;
Make not your rosary of yew-berries,
   Nor let the beetle, nor the death-moth be
      Your mournful Psyche, nor the downy owl
A partner in your sorrow's mysteries;
   For shade to shade will come too drowsily,
      And drown the wakeful anguish of the soul.

II

But when the melancholy fit shall fall
   Sudden from heaven like a weeping cloud,
That fosters the droop-headed flowers all,
   And hides the green hill in an April shroud;
Then glut thy sorrow on a morning rose,
   Or on the rainbow of the salt sand-wave,
   Or on the wealth of globed peonies;
Or if thy mistress some rich anger shows,
   Emprison her soft hand, and let her rave,
      And feed deep, upon her peerless eyes.

III

She dwells with Beauty – Beauty that must die;
   And Joy, whose hand is ever at his lips
Bidding adieu; and aching Pleasure nigh,
   Turning to Poison while the bee-mouth sips:
Ay, in the very temple of delight
   Veil'd Melancholy has her sovran shrine,
      Though seen of none save him whose strenuous tongue
Can burst Joy's grape against his palate fine;
   His soul shall taste the sadness of her might,
      And be among her cloudy trophies hung.

John Keats (1795–1821)

243

The Woman who obeyed a Gang of Ghosts

THIS MOST amazing of all ghost stories was related by a woman at the end of the last century to several eminent men who took it seriously. Lord Bute, Andrew Lang, the literary historian, and his friend Dr Ferrier collected the details of how a 'Mrs Claughton' (a pseudonym) was visited by a party of ghosts and given instructions and an appointment to meet them again. Only the real names of places and certain people were changed to avoid embarrassment to living people, but the names were given to the investigators.

Dr Ferrier was dining with Andrew Lang and some friends in 'Rapingham' (a pseudonym) in October, 1893, and during conversation, Dr Ferrier asked if they had heard about the haunted house in Blake Street which belonged to some friends of his named Appleby. These had let the house and the new tenants, a Mr Buckley and his mother and sister, had been puzzled by ghostly happenings there. Dr Ferrier said that he himself had been in the house years before, and while the family were in the dining-room they heard queer noises in the room overhead, which was empty.

Besides noises there were other puzzling things. Buckley's sister was alone in an attic, kneeling by a trunk, when water was swished over her face. When Mr Buckley was carrying an inkwell upstairs one evening he suddenly felt liquid in his hand and feared that he had spilled ink. Reaching his room he went to the window and found that his hand held not ink but water.

These incidents might belong to any old ghost story, but they were to prove only the preliminary operations of the ghosts in the Blake Street house in Rapingham, who apparently were trying to engage the attention of a living person. And their opportunity came with the arrival of Mrs Claughton, a widow, and two of her children, to stay with the Buckleys. She had not been there more than a few days before she went to consult Dr Ferrier and told him that the previous night, while asleep with one of her children in the same bed, she had been awakened by footsteps on the stairs. At last she lit her candle and went to look. By the clock on the landing the time was twenty past one. Nobody was on the stairs. She went back to bed and started to read but fell asleep. When she woke the candle was burnt low and the sound of a sigh made her look up. A woman wrapped in a white shawl was leaning over her.

Mrs Claughton heard the words 'Follow me' and took hold of the candlestick. She may have dreamed what happened next except for one thing. She followed the apparition past the landing and into the drawing-room, which was on the same floor but had been locked by the maid. As her candle was nearly out she replaced it by a pink one from an ornamental cupboard in the drawing-room. Meanwhile she saw the ghost go towards the window, turn round, and say 'Tomorrow'. Then it vanished. When she got back to bed her child sleepily asked, 'Who is the lady in white?' She eventually fell asleep again. In the morning she saw the pink candle in her candlestick.

Mr Buckley arranged for Mrs Claughton to have an electric alarm communicating with his sister's room, in case she was frightened in the night.

This is still like an ordinary ghost story. But Dr Ferrier went to to tell his friends that Mrs Claughton had suddenly left Rapingham to obey the instructions of three ghosts who, again at night when she was in bed, had appeared to her. They had ordered her to go to 'Meresby'. Whereas Rapingham was in the Midlands, Meresby was an obscure village several hours by train on the south side of London. Buckley's sister the previous night, about one o'clock had been aroused by the electric alarm. She and her brother had found Mrs Claughton lying on the floor of her bedroom in a faint.

Nobody expected to hear any further incidents in this story, and a report of the occurrences, so far as they knew them, was sent to the Psychical Research Society.

The night that she had rung the alarm bell, Mrs Claughton did not get into bed but lay on it in her dressing-gown, intending to read. But she fell asleep, then woke (as she believed) to see the white-shawled woman bending over her. Then another figure appeared beside her, a tall, dark man in good health, who was sixty. He told her his name was George Howard, and that he had been buried in Meresby Churchyard. (Neither Mrs Claughton nor the Buckleys had ever heard of Meresby.) This ghost gave her notes of his marriage and death and impelled her to put them down in her notebook. She must, he said, go to Meresby to check these dates, and if she found them correct, she must wait alone in the church there at 1.15 at night beside the grave of Richard Harte. Mrs Claughton had never heard of Harte or Howard. But the ghostly Howard told her she would find Harte's grave at the south-west corner of the south aisle. The ghost then described to her the parish clerk, one Joseph Wright, who would, he said, help her. When Howard finished talking, Mrs Claughton saw a third phantom, who seemed to be in great grief. She told the investigators that she was not free to repeat his name.

The three ghosts made her understand that if she obeyed them, they would meet her again at Meresby Church at the time indicated. Then as they vanished she got up to look at the time by the landing clock. Feeling that she was going to faint, she rang the alarm. (Her condition suggests that she had been asleep.)

Mrs Claughton left for London on the Thursday, slept in London on the Friday night and this time knew that she merely *dreamed* of the ghosts, who gave her other particulars and told her that her half ticket to Meresby would not be collected. They also added to their previous instructions that she would seek out a Mr Francis, who knew about the private affairs which the ghosts wanted straightened out. All of which was realised in fact.

When she reached Meresby on the Saturday the clerk, Wright, got her the registers and she checked up the dates in her notebook. Wright testified afterwards that she correctly described George Howard, whom he had known. Inside the church she found the grave of Richard Harte, who had died in 1745, and was apparently only useful as a meeting-place.

The curate was surprised at her request to be allowed to go into the church alone that night, but eventually he left the matter in the hands of the parish clerk, who unlocked the church for her and locked her in from 1.20 until 1.45 am on Saturday, October 14, 1893.

Whether or not Mrs Claughton really met the ghosts again in the church, as she maintained, it is a fact that she was supplied with accurate details of the private affairs of people who were strangers to her. On the following Monday she visited the daughter of George Howard and passed on to her the ghostly messages. Howard's daughter recognised the importance and reasonableness of their requests, though the details were too private to publish. She sent the uncollected half ticket to Meresby to Dr Ferrier, who gave it to Andrew Lang. Lang got the railway company to check the date of issue. None of the ghosts was ever heard of again.

One might well ask what kind of telepathy was this! Spiritualists would not hesitate to regard it as direct communication from persons who had died to a living person whose mind was in the twilight state of dream resembling a trance. Each reader may select a theory where no theory can be substantiated, but one course I do not believe can reasonably be followed, and that is to dismiss such investigated stories as mere superstitious twaddle.

From THE DREAM WORLD, *by R. L. Megroz*

The Witches' Charms

1 *Charm.*   Dame, dame! the watch is set:
Quickly come, we all are met.
From the lakes and from the fens,
From the rocks and from the dens,
From the woods and from the caves,
From the churchyards, from the graves,
From the dungeon, from the tree
That they die on, here are we!

        Comes she not yet?
        Strike another heat!

2 *Charm.*   The weather is fair, the wind is good:
Up, dame, o' your horse of wood!
Or else tuck up your gray frock,
And saddle your goat or your green cock,
To roll up how many miles you have rid.
Quickly come away,
For we all stay.

        Nor yet? nay then
        We'll try her again.

3 *Charm.*   The owl is abroad, the bat and the toad,
      And so is the cat-a-mountain;
The ant and the mole sit both in a hole,
      And frog peeps out o' the fountain.
The dogs they do bay, and the timbrels play,
      The spindle is now a-turning;
The moon it is red, and the stars are fled,
      But all the sky is a-burning:
The ditch is made, and our nails the spade:
With pictures full, of wax and of wool,
Their livers I stick with needles quick;
There lacks but the blood to make up the flood.
Quickly, dame, then bring your part in!
Spur, spur, upon little Martin!
Merrily, merrily, make him sail,
A worm in his mouth and a thorn in his tail,
Fire above, and fire below,
With a whip in your hand to make him go!

          O now she's come!
          Let all be dumb.

          THE MASQUE OF QUEENS, *Ben Jonson* (1572–1637)

Mary's Ghost

Twas in the middle of the night.
   To sleep young William tried;
When Mary's ghost came stealing in,
   And stood at his bed-side.

O William dear! O William dear!
   My rest eternal ceases;
Alas! my everlasting peace
   Is broken into pieces.

I thought the last of all my cares
   Would end with my last minute;
But though I went to my long home,
   I didn't stay long in it.

The body-snatchers they have come,
   And made a snatch at me;
It's very hard them kind of men
   Won't let a body be!

You thought that I was buried deep,
   Quite decent like and chary,
But from her grave in Mary-bone,
   They've come and boned your Mary.

The arm that used to take your arm
   Is took to Dr Vyse;
And both my legs are gone to walk
   The hospital at Guy's.

I vowed that you should have my hand,
   But fate gives us denial;
You'll find it there, at Dr Bell's,
   In spirits and a phial.

As for my feet, the little feet
   You used to call so pretty,
There's one, I know, in Bedford Row,
   The t'other's in the City.

I can't tell where my head is gone,
   But Dr Carpue can;
As for my trunk it's all packed up
   To go by Pickford's van.

I wish you'd go to Mr P.
   And save me such a ride;
I don't half like the outside place,
   They've took for my inside.

The cock it crows – I must be gone!
   My William, we must part!
But I'll be yours in death, altho'
   Sir Astley has my heart.

Don't go to weep upon my grave,
   And think that there I be;
They haven't left an atom there
   Of my anatomie.

Thomas Hood (1799–1845)

GHOSTS ON A WET NIGHT: Glasgow, *by Guy Gravett*

THREE WOMEN
OF DUNDEE
by Michael Peto

Haunted Houses

All houses wherein men have lived and died
   Are haunted houses. Through the open doors
The harmless phantoms on their errands glide,
   With feet that make no sound upon the floors.

We meet them at the doorway, on the stair,
   Along the passages they come and go,
Impalpable impressions on the air,
   A sense of something moving to and fro.

There are more guests at table, than the hosts
   Invited; the illuminated hall
Is thronged with quiet, inoffensive ghosts,
   As silent as the pictures on the wall.

The stranger at my fireside cannot see
   The forms I see, nor hear the sounds I hear;
He but perceives what is; while unto me
   All that has been is visible and clear.

We have no title-deeds to house or lands;
   Owners and occupants of earlier dates
From graves forgotten stretch their dusty hands,
   And hold in mortmain still their old estates.

The spirit world around this world of sense
   Floats like an atmosphere, and everywhere
Wafts through these earthly mists and vapours dense
   A vital breath of more ethereal air.

Our little lives are kept in equipoise
   By opposite attractions and desires;
The struggle of the instinct that enjoys,
   And the more noble instinct that aspires.

GHOST ROAD etched by headlights during the
   Monte Carlo Rally, *by Alexander Low*
GYMNASIUM, *by Guy Gravett*

These perturbations, this perpetual jar
   Of earthly wants and aspirations high,
Come from the influence of an unseen star,
   An undiscovered planet in our sky.

And as the moon from some dark gate of cloud
   Throws o'er the sea a floating bridge of light,
Across whose trembling planks our fancies crowd
   Into the realm of mystery and night,—

So from the world of spirits there descends
   A bridge of light, connecting it with this,
O'er whose unsteady floor, that sways and bends,
   Wander our thoughts above the dark abyss.

                      Longfellow

Night-hag

Nor uglier follow the Night-hag, when call'd
In secret riding through the air she comes,
Lured with the smell of infant blood, to dance
With Lapland witches. . . .

              PARADISE LOST: *John Milton*

                      Come, seeling night,
Scarf up the tender eye of pitiful day,
And with thy bloody and invisible hand
Cancel and tear to pieces that great bond
Which keeps me pale! Light thickens, and the crow
Makes wing to the rooky wood:
Good things of day begin to droop and drowse,
Whiles night's black agents to their preys do rouse.

                 MACBETH: *Shakespeare*

SHAKESPEARE

The Night before Agincourt

Chorus.   Now entertain conjecture of a time
When creeping murmur and the poring dark
Fills the wide vessel of the universe.
From camp to camp through the foul womb of night
The hum of either army stilly sounds,
That the fix'd sentinels almost receive
The secret whispers of each other's watch:
Fire answers fire, and through their paly flames
Each battle sees the other's umber'd face;
Steed threatens steed, in high and boastful neighs
Piercing the night's dull ear; and from the tents
The armourers, accomplishing the knights,
With busy hammers closing rivets up,
Give dreadful note of preparation:
The country cocks do crow, the clocks do toll,
And the third hour of drowsy morning name.
Proud of their numbers and secure in soul,
The confident and over-lusty French
Do the low-rated English play at dice;
And chide the crippled tardy-gaited night
Who, like a foul and ugly witch, doth limp
So tediously away. The poor condemned English,
Like sacrifices, by their watchful fires
Sit patiently and inly ruminate
The morning's danger, and their gesture sad
Investing lank-lean cheeks and war-worn coats
Presenteth them unto the gazing moon
So many horrid ghosts. O now, who will behold
The royal captain of this ruin'd band
Walking from watch to watch, from tent to tent,
Let him cry 'Praise and glory on his head!'
For forth he goes and visits all his host,
Bids them good morrow with a modest smile,
And calls them brothers, friends and countrymen.
Upon his royal face there is no note

How dread an army hath enrounded him;
Nor doth he dedicate one jot of colour
Unto the weary and all-watched night,
But freshly looks and over-bears attaint
With cheerful semblance and sweet majesty;
That every wretch, pining and pale before,
Beholding him, plucks comfort from his looks:
A largess universal like the sun
His liberal eye doth give to every one,
Thawing cold fear, that mean and gentle all
Behold, as may unworthiness define,
A little touch of Harry in the night.
And so our scene must to the battle fly;
Where – O for pity! – we shall much disgrace
With four or five most vile and ragged foils,
Right ill-disposed in brawl ridiculous,
The name of Agincourt. Yet sit and see,
Minding true things by what their mockeries be.

THE LIFE OF HENRY V: *William Shakespeare*

W. H. PRESCOTT

Cortés and the Melancholy Night

In the year 1520 Herman Cortés, the Spanish conqueror of Mexico, and his tiny force had to fight their way out of the city of Tlacopan. This is how the American historian W. H. Prescott describes 'Noche Triste', the melancholy night of the evacuation:

THERE WAS no longer any question as to the expediency of evacuating the capital. The only doubt was as to the time of doing so, and the route. The Spanish commander called a council of officers to deliberate on these matters. It was his purpose to retreat on Tlascala and in that capital to decide according to circumstances on his future operations. After some discussion, they agreed on the causeway of Tlacopan as the avenue by which to leave the city. It would, indeed, take them back by a circuitous route, considerably longer than either of those by which they had approached the capital. But, for that reason, it would be less likely to be guarded, as least suspected; and the causeway itself, being shorter than either of the other entrances, would sooner place the army in comparative security on the main land.

There was some difference of opinion in respect to the hour of departure. The day-time, it was argued by some, would be preferable, since it would enable them to see the nature and extent of their danger, and to provide against it. Darkness would be much more likely to embarrass their own movements than those of the enemy, who were familiar with the ground. A thousand impediments would occur in the night, which might prevent their acting in concert, or obeying, or even ascertaining, the orders of the commander. But on the other hand it was urged, that the night presented many obvious advantages in dealing with a foe who rarely carried his hostilities beyond the day. The late active operations of the Spaniards had thrown the Mexicans off their guard, and it was improbable they would anticipate so speedy a departure of their enemies. With celerity and caution they might succeed, therefore, in making their escape from the town, possibly over the causeway, before their retreat should be discovered; and, could they once get beyond that pass of peril, they felt little apprehension for the rest.

These views were fortified, it is said, by the counsels of a soldier named Botello, who professed the mysterious science of judicial astrology. He had gained credit with the army by some predictions which had been verified by the events; those lucky hits which make chance pass for calculation with the credulous multitude. This man recommended to his countrymen by all means to evacuate the place in the night, as the hour most propitious to them, although he should perish in it. The event proved the astrologer better acquainted with his own horoscope than with that of others.

It is possible Botello's predictions had some weight in determining the opinion of

Cortés. Superstition was the feature of the age, and the Spanish general, as we have seen, had a full measure of its bigotry. Seasons of gloom, moreover, disposed the mind to a ready acquiescence in the marvellous. It is, however, quite as probable that he made use of the astrologer's opinion, finding it coincided with his own, to influence that of his men, and inspire them with higher confidence. At all events it was decided to abandon the city that very night.

The general's first care was to provide for the safe transportation of the treasure. Many of the common soldiers had converted their share of the prize, as we have seen, into gold chains, collars, or other ornaments, which they easily carried about their persons. But the royal fifth, together with that of Cortés himself, and much of the rich booty of the principal cavaliers had been converted into bars and wedges of solid gold, and deposited in one of the strong apartments of the palace. Cortés delivered the share belonging to the crown to the royal officers, assigning them one of the strongest horses, and a guard of Castilian soldiers to transport it. Still, much of the treasure belonging both to the crown and to individuals was necessarily abandoned, from the want of adequate means of conveyance. The metal lay scattered in shining heaps along the floor, exciting the cupidity of the soldiers. 'Take what you will of it,' said Cortés to his men. 'Better you should have it than these Mexican hounds. But be careful not to overload yourselves. He travels safest in the dark night who travels lightest.' His own more wary followers took heed to his counsel, helping themselves to a few articles of least bulk, though, it might be, of greatest value. But the troops of Narvaez, pining for riches, of which they had heard so much, and hitherto seen so little, showed no such discretion. To them it seemed as if the very mines of Mexico were turned up before them, and, rushing on the treacherous spoil, they greedily loaded themselves with as much of it, not merely as they could accommodate about their persons, but as they could stow away in wallets, boxes, or any other mode of conveyance at their disposal.

Cortés next arranged the order of march. The van, composed of two hundred Spanish foot, he placed under the command of the valiant Gonzalo de Sandoval, supported by Diego de Ordaz, Francisco de Lujo, and about twenty other cavaliers. The rearguard, constituting the strength of the infantry, was intrusted to Pedro de Alvarado and Velasquez de Leon. The general himself took charge of the 'battle', or centre, in which went the baggage, some of the heavy guns, most of which, however, remained in the rear, the treasure, and the prisoners. These consisted of a son and two daughters of Montezuma, Cacama, the deposed lord of Tezcuco, and several other nobles, whom Cortés retained as important pledges in his future negotiations with the enemy. The Tlascalans were distributed pretty equally among the three divisions; and Cortés had under his immediate command a hundred picked soldiers, his own veterans most attached to his service, who, with Christoval de Olid, Francisco de Morla, Alonso de Avila, and two or three other cavaliers, formed a select corps to act wherever occasion might require.

The general had already superintended the construction of a portable bridge to be laid over the open canals in the causeway. This was given in charge to an officer named Magarino, with forty soldiers under his orders, all pledged to defend the passage to the last extremity. The bridge was to be taken up when the entire army had crossed one of the breaches, and transported to the next. There were three of these openings in the causeway, and most fortunate would it have been for the expedition, if the foresight of the commander had provided the same number of bridges. But the labour would have been great, and time was short.

At midnight the troops were under arms, in readiness for the march. Mass was performed by Father Olmedo, who invoked the protection of the Almighty through the awful perils of the night. The gates were thrown open, and, on the first of July, 1520, the Spaniards for the last time sallied forth from the walls of the ancient fortress, the scene of so much suffering and such indomitable courage.

The night was cloudy, and a drizzling rain, which fell without intermission, added to the obscurity. The great square before the palace was deserted, as, indeed, it had been since the fall of Montezuma. Steadily, and as noiselessly as possible, the Spaniards held their way along the great street of Tlacopan, which so lately had resounded to the tumult of battle. All was now hushed in silence; and they were only reminded of the past by the occasional presence of some solitary corpse, or a dark heap of the slain, which too plainly told where the strife had been hottest. As they passed along the lanes and alleys which opened into the great street, or looked down the canals, whose polished surface gleamed with a sort of ebon lustre through the obscurity of night, they easily fancied that they discerned the shadowy forms of their foe lurking in ambush, and ready to spring on them. But it was only fancy; and the city slept undisturbed even by the prolonged echoes of the tramp of the horses, and the hoarse rumbling of the artillery and baggage trains. At length a lighter space beyond the dusky line of buildings showed the van of the army that it was emerging on the open causeway. They might well have congratulated themselves on having thus escaped the dangers of an assault in the city itself, and that a brief time would place them in comparative safety on the opposite shore. But the Mexicans were not all asleep.

As the Spaniards drew near the spot where the street opened on the causeway, and were preparing to lay the portable bridge across the uncovered breach which now met their eyes, several Indian sentinels, who had been stationed at this, as at the other approaches to the city, took the alarm, and fled, rousing their countrymen by their cries. The priests, keeping their night watch on the summit of the *teocallis*, instantly caught the tidings and sounded their shells, while the huge drum in the desolate temple of the war-god sent forth those solemn tones, which, heard only in seasons of calamity, vibrated through every corner of the capital. The Spaniards saw that no time was to be lost. The bridge was brought forward and fitted with all possible expedition. Sandoval was the first to try its strength, and, riding across, was followed by his little body of chivalry, his infantry, and Tlascalan allies, who formed the first division of the army. Then came Cortés and his squadrons, with the baggage, ammunition waggons, and a part of the artillery. But before they had time to defile across the narrow passage, a gathering sound was heard, like that of a mighty forest agitated by the winds. It grew louder and louder, while on the dark waters of the lake was heard a splashing noise, as of many oars. Then came a few stones and arrows striking at random among the hurrying troops. They fell every moment faster and more furious, till they thickened into a terrible tempest, while the very heavens were rent with the yells and war-cries of myriads of combatants, who seemed all at once to be swarming over land and lake!

The Spaniards pushed steadily on through this arrowy sleet, though the barbarians, dashing their canoes against the sides of the causeway, clambered up and broke in upon their ranks. But the Christians, anxious only to make their escape, declined all combat except for self-preservation. The cavaliers, spurring forward their steeds, shook off their assailants, and rode over their prostrate bodies, while the men on foot with their good swords or the butts of their pieces drove them headlong again down the sides of the dike.

But the advance of several thousand men, marching, probably, on a front of not more than fifteen or twenty abreast, necessarily required much time, and the leading files had already reached the second breach in the causeway before those in the rear had entirely traversed the first. Here they halted; as they had no means of effecting a passage, smarting all the while under unintermitting volleys from the enemy, who were clustered thick on the waters around this second opening. Sorely distressed, the vanguard sent repeated messages to the rear to demand the portable bridge. At length the last of the army had crossed, and Magarino and his sturdy followers endeavoured to raise the ponderous framework. But it stuck fast in the sides of the dike. In vain they strained every nerve. The weight of so many men and horses, and above all of the heavy artillery, had wedged the timbers so firmly in the stones and earth, that it was beyond their power to dislodge them. Still they laboured amidst a torrent of missiles, until, many of them slain, and all wounded, they were obliged to abandon the attempt.

The tidings soon spread from man to man, and no sooner was their dreadful import comprehended, than a cry of despair arose, which for a moment drowned all the noise of conflict. All means of retreat were cut off. Scarcely hope was left. The only hope was in such desperate exertions as each could make for himself. Order and subordination were at an end. Intense danger produced intense selfishness. Each thought only of his own life. Pressing forward, he trampled down the weak and the wounded, heedless whether it were friend or foe. The leading files, urged on by the rear, were crowded on the brink of the gulf. Sandoval, Ordaz, and the other cavaliers dashed into the water. Some succeeded in swimming their horses across; others failed, and some, who reached the opposite bank, being over-turned in the ascent, rolled headlong with their steeds into the lake. The infantry followed pellmell, heaped promiscuously on one another, frequently pierced by the shafts, or struck down by the war-clubs of the Aztecs; while many an unfortunate victim was dragged half-stunned on board their canoes, to be reserved for a protracted, but more dreadful death.

The carnage raged fearfully along the length of the causeway. Its shadowy bulk presented a mark of sufficient distinctness for the enemy's missiles, which often prostrated their own countrymen in the blind fury of the tempest. Those nearest the dike, running their canoes alongside, with a force that shattered them to pieces, leaped on the land and grappled with the Christians, until both came rolling down the side of the causeway together. But the Aztec fell among his friends, while his antagonist was borne away in triumph to the sacrifice. The struggle was long and deadly. The Mexicans were recognised by their white cotton tunics, which showed faint through the darkness. Above the combatants rose a wild and discordant clamour, in which horrid shouts of vengeance were mingled with groans of agony, with invocations of the saints and the blessed Virgin, and with the screams of women; for there were several women, both native and Spaniards, who had accompanied the Christian camp. Among these, one named María de Estrada is particularly noticed for the courage she displayed, battling with broad-sword and target like the staunchest of the warriors.

The opening in the causeway, meanwhile, was filled up with the wreck of matter which had been forced into it, ammunition-waggons, heavy guns, bales of rich stuffs scattered over the waters, chests of solid ingots, and bodies of men and horses, till over this dismal ruin a passage was gradually formed by which those in the rear were enabled to clamber to the other side. Cortés, it is said, found a place that was fordable, where halting with the water up to his saddle-girths, he endeavoured to check the confusion, and lead his followers by a safer path to the opposite bank. But his voice was lost in the wild uproar, and finally, hurrying on with the tide, he pressed forwards with a few trusty cavaliers, who remained near his person, to the van; but not before he had seen his favourite page, Juan de Salazar, struck down, a corpse, by his side. Here he found Sandoval and his companions, halting before the third and last breach, endeavouring to cheer on their followers to surmount it. But their resolution faltered. It was wide and deep; though the passage was not so closely beset by the enemy as the preceding ones. The cavaliers again set the example by plunging into the water. Horse and foot followed as they could, some swimming, others with dying grasp clinging to the manes and tails of the struggling animals. Those fared best, as the general had predicted, who travelled lightest; and many were the unfortunate wretches, who, weighed down by the fatal gold which they loved so well, were buried with it in the salt floods of the lake. Cortes, with his gallant comrades, Olid, Morla, Sandoval, and some few others, still kept in the advance, leading his broken remnant off the fatal causeway. The din of battle lessened in the distance; when the rumour reached them, that the rear-guard would be wholly overwhelmed without speedy relief. It seemed almost an act of desperation; but the generous hearts of the Spanish cavaliers did not stop to calculate danger when the cry for succour reached them. Turning their horses' bridles, they galloped back to the theatre of action, worked their way through the press, swam the canal, and placed themselves in the thick of the *mêlée* on the opposite bank.

The first grey of the morning was now coming over the waters. It showed the hideous confusion of the scene which had been shrouded in the obscurity of night. The dark masses of combatants, stretching along the dike, were seen struggling for mastery, until the very causeway on which they stood appeared to tremble, and reel to and fro, as if shaken by an earthquake; while the bosom of the lake, as far as the eye could reach, was darkened by canoes crowded with warriors, whose spears and bludgeons, armed with blades of 'volcanic glass', gleamed in the morning light.

From THE CONQUEST OF MEXICO, *by* W. H. Prescott

Anthem for Doomed Youth

What passing-bells for these who die as cattle?
Only the monstrous anger of the guns.
   Only the stuttering rifles' rapid rattle
Can patter out their hasty orisons.
No mockeries for them from prayers or bells,
   Nor any voice of mourning save the choirs, –
The shrill, demented choirs of wailing shells;
   And bugles calling for them from sad shires.

What candles may be held to speed them all?
   Not in the hands of boys, but in their eyes
Shall shine the holy glimmers of good-byes.
   The pallor of girls' brows shall be their pall;
Their flowers the tenderness of silent minds,
And each slow dusk a drawing-down of blinds.

Wilfrid Owen (1893–1918)

Bayonet Charge

Suddenly he awoke and was running – raw
In raw-seamed hot khaki, his sweat heavy,
Stumbling across a field of clods towards a green hedge
That dazzled with rifle fire, hearing
Bullets smacking the belly out of the air –
He lugged a rifle numb as a smashed arm;
The patriotic tear that had brimmed in his eye
Sweating like molten iron from the centre of his chest, –

In bewilderment then he almost stopped –
In what cold clockwork of the stars and the nations
Was he the hand pointing that second? He was running
Like a man who has jumped up in the dark and runs
Listening between his footfalls for the reason
Of his still running, and his foot hung like
Statuary in mid-stride. Then the shot-slashed furrows

Threw up a yellow hare that rolled like a flame
And crawled in a threshing circle, its mouth wide
Open silent, its eyes standing out.
He plunged past with his bayonet towards the green hedge,
King, honour, human dignity etcetera
Dropped like luxuries in a yelling alarm
To get out of that blue cracking air
His terror's touchy dynamite.

From THE HAWK IN THE RAIN, *the early poems of Ted Hughes*

Bombers over Berlin

ENEMY air activity over Berlin has again increased very considerably. During the week-end alone there were four alarms. During one of the attacks we were with Dicki Wrede, who provides accommodation, night after night, in her 'catacomb' in the Rauchstrasse for men on leave from the front, and on this occasion was celebrating the arrival of some of them with a bottle-party. Twenty guests, nearly all of them badly wounded officers, some with a wooden leg or on crutches, and decorated with the Golden Cross or the Knight's Cross, turned up, laden with bottles; among them was Knyphausen, Hanstein, Brandis and Rumohr. When the alarm sounded, not one of them showed the slightest sign of nervousness. The flak in the Zoo opened a furious rapid fire. Then down crashed the bombs, and there ensued the heaviest gunfire and the most concentrated bombing that I have ever witnessed in the Tiergarten area. The greater the fury of the explosions, the merrier became our mood. The music did not stop for a moment. When one young girl in a moment of panic wanted to rush out into the street, the roars of laughter quickly brought her to her senses and she returned to the party. But how very stupid it was to have closed the night clubs in all the cities. I wonder if any of the reunions held by order of the regime would have shown the same spirit during a heavy air raid as did these young people, whose love of life had been unimpaired by their terrible injuries and who laughed at the threat of death.

Wednesday, March 14, 1945

The Ministry of Propaganda was hit by a mine yesterday at 9.00 p.m. The explosion destroyed that part of the Ministry which is situated in Prince Ferdinand of Prussia's palace. The palace was one of the most beautiful in Berlin. It was built in the eighteenth century and was remodelled in the classical style by Schinkel. Goebbels had always been proud of the fact that his house had been practically undamaged by the war in the air. He looked upon it as a good omen. No one was killed, but the Wilhelmstrasse was closed – for the first time in the war – in order to facilitate the work of the fire brigade and demolition parties. The new Propaganda Ministry building next to the palace can still be used. Today at midday Frau Goebbels arrived, accompanied by three of her children and an Air Force orderly, to view the damage. In her mink coat and green velvet hat, she looked as though she were going to a cocktail party.

From WHILE BERLIN BURNS, *the diary of Hans-Georg von Studnitz,*
1943–1945, translated from the German by R. H. Stevens

A letter from the blitz

October 13, 1940

MY DEAR: Please note new address: Hitler has evicted us again – nobody will live at No 53 any more, until the war's over. . . .

When I got home on Friday evening the builder's men had practically finished their repairs after last week's bomb damage: all the ceilings had been replaced, a dividing wall made good and the window-frames made part of the house again. It had been planned that until the house was shipshape I was to sleep on the kitchen floor of No 10 with Ron and Mona while the rest of the family disposed themselves in the downstairs rooms of 53 – Mother and Florence in the dining-room and Dad on the kitchen floor. Uncle insisted on remaining upstairs in his own bedroom, as usual.

The folks turned in early, but Johnnie the sergeant called round to No. 10 and invited Ron and me along to the Mess – he said it was ladies' night, and would Mona come too. She came too. We yarned until we yawned and about 12.30 began to think about going home. By this time the nightly raid had been going on for some time, but although the barrage was heavy, nothing dropped – until *now*.

We heard the swoosh of a bomb louder than I've ever known before. We flung ourselves on to the floor. The swoosh lasted probably four seconds, then there was a terrific explosion. We got up and grinned at each other the way one does, put on our coats and hats and went out to see where the thing had dropped. In the street we heard the warden's whistle and saw signs of activity in the moonlight outside No. 53. We pushed past some people through the gaping garage doors. Someone said, 'The old lady's buried somewhere under there.' But as we got to the kitchen door we heard Mother's voice and saw her picking her way through the debris. She was asking where was Dad and Uncle and the old couple next door – a bit distraught, poor darling.

Then we saw Dad on his hands and knees, looking for his hat. We shuddered at the unholy mess in the kitchen where he'd been lying. It was he who'd been buried – under plaster and glass, bits of gas-stove and broken crockery and – pea soup! The window frame was hanging down only about two feet from where his head had been. At the explosion he'd found himself covered in the mess of it all, found his head wet and sticky and naturally thought it was his own blood. A taste of it put his mind to rest – it was just that pea soup of Mother's, blasted off the stove all over the poor man.

'Look after your mother,' he said: 'I'll come when I've found my hat.' (He always sleeps in his trilby as an extra protection.) But I jammed mine on his head and got him to his feet. Meantime Mona had found Uncle sitting on a pile of plaster (debris from the previous blow-up) on the pavement outside. The frame on his window had blown out on to his back as he lay in bed. He was badly bruised but not broken in any way. A diminutive warden had somehow managed to drag him down the stairs and dump him on the plaster pile. Florence was safe, too – the dining-room hadn't suffered much: only the ceiling down, the windows broken and the door torn off its hinges and flung across Mother's bed, without harming her.

We put blankets around them all, got them past the wardens and ambulance-men – who *so* much wanted to treat someone for something! – and bundled them across to No 10. Black coffee and whisky took the shock out of them. I had a sense of intense elation – it was so marvellous to have them all here, whole and unbloodied; it was a real sharp pleasure such as one seldom feels. After we'd tucked them in, Ron and I went back to see the extent of the damage.

The bomb had dropped plumb on the railway line just those few yards directly behind the house: we saw the gaping hole in the bright moonlight; bits of the rail had been thrown half-a-mile to land in the High Street. 53 was still standing, but the damage was pretty considerable and the rooms ugly with wreckage. Small bits of the bomb were embedded in the outer walls, glass fragments stuck like daggers an inch deep in the inner walls – some of the furniture, too, had the glass splinters buried in it. Smashed woodwork littered the place, and the floors were a foot deep in crumpled plaster . . . all the work the men had finished that day lay on the floors again, with a lot more besides, and all the tiles were off the roof again.

The 'all clear' siren came at 2.30. Next morning the papers reported a very quiet night . . . .

JIM

JOHN HERSEY

The Night of Hiroshima

BY NIGHTFALL, ten thousand victims of the explosion had invaded the Red Cross Hospital, and Dr Sasaki, worn out, was wandering aimlessly and dully up and down the stinking corridors with wads of bandage and bottles of mercurochrome, still wearing the glasses he had taken from the wounded nurse, binding up the worst cuts as he came to them. Other doctors were putting compresses of saline solution on the worst burns. That was all they could do. After dark, they worked by the light of the city's fires and by candles the ten remaining nurses held for them. Dr Sasaki had not looked outside the hospital all day; the scene inside was so terrible and so compelling that it had not occurred to him to ask any questions about what had happened beyond the windows and doors. Ceilings and partitions had fallen; plaster, dust, blood, and vomit were everywhere. Patients were dying by the hundreds but there was nobody to carry away the corpses. Some of the hospital staff distributed biscuits and rice balls, but the charnel-house smell was so strong that few were hungry. By three o'clock next morning, after nineteen straight hours of his gruesome work, Dr Sasaki was incapable of dressing another wound. He and some other survivors of the hospital staff got straw mats and went outdoors – thousands of patients and hundreds of dead were in the yard and on the drive way – and hurried around behind the hospital and lay down in hiding to snatch some sleep. But within an hour wounded people had found them; a complaining circle formed around them: 'Doctors! Help us! How can you sleep?' Dr Sasaki got up again and went back to work. Early in the day, he thought for the first time of his mother at their country home in Mukaihara, thirty miles from town. He usually went home every night. He was afraid she would think he was dead.

From HIROSHIMA, *by John Hersey*

The night of King Lear

. . . This night, wherein the cub-drawn bear would couch,
The lion and the belly-pinched wolf
Keep their fur dry, unbonnetted he runs,
And bids what will take all.

Lear: Blow, winds, and crack your cheeks! rage! blow!
  You cataracts and hurricanoes, spout
  Till you have drench'd our steeples, drown'd the cocks!
  You sulphurous and thought-executing fires,
  Vaunt-couriers to oak-cleaving thunderbolts,
  Singe my white head! And thou, all-shaking thunder,
  Smite flat the thick rotundity o' the world!
  Crack nature's moulds, all germins spill at once
  That make ingrateful man!

Paul Scofield and Alec McCowen in a Royal Shakespeare Company production of 'King Lear', photographed by Zoë Dominic

NIGHT BOMBER BOUND FOR BERLIN, 1943
by Fl.-Lt. Peter Clark

COMMANDO ATTACK, Norway, 1941
by Captain Reynolds

LONDON'S BURNING, 1940
by Bert Mason

PINK AND GREEN SLEEPERS
by Henry Moore (Tate Gallery, London)

THIEVES! *by George Cruikshank*

HENRY MAYHEW

A Visit to the Dens of Thieves

. . . ON ENTERING into a public-house in another alley near Union Street we came to one of the most dangerous thieves' dens we have visited in the course of our rambles. As we approached the door of the house we saw a dissipated-looking man stealthily whispering outside the door to the ruffian-looking landlord, who appeared to be a fighting man, from his large coarse head and broken nose. The officer by our side hinted to us that the latter was a fence, or receiver of stolen property, and was probably speaking to his companion on some business of this nature. As we went forward they sneaked away, the one through a neighbouring archway, and the other into his house. We followed the latter into the public-house, and found two or three brutal-looking men loafing about the bar. We passed through a small yard behind the house, where we found a number of fighting dogs chained to their kennels. Some were close to our feet as we passed along, and others, kept in an outhouse beside them, could almost snap at our face. We went to another outhouse beyond, where between thirty and forty persons were assembled round a wooden enclosure looking on, while some of their dogs were killing rats. They consisted of burglars, pickpockets, and the associates of thieves, along with one or two receivers of stolen property. Many of them were coarse and brutal in their appearance, and appeared to be in their element as they urged on their dogs to destroy the rats, which were taken out one after another from a small wooden box. These men apparently ranged from twenty-two to forty years of age. Many of them had the rough stamp of the criminal in their countenances, and when inflamed with strong drink, would possibly be fit for any deed of atrocious villainy. Some of the dogs were strong and vigorous, and soon disposed of the rats as they ran round the wooden enclosure, surrounded by this redoubtable band of ruffians, who made the rafters ring with merriment when the dog caught hold of its prey, or when the rat turned desperate on its adversary. . . .

This is one of the most dangerous thieves' dens we have seen in London. Were any unfortunate man to be inveigled into it in the evening, or at midnight, when the desperadoes who haunt it are inflamed with strong drink, he would be completely in their power, even were he the bravest soldier in the British service, and armed with a revolver. Were he to fight his way desperately through the large ferocious gang in this outhouse, the fighting-dogs in the yard might be let loose on him, and were he to cleave his way through them, he would have to pass through the public-house frequented by similar low characters. . . .

. . . The rookery in Spitalfields we proposed to visit is comprised within the space of about 400 square yards. It is bounded by Church Street, Whitechapel, East Brick Lane, and West Commercial Street, and contains 800 thieves, vagabonds, beggars and prostitutes, a large proportion of whom may be traced to the old criminal inhabitants of the now extinct Essex Street and old Rose Lane.

For instance, a man and woman lived for many years in George Yard, Whitechapel, a narrow, dirty and overcrowded street leading from Whitechapel into Wentworth Street. The man was usually seen among crowds of thieves, gambling and associating with them. As his family increased, in the course of time he took a beershop and lodging-house for thieves in Thrall Street. His family consisted of three boys and three girls. His wife usually addressed the young thieves as they left her lodging-house in the morning, in the hearing of her own children, in this manner: 'Now, my little dears, do the best you can, and may God bless you!'

The following is a brief account of their children: –

The eldest son married a girl whose father died during his transportation. He and his wife gained their living by thieving, and were frequently in custody. At last he connected himself with burglars, was tried, convicted, and sentenced to six years' penal servitude. He is now at Gibraltar, ten months of his sentence being unexpired. His wife has been left with three young children; since his transportation she has been frequently in custody for robbing drunken men, and has had an illegitimate child since her husband left. Her eldest daughter was taken from her about twelve months ago by Mr Ashcroft, secretary of the Refuge Aid Society, and placed in a refuge in Albert Street, Mile End New Town, where the Society maintains her. The girl is eleven years of age, and appeared pleased that she was taken away from her filthy abode and bad companions in George Street. The second son has been repeatedly in custody for uttering base coin, and was at last convicted and transported for four years. The eldest daughter married a man who was also transported, and is now a returned convict. She was apprehended, convicted, and sentenced to four years' penal servitude. While in Newgate jail she was delivered of twins, and received a reprieve, and has since been in custody for shoplifting.

. . . We next went to a brothel in Wentworth Street, kept by a woman, a notorious character. She has been repeatedly in custody for robbing drunken men, and her husband is now in prison for felony. She is a strong, coarse-looking woman, with her countenance bearing marked traces of unbrided passion – the type of person we would expect as the keeper of a low brothel. She had been stabbed on the cheek a few days previously by another woman, and bore the scar of the fresh wound at the time of our visit. The rooms of her house were wretchedly furnished, suitable to the low orgies of this foul abode. One or two withered prostitutes were lounging about the kitchen. . . .

We visited another lodging-house of the lowest description, belonging to an infamous man whom we have already referred to. We were shown upstairs to a large room filled with beds, by a coarse-featured hideous old hag with a dark moustache. Her hair was grey, and her face seamed and scarred with dark passions, as she stood before us with her protruding breasts and bloated figure. Her eyes were dark and muddy. She had two gold rings on one of her fingers, and was dressed in a dirty light cotton gown sadly tattered, a red spotted soiled handkerchief round her neck, and a dirty light apron, almost black. On observing us looking at her, she remarked, 'I am an old woman, and am not so young as I have been. Instead of enjoying the fruit of my hard-wrought life, some other person has done it.'

On examining one of the beds in the room, we found the bedding to consist of two rugs, two sheets and a flock bed, with a pillow and pillow-case, let at 3*d*. a night. This house is registered for thirty lodgers. Young and middle-aged women, the lowest prostitutes, and thieves frequent this house; some with holes cut with disease into their brow. D—bl—n B—ll is the proprietor of this infamous abode. We saw him as we passed through the house: a sinister-looking, middle-aged man, about 5 feet 7 inches in height. On leaving the house, the old hag stood at the foot of the stair, a picture of horrid misery.

from 'THOSE THAT WILL NOT WORK', *the fourth volume of* LONDON LABOUR AND THE LONDON POOR, *published in* 1862. *By Henry Mayhew*

SHAKESPEARE

The Hateful Night

In this hateful night Lucrece, the virtuous wife of Collatinus, has been ravished by the treacherous Sextus Tarquinius.

He like a thievish dog creeps sadly thence;
She like a wearied lamb lies panting there;
He scowls, and hates himself for his offence;
She, desperate, with her nails her flesh doth tear;
He faintly flies, sweating with guilty fear;
 She stays, exclaiming on the direful night;
 He runs, and chides his vanish'd, loathed delight.

He thence departs a heavy convertite;
She there remains a hopeless cast-away;
He in his speed looks for the morning light;
She prays she never may behold the day,
'For day,' quoth she, 'night's 'scapes doth open lay,
 And my true eyes have never practised how
 To cloak offences with a cunning brow.

275

'They think not but that every eye can see
The same disgrace which they themselves behold;
And therefore would they still in darkness be,
To have their unseen sin remain untold;
For they their guilt with weeping will unfold,
　　And grave, like water that doth eat in steel,
　　Upon my cheeks what helpless shame I feel.'

Here she exclaims against repose and rest,
And bids her eyes thereafter still be blind.
She wakes her heart by beating on her breast,
And bids it leap from thence, where it may find
Some purer chest to close so pure a mind.
　　Frantic with grief thus breathes she forth her spite
　　Against the unseen secrecy of night:

'O comfort-killing Night, image of hell!
Dim register and notary of shame!
Black stage for tragedies and murders fell!
Vast sin-concealing chaos! nurse of blame!
Blind muffled bawd! dark harbour for defame!
　　Grim cave of death! whispering conspirator
　　With close-tongued treason and the ravisher!

'O hateful, vaporous and foggy Night!
Since thou art guilty of my cureless crime,
Muster thy mists to meet the eastern light,
Make war against proportion'd course of time;
Or if thou wilt permit the sun to climb
　　His wonted height, yet ere he go to bed,
　　Knit poisonous clouds about his golden head.

'With rotten damps ravish the morning air;
Let their exhaled unwholesome breaths make sick
The life of purity, the supreme fair,
Ere he arrive his weary noon-tide prick;
And let thy misty vapours march so thick
　　That in their smoky ranks his smother'd light
　　May set at noon and make perpetual night . . .'

From THE RAPE OF LUCRECE, *by William Shakespeare*

The Murder of PC 43

JOHN SMITH, *alias* WILLIAM SAPWELL
Executed for the Murder of a Policeman

THE COLD-BLOODED and atrocious murder of which this man was convicted, showed him to merit most fully the awful punishment which befell him.

The object of the dreadful crime of which he was guilty, was a constable of the G division of the Metropolitan Police Force, then only recently established in London and its vicinity. In laying before our readers the circumstances of the case, it will not perhaps be considered out of place if we shortly recite the manner in which that most admirable body was first called into existence and operation.

The necessity of some improvement in the police of the metropolis had long been felt, and the utter inadequacy of the few Bow Street patrols hitherto employed to guard the streets of London by day, and of the watchmen, upon whom the same duty devolved by night, had for a considerable time attracted the attention of the public and of parliament. Committees of the House of Commons sat for the purpose of receiving evidence upon the subject, and a vast number of suggestions were thrown out upon the proper measures which should be taken with a view to obviate the existing difficulty. . . .

In the session of parliament of the year 1829 Mr Peel, at that time Secretary of State for the Home Department, introduced a bill to the House of Commons . . . The general scheme which was put forth as being most desirable, was that of making a police throughout England, the centre and focus of which was to be fixed in London. The great towns throughout the kingdom would act as corresponding agents for the diffusion of that intelligence, the rapid and regular transmission of which was properly looked upon as so important to the success of any system of this description. In London, again, a smaller focus was to be formed under a board of commissioners, who would have daily communication with every division of the metropolis in which the police should be established, as well as with those country districts to which we have already alluded.

The minor details of the measure were to be carried out by the marking out of divisions, to be governed by superintendants, inspectors, serjeants, and privates in their various grades, constant communication being kept up throughout the metropolis, by day as well as by night, between each division. . . .

Mr Peel lost no time in proposing a bill in parliament, which should have for its object the immediate appointment of a body of men capable of performing all the police duties of the metropolis. The proposition was at once assented to by both houses of the legislature, and on Tuesday the 29th September 1829, the 'new policemen' first entered upon their duties. Their dress, their supposed military character, and the extreme jealousy with which all classes of Englishmen view anything which may be supposed to derogate from their rights and privileges, long conspired to make this most useful force in the highest degree unpopular. Epithets of the most odious character were heaped upon them, attacks both abusive and violent were levelled at them from all quarters, and a few instances of irregularity amongst their numbers were eagerly seized hold of, as arguments to be employed against the general body. But at length, the increased safety obtained for the community, the quiet and orderly manner of the men themselves, as well as the improvement in the general conduct of the lower classes, obtained for them a reputation of the very highest description. The system which, first, was confined to the limits of the metropolis, has been joyfully extended to all large towns and to manufacturing neighbourhoods, and so anxious have even the most remote rural districts become for this new safeguard for their property and their lives, that almost every month sees the adoption of the plan in some new quarter. The improvement of the morals of the lower orders is no less than that which has taken place in their manners, and many of the crimes by which society was formerly so frequently disgraced, have now happily disappeared from the dreadful catalogue which the life of degraded man presents.

There can be no doubt that the offence of which we are about to enter into a description was in some degree attributable to that feeling of hatred for the police which was so peculiarly exemplified among the lower orders of the people. Long, the unfortunate object of the attack of this determined murderer, was a police-constable, No. 43 of the G division, and occupied a beat in Gray's Inn Lane. On the night of Monday the 16th August 1830, he was engaged in the performance of his duty when, at about half-past twelve o'clock, he observed three men of suspicious appearance lurking about the vicinity. Entertaining an apprehension of their intention to commit a burglary, he communicated his opinions to a brother constable on the adjoining beat, and it was determined that the men should be watched. They remained within Long's district of duty, and he followed them as far as the burial-ground of St Andrew's parish, which is situated at the back of Mecklenburgh Square. Here they stopped and remained in conversation for some time, and Long, believing this to be a favourable opportunity for convincing them of his intention to prevent the success of any marauding schemes which they might have in view, warned them to retire. The words had scarcely escaped the lips of the unfortunate man, ere he was violently seized by the arm by two of the party, while the third stabbed him to the heart. So desperate was the wound, that the murderer was unable to withdraw the weapon with which it was inflicted; but in his effort to do so, he pulled away the handle, and then all three ran off. This diabolical act was witnessed by more than one person, and several individuals instantly rushed to the spot. Long had fallen to the ground, with an exclamation that he was 'a dead man', and upon his head being raised upon the knee of one of the witnesses, he immediately expired. In the meantime, Newton, the constable to whom the unfortunate man had communicated his suspicions, had followed the assassins, and Smith was secured by him, having run a considerable distance and being in a state of the greatest agitation and alarm. Two other persons were also taken into custody, but it turned out that they were unconnected with the dreadful occurrence, and they were set at liberty. The truth of the suspicions of the constable was amply exhibited by the discovery of a number of housebreaking implements near the spot, which it was evident the thieves had intended to employ, but had thrown away in their flight. The handle of the knife was also discovered lying in the road at about one hundred yards from the spot where the murder was committed.

Several examinations of the prisoner subsequently took place before the magistrates at Hatton Garden, and witnesses were called who swore positively that his was the hand by which the wound was given which had caused the death of the deceased. During his imprisonment, he continued firm in his denial of participation in the murder, and maintained a sullen silence as to his occupation in life as well as his connections. He appeared to associate with none of his fellow-prisoners.

His trial took place at the Old Bailey sessions, on Friday the 17th of September, when it turned out that his name was Sapwell and that he was a baker by trade. He still protested his innocence, but the evidence of the witnesses being of the most conclusive description, a verdict of guilty was returned, and he was sentenced to be executed on the following Monday.

On the day after his conviction he was visited by his wife and his six children, to whom, as well as to the officers of the jail, he continued loud in his declarations of his having been wrongfully convicted. He asserted that he had been to the Bedford Tea Gardens at Camden Town on the night of the murder, and that on his way home he heard a cry of 'Stop thief', and had joined in the pursuit of four men whom he saw running away, when he was himself taken into custody. He was exhorted by the Rev. Mr Cotton, the ordinary of the prison, to whose humane advice he paid some attention; but he declined to receive the sacrament. . . .

On the morning of his execution (the 20th of September 1830), he entered freely into conversation with Sheriff Ward, and with new asseverations that he was not guilty of the crime for which he was about to suffer, declared, in an imaginary dialogue with the Almighty, that on his arrival at the gates of heaven, he should be unable to account for his standing there, and that the Almighty would give him admission; protesting, however, that he ought not to have been sent there so soon. He appeared sensible of his situation, and requested that the proceedings on the scaffold might occupy as little time as possible. He was turned off at the usual hour, and his remains were given to the directors of St George's Hospital for dissection.

The wretched man occupied the greater part of Saturday and Sunday, previous to his death, in drawing up statements of the manner in which he was by mistake drawn into the situation in which he stood, which amounted simply to a repetition of the story he had related to his family. He appears to have been very illiterate, his letters being both ill-spelt and ill-written, and he expressed none of those fears usually exhibited by persons in his situation.

Long, the constable, appears to have been a man of excellent character, having for a considerable time occupied a situation as watchman before he entered the police. He left a wife and several children, for whom a liberal public subscription was afterwards raised.

THE NEWGATE CALENDAR

EDGAR ALLAN POE

The Cask of Amontillado

THE THOUSAND injuries of Fortunato I had borne as I best could; but when he ventured upon insult, I vowed revenge. You, who so well know the nature of my soul, will not suppose, however, that I gave utterance to a threat. *At length* I would be avenged; this was a point definitely settled – but the very definitiveness with which it was resolved, precluded the idea of risk. I must not only punish, but punish with impunity. A wrong is unredressed when retribution overtakes its redresser. It is equally unredressed when the avenger fails to make himself felt as such to him who has done the wrong.

It must be understood, that neither by word nor deed had I given Fortunato cause to doubt my goodwill. I continued, as was my wont, to smile in his face, and he did not perceive that my smile *now* was at the thought of his immolation.

He had a weak point – this Fortunato – although in other regards he was a man to be respected and even feared. He prided himself on his connoisseurship in wine. Few Italians have the true virtuoso spirit. For the most part their enthusiasm is adapted to suit the time and opportunity – to practise imposture upon the British and Austrian millionaires. In painting and gemmary Fortunato, like his countrymen, was a quack – but in the matter of old wines he was sincere. In this respect I did not differ from him materially: I was skilful in the Italian vintages myself, and bought largely whenever I could.

It was about dusk, one evening during the supreme madness of the Carnival season, that I encountered my friend. He accosted me with excessive warmth, for he had been drinking much. The man wore motley. He had on a tight-fitting parti-striped dress, and his head was surmounted by the conical cap and bells. I was so pleased to see him, that I thought I should never have done wringing his hand.

I said to him: 'My dear Fortunato, you are luckily met. How remarkably well you are looking today! But I have received a pipe of what passes for Amontillado, and I have my doubts.'

'How?' said he; 'Amontillado? A pipe? Impossible! And in the middle of the Carnival!'

'I have my doubts,' I replied; 'and I was silly enough to pay the full Amontillado price without consulting you in the matter. You were not to be found, and I was fearful of losing a bargain.'

'Amontillado!'

'I have my doubts.'

'Amontillado!'

'And I must satisfy them.'

'Amontillado!'

'As you are engaged, I am on my way to Luchesi. If any one has a critical turn, it is he. He will tell me——'

'Luchesi cannot tell Amontillado from Sherry.'

'And yet some fools will have it that his taste is a match for your own.'

'Come, let us go.'

'Whither?'

'To your vaults.'

'My friend, no; I will not impose upon your good-nature. I perceive you have an engagement. Luchesi——'

'I have no engagement; come.'

'My friend, no. It is not the engagement, but the severe cold with which I perceive you are afflicted. The vaults are insufferably damp. They are encrusted with nitre.'

'Let us go nevertheless. The cold is merely nothing. Amontillado! You have been imposed upon. And as for Luchesi – he cannot distinguish Sherry from Amontillado.'

Thus speaking, Fortunato possessed himself of my arm. Putting on a mask of black silk, and drawing a *roquelaire* closely about my person, I suffered him to hurry me to my palazzo.

There were no attendants at home; they had absconded to make merry in honour of the time. I had told them that I should not return until the morning, and had given them explicit orders not to stir from the house. These orders were sufficient, I well knew, to ensure their immediate disappearance, one and all, as soon as my back was turned.

I took from their sconces two flambeaux, and giving one to Fortunato, bowed him through several suites of rooms to the archway that led into the vaults. I passed down a long and winding staircase, requesting him to be cautious as he followed. We came at length to the foot of the descent, and stood together on the damp ground of the catacombs of the Montresors.

The gait of my friend was unsteady, and the bells upon his cap jingled as he strode.

'The pipe,' said he.

'It is farther on,' said I; 'but observe the white webwork which gleams from these cavern walls.'

He turned towards me, and looked into my eyes with two filmy orbs that distilled the rheum of intoxication.

'Nitre,' I replied. 'How long have you had that cough?'

'Ugh! ugh! ugh! – ugh! ugh! ugh! – ugh! ugh! ugh! – ugh! ugh! ugh – ugh! ugh! ugh!' My poor friend found it impossible to reply for many minutes.

'It is nothing,' he said, at last.

'Come,' I said, with decision, 'we will go back; your health is precious. You are rich, respected, admired, beloved; you are happy, as once I was. You are a man to be missed. For me it is no matter. We will go back; you will be ill, and I cannot be responsible. Besides, there is Luchesi——'

'Enough,' he said, 'the cough is a mere nothing; it will not kill me. I shall not die of a cough.'

'True – true,' I replied; 'and, indeed, I had no intention of alarming you unnecessarily – but you should use all proper caution. A draught of this Medoc will defend us from the damps.'

Here I knocked off the neck of a bottle which I drew from a long row of its fellows that lay upon the mould.

'Drink,' I said, presenting him the wine.

He raised it to his lips with a leer. He paused and nodded to me familiarly, while his bells jingled.

'I drink,' he said, 'to the buried that repose around us.'

'And I to your long life.'

He again took my arm, and we proceeded.

'These vaults,' he said, 'are extensive.'

'The Montresors,' I replied, 'were a great and numerous family.'

'I forget your arms.'

'A huge human foot d'or, in a field azure; the foot crushes a serpent rampant whose fangs are embedded in the heel.'

'And the motto?'

'*Nemo me impune lacessit.*'

'Good!' he said.

The wine sparkled in his eyes and the bells jingled. My own fancy grew warm with the Medoc. We had passed through walls of piled bones, with casks and puncheons inter-mingling, into the inmost recesses of the catacombs. I paused again, and this time I made bold to seize Fortunato by an arm above the elbow.

'The nitre!' I said; 'see, it increases. It hangs like moss upon the vaults. We are below the river's bed. The drops of moisture trickle among the bones. Come, we will go back ere it is too late. Your cough——'

'It is nothing,' he said; 'let us go on. But first, another draught of the Medoc.'

I broke and reached him a flagon of De Grâve. He emptied it at a breath. His eyes flashed with a fierce light. He laughed and threw the bottle upwards with a gesticulation I did not understand.

I looked at him in surprise. He repeated the movement – a grotesque one.

'You do not comprehend?' he said.

'Not I,' I replied.

'Then you are not of the brotherhood.'

'How?'

'You are not of the masons.'

'Yes, yes,' I said; 'yes, yes.'

'You? Impossible! A mason?'

'A mason,' I replied.

'A sign,' he said.

'It is this,' I answered, producing a trowel from beneath the folds of my *roquelaire*.

'You jest,' he exclaimed, recoiling a few paces. 'But let us proceed to the Amontillado.'

'Be it so,' I said, replacing the tool beneath the cloak, and again offering him my arm. He leaned upon it heavily. We continued our route in search of the Amontillado. We passed through a range of low arches, descended, passed on, and descending again, arrived at a deep crypt, in which the foulness of the air caused our flambeaux to glow rather than flame.

At the most remote end of the crypt there appeared another less spacious. Its walls had been lined with human remains, piled to the vault overhead, in the fashion of the great catacombs of Paris. Three sides of this interior crypt were still ornamented in this manner. From the fourth the bones had been thrown down, and lay promiscuously upon the earth, forming at one point a mound of some size. Within the wall thus exposed by the displacing of the bones, we perceived a still interior recess, in depth about four feet, in width three, in height six or seven. It seemed to have been constructed for no especial use within itself, but formed merely the interval between two of the colossal supports of the roof of the catacombs, and was backed by one of their circumscribing walls of solid granite.

It was in vain that Fortunato, uplifting his dull torch, endeavoured to pry into the depth of the recess. Its termination the feeble light did not enable us to see.

'Proceed,' I said; 'herein is the Amontillado. As for Luchesi——'

'He is an ignoramus,' interrupted my friend, as he stepped unsteadily forward, while I followed immediately at his heels. In an instant he had reached the extremity of the niche, and finding his progress arrested by the rock, stood stupidly bewildered. A moment more and I had fettered him to the granite. In its surface were two iron staples, distant from each other about two feet, horizontally. From one of these depended a short chain, from the other a padlock. Throwing the links about his waist, it was but the work of a few seconds to secure it. He was too much astounded to resist. Withdrawing the key, I stepped back from the recess.

'Pass your hand,' I said, 'over the wall; you cannot help feeling the nitre. Indeed it is *very* damp. Once more let me *implore* you to return. No? Then I must positively leave you. But I must first render you all the little attentions in my power.'

'The Amontillado!' ejaculated my friend, not yet recovered from his astonishment.

'True,' I replied, 'the Amontillado.'

As I said these words I busied myself among the pile of bones of which I have before spoken. Throwing them aside, I soon uncovered a quantity of building stone and mortar. With these materials, and with the aid of my trowel, I began vigorously to wall up the entrance of the niche.

I had scarcely laid the first tier of the masonry when I discovered that the intoxication of Fortunato had in a great measure worn off. The earliest indication I had of this was a low moaning cry from the depth of the recess. It was *not* the cry of a drunken man. There was then a long and obstinate silence. I laid the second tier, and the third, and the fourth; and then I heard the furious vibrations of the chain. The noise lasted for several minutes, during which, that I might hearken to it with the more satisfaction, I ceased my labour and sat down upon the bones. When at last the clanking subsided, I resumed the trowel, and finished without interruption the fifth, the sixth, and the seventh tier. The wall was now nearly upon a level with my breast. I again paused, and holding the flambeaux over the mason-work, threw a few feeble rays upon the figure within.

A succession of loud and shrill screams, bursting suddenly from the throat of the chained form, seemed to thrust me violently back. For a brief moment I hesitated – I trembled. Unsheathing my rapier, I began to grope with it about the recess; but the thought of an instant reassured me. I placed my hand upon the solid fabric of the catacombs, and felt satisfied. I reapproached the wall. I replied to the yells of him who clamoured. I re-echoed – I aided – I surpassed them in volume and in strength. I did this, and the clamourer grew still.

It was now midnight, and my task was drawing to a close. I had completed the eighth, the ninth, and the tenth tier. I had finished a portion of the last and the eleventh; there remained but a single stone to be fitted and plastered in. I struggled with its weight; I placed it partially in its destined position. But now there came from out the niche a low laugh that erected the hairs upon my head. It was succeeded by a sad voice, which I had difficulty in recognising as that of the noble Fortunato. The voice said –

'Ha! ha! ha! – he! he! – a very good joke indeed – and excellent jest. We will have many a rich laugh about it at the palazzo – he! he! he! – over our wine – he! he! he!'

'The Amontillado!' I said.

'He! he! he! – he! he! he! – yes, the Amontillado. But is it not getting late? Will not they be awaiting us at the palazzo, the Lady Fortunato and the rest? Let us be gone.'

'Yes,' I said, 'let us be gone.'

'*For the love of God, Montresor!*'

'Yes,' I said, 'for the love of God!'

But to these words I hearkened in vain for a reply. I grew impatient. I called aloud –
'Fortunato!'

No answer. I called again –
'Fortunato!'

No answer still. I thrust a torch through the remaining aperture and let it fall within. There came forth in return only a jingling of the bells. My heart grew sick – on account of the dampness of the catacombs. I hastened to make an end of my labour. I forced the last stone into its position; I plastered it up. Against the new masonry I re-erected the old rampart of bones. For the half of a century no mortal has disturbed them. *In pace requiescat!*

From TALES OF MYSTERY AND IMAGINATION, by Edgar Allan Poe (1809–1849)

NIGHT, *by Hogarth*

INTERROGATION, *by John Cowan*

NIGHT BEAT, *by Bill Brandt*

SHEEP TO THE SLAUGHTER: Caledonian Cattle Market, *by Donald McCullin*

NIGHT IS FOR ENDINGS

HOMECOMING: Eight members of the Manchester United football team were killed when their plane crash

Munich. On a wet night in 1958 their bodies come back to Manchester. *A photograph by Joseph McKeown*

From *Murder in the Cathedral*

T. S. ELIOT

Thomas

Now to Almighty God, to the Blessed Mary ever
Virgin, to the blessed John the Baptist, the holy apostles
Peter and Paul, to the blessed martyr Denys, and to all
the Saints, I commend my cause and that of the Church.

While the Knights *kill him, we hear the*
Chorus

Clear the air! clean the sky! wash the wind! take stone
   from stone and wash them.
The land is foul, the water is foul, our beasts and ourselves defiled with blood.
A rain of blood has blinded my eyes. Where is England?
   where is Kent? where is Canterbury?
O far far far far in the past; and I wander in a land of
   barren boughs: if I break them, they bleed; I wander
   in a land of dry stones: if I touch them they bleed.
How how can I ever return, to the soft quiet seasons?
Night stay with us, stop sun, hold season, let the day
   not come, let the spring not come.
Can I look again at the day and its common things, and
   see them all smeared with blood, through a curtain
   of falling blood?
We did not wish anything to happen.
We understood the private catastrophe,
The personal loss, the general misery,
Living and partly living;
The terror by night that ends in daily action,
The terror by day that ends in sleep;
But the talk in the market-place, the hand on the broom,
The nighttime heaping of the ashes,
The fuel laid on the fire at daybreak,
These acts marked a limit to our suffering.
Every horror had its definition,
Every sorrow had a kind of end:
In life there is not time to grieve long.
But this, this is out of life, this is out of time,

293

THE CARDINAL *by Manzu. Beyond:* RECLINING
FIGURE *by Henry Moore. Photographed at the
Festival of Two Worlds, Spoleto, by Roloff Beny*

An instant eternity of evil and wrong.
We are soiled by a filth that we cannot clean, united to
    supernatural vermin,
It is not we alone, it is not the house, it is not the city
    that is defiled,
But the world that is wholly foul.
Clear the air! clean the sky! wash the wind! take the stone
    from the stone, take the skin from the arm, take
    the muscle from the bone, and wash them. Wash the stone,
    wash the bone, wash the brain, wash the soul, wash them
    wash them!

[*The* KNIGHTS, *having completed the murder, advance to the
front to the stage and address the audience . . .*]

From MURDER IN THE CATHEDRAL, *by T. S. Eliot*

Cruel Necessity

Pope is the authority given in Spence's 'Anecdotes' for the following:

THE NIGHT after King Charles the first was beheaded, my Lord Southampton and a friend of his got leave to sit up by the body, in the banqueting-house at Whitehall. As they were sitting very melancholy there, about two o'clock in the morning, they heard the tread of somebody coming very slowly upstairs. By-and-by the door opened, and a man entered, very much muffled up in his cloak, and his face quite hid by it. He approached the body, considered it very attentively for some time, and then shook his head and sighed out the words 'Cruel necessity!' He then departed in the same slow and concealed manner as he had come in. Lord Southampton used to say that he could not distinguish anything of his face; but that by his voice and gait he took him to be Oliver Cromwell.

From A BOOK OF ANECDOTES, *selected and edited by Daniel George*

The Sadness of a King

This letter from Henry VIII to Anne Boleyn is undated. He married her in 1533.

MINE OWN SWEETHEART, this shall be to advertise you of the great melancholy that I find here since your departing; for, I ensure you, methinketh the time longer since your departing now last than I was wont to do a whole fortnight. I think your kindness and my fervency of love causeth it; for, otherwise I would not have thought it possible that for so little a while it should have grieved me. But now I am coming towards you, methinketh my pains by half removed; and also I am right well comforted insomuch that my book maketh substantially for my matter; in looking whereof I have spent above four hours this day, which causeth me now to write the shorter letter to you at this time, because of some pain in my head. Wishing myself (especially an evening) in my sweetheart's arms whose pretty duckies I trust shortly to kiss. Written by the hand of him that was, is, and shall be yours by his own will,

H. R.

The Sadness of a Queen

In 1536 Anne Boleyn was beheaded on Tower Green. Thirteen days before her death she wrote this letter to Henry VIII:

SIR, Your Grace's displeasure and my imprisonment are things so strange unto me, as what to write, or what to excuse, I am altogether ignorant. Whereas you send unto me (willing [me] to confess a truth, and to obtain your favour) by such an one whom you know to be mine ancient professed enemy, I no sooner conceived this message by him, than I rightly conceived your meaning; and if, as you say, confessing a truth indeed may procure my safety, I shall with all willingness and duty perform your command.

But let not your Grace ever imagine that your poor wife will ever be brought to acknowledge a fault where not so much as a thought thereof proceeded. And to speak a truth, never prince had wife more loyal in all duty, and in all true affection, than you have found in Anne Boleyn; with which name and place I could willingly have contented myself, if God and your Grace's pleasure had been so pleased. Neither did I at any time so far forget myself in my exaltation or received queenship, but that I always looked for such an alteration as now I find: for the ground of my preferment being on no surer foundation than your Grace's fancy, the least alteration I knew was fit and sufficient to draw that fancy to some other subject. You have chosen me from a low estate to be your queen and companion, far beyond my desert or desire. If then you found me worthy of such honour, good your Grace, let not any light fancy or bad counsel of mine enemies withdraw your princely favour from me; neither let that stain, that unworthy stain, of a disloyal heart towards your good Grace, ever cast so foul a blot on your most dutiful wife, and the infant princess, your daughter.

Try me, good king, but let me have a lawful trial; and let not my sworn enemies sit as my accusers and my judges; yea, let me receive an open trial, for my truth shall fear no open shame. Then shall you see either mine innocency cleared, your suspicions and conscience satisfied, the ignominy and slander of the world stopped, or my guilt openly declared; so that, whatsoever God or you may determine of me, your Grace may be freed from an open censure; and mine offence being so lawfully proved, your Grace is at liberty, both before God and man, not only to execute worthy punishment on me, as an unlawful wife, but to follow your affection already settled on that party for whose sake I am now as I am, whose name I could some good while since have pointed unto; your Grace not being ignorant of my suspicion therein.

But if you have already determined of me; and that not only my death, but an infamous slander, must bring you the enjoying of your desired happiness; then I desire of God that he will pardon your great sin therein, and likewise my enemies the instruments thereof; and that He will not call you to a strict account for your unprincely and cruel usage of me, at his general judgment-seat, where both you and myself must shortly appear; and in whose judgment, I doubt not, whatsoever the world may think of me, mine innocence shall be openly known and sufficiently cleared.

My last and only request shall be, that myself may only bear the burden of your Grace's displeasure, and that it may not touch the innocent souls of those poor gentlemen who, as I understand, are likewise in strait imprisonment for my sake. If ever I have found favour in your sight, if ever the name of Anne Boleyn hath been pleasing in your ears, then let me obtain this request; and I will so leave to trouble your Grace any further; with mine earnest prayers to the Trinity, to have your Grace in his good keeping, and to direct you in all your actions. From my doleful prison in the Tower, this 6th of May. Your most loyal and ever faithful wife,

ANNE BOLEYN

Even such is time

Even such is Time, which takes in trust
  Our youth, and joys, and all we have;
And pays us but with age and dust,
  Which, in the dark and silent grave,
When we have wandered all our ways,
Shuts up the story of our days:
  And from which earth, and grave, and dust,
  The Lord shall raise me up, I trust.

Sir Walter Ralegh, written on the eve of his execution, 1618

AFTER THE SHIFT: *by Michael Peto*

'When the miners reach the surface after the day's shift underground they just slump down there at the pithead, too cramped and tired to go any farther. They stretch out, light their first cigarettes. It will be twenty minutes or so before they are ready to start walking home': *Michael Peto's note about his photograph taken in Ystradgynlais, South Wales*

THE END OF THE ROAD, Shetlands, *by Michael Pet...*

rain or hail
sam done
the best he kin
till they digged his hole

:sam was a man

stout as a bridge
rugged as a bear
slickern a weazel
how be you

(sun or snow)

gone into what
like all them kings
you read about
and on him sings

a whippoorwill;

heart was big
as the world aint square
with room for the devil
and his angels too

yes,sir

what may be better
or what may be worse
and what may be clover
clover clover

(nobody'll know)

sam was a man
grinned his grin
done his chores
laid him down.

Sleep well
       e.e.cummings

The Last Hours of Socrates

In Athens in the year 399 B.C. Socrates was accused of heresy and of 'corrupting the minds of the young' by his doctrines. He was found guilty and sentenced to death. The account of his last day in prison and how, as the sun was about to set, he drank the poison, was given by an eye-witness, Phaedo of Elis, to a group of friends, and was reported by Plato in his 'Dialogues'.

Socrates is speaking . . .

'. . . There is one way then, in which a man can be free from all anxiety about the fate of his soul; if in life he has abandoned bodily pleasures and adornments, as foreign to his purpose and likely to do more harm than good, and has devoted himself to the pleasures of acquiring knowledge; and so by decking his soul not with a borrowed beauty but with its own – with self-control, and goodness, and courage, and liberality, and truth – has fitted himself to await his journey to the next world. You, Simmias and Cebes and the rest, will each make this journey some day in the future; but "for me the fated hour" (as a tragic character might say) "calls even now". In other words, it is about time that I took my bath. I prefer to have a bath before drinking the poison, rather than give the women the trouble of washing me when I am dead.'

When he had finished speaking, Crito said 'Very well, Socrates. But have you no directions for the others or myself about your children or anything else? What can we do to please you best?'

'Nothing new, Crito,' said Socrates; 'just what I am always telling you. If you look after yourselves, whatever you do will please me and mine and you too, even if you don't agree with me now. On the other hand, if you neglect yourselves and fail to follow the line of life as I have laid it down both now and in the past, however fervently you agree with me now, it will do no good at all.'

'We shall try our best to do as you say,' said Crito. 'But how shall we bury you?'

'Any way you like,' replied Socrates, 'that is, if you can catch me and I don't slip through your fingers.' He laughed gently as he spoke, and turning to us went on: 'I can't persuade Crito that I am this Socrates here who is talking to you now and marshalling all the arguments; he thinks that I am the one whom he will see presently lying dead; and he asks how he is to bury me! As for my long and elaborate explanation that when I have drunk the poison I shall remain with you no longer, but depart to a state of heavenly happiness, this attempt to console both you and myself seems to be wasted on him. You must give an assurance to Crito for me – the opposite of the one which he gave to the court which tried me. He undertook that I should stay; but you must assure him that when I am dead I shall not stay, but depart and be gone. That will help Crito to bear it more easily, and keep him from being distressed on my account when he sees my body being burned or buried, as if something dreadful were happening to me; or from saying at the funeral that it is Socrates whom he is laying out or carrying to the grave or burying. Believe me, my dear friend Crito: mis-statements are not merely jarring in their immediate context; they also have a bad effect upon the soul. No, you must keep up your spirits and say that it is only my body that you are burying; and you can bury it as you please, in whatever way you think is most proper.'

With these words he got up and went into another room to bathe; and Crito went after him, but told us to wait. So we waited, discussing and reviewing what had been said, or else dwelling upon the greatness of the calamity which had befallen us; for we felt just as though we were losing a father and should be orphans for the rest of our lives. Meanwhile, when Socrates had taken his bath, his children were brought to see him – he had two little sons and one big boy – and the women of his household – you know – arrived. He talked to them in Crito's presence and gave them directions about carrying out his wishes; then he told the women and children to go away, and came back himself to join us.

It was now nearly sunset, because he had spent a long time inside. He came and sat down, fresh from the bath; and he had only been talking for a few minutes when the prison officer came in, and walked up to him. 'Socrates,' he said, 'at any rate I shall not have to find fault with you, as I do with others, for getting angry with me and cursing when I tell them to drink the poison – carrying out Government orders. I have come to know during this time that you are the noblest and the gentlest and the bravest of all the men that have ever come here, and now especially I am sure that you are not angry with me, but with them; because you know who are responsible. So now – you know what I have come to say – goodbye and try to bear what must be as easily as you can.' As he spoke he burst into tears, and turning round, went away.

Socrates looked up at him and said 'Goodbye to you, too; we will do as you say.' Then addressing us he went on 'What a charming person! All the time I have been here he has visited me, and sometimes had discussions with me, and shown me the greatest kindness; and how generous of him now to shed tears for me at parting! But come, Crito, let us do as he says. Someone had better bring the poison, if it is ready prepared; if not, tell the man to prepare it.'

'But surely, Socrates,' said Crito, 'the sun is still upon the mountains; it has not gone down yet. Besides, I know that in other cases people have dinner and enjoy their wine, and sometimes the company of those whom they love, long after they receive the warning; and only drink the poison quite late at night. No need to hurry; there is still plenty of time.'

'It is natural that these people whom you speak of should act in that way, Crito,' said Socrates, 'because they think that they gain by it. And it is also natural that I should not; because I believe that I should gain nothing by drinking the poison a little later – I should only make myself ridiculous in my own eyes if I clung to life and hugged it when it has no more to offer. Come, do as I say and don't make difficulties.'

At this Crito made a sign to his servant, who was standing near by. The servant went out and after spending a considerable time returned with the man who was to administer the poison; he was carrying it ready prepared in a cup. When Socrates saw him he said 'Well, my good fellow, you understand these things; what ought I to do?'

'Just drink it,' he said, 'and then walk about until you feel a weight in your legs, and then lie down. Then it will act of its own accord.'

As he spoke he handed the cup to Socrates, who received it quite cheerfully, Echecrates, without a tremor, without any change of colour or expression, and said, looking up under his brows with his usual steady gaze 'What do you say about pouring a libation from this drink? Is it permitted, or not?'

'We only prepare what we regard as the normal dose, Socrates,' he replied.

'I see,' said Socrates. 'But I suppose I am allowed, or rather bound, to pray the gods that my removal from this world to the other may be prosperous. This is my prayer, then; and I hope that it may be granted.' With these words, quite calmly and with no sign of distaste, he drained the cup in one breath.

Up till this time most of us had been fairly successful in keeping back our tears; but when we saw that he was drinking, that he had actually drunk it, we could do so no longer; in spite of myself the tears came pouring out, so that I covered my face and wept broken-heartedly – not for him, but for my own calamity in losing such a friend. Crito had given up even before me, and had gone out when he could not restrain his tears. But Apollodorus, who had never stopped crying even before, now broke out into such a storm of passionate weeping that he made everyone in the room break down, except Socrates himself, who said:

'Really, my friends, what a way to behave! Why, that was my main reason for sending away the women, to prevent this sort of disturbance; because I am told that one should make one's end in a tranquil frame of mind. Calm yourselves and try to be brave.'

This made us feel ashamed, and we controlled our tears. Socrates walked about, and presently, saying that his legs were heavy, lay down on his back – that was what the man recommended. The man (he was the same one who had administered the poison) kept his hand upon Socrates, and after a little while examined his feet and legs; then pinched his foot hard and asked if he felt it. Socrates said no. Then he did the same to his legs; and moving gradually upwards in this way let us see that he was getting cold and numb. Presently he felt him again and said that when it reached the heart, Socrates would be gone.

The coldness was spreading about as far as his waist when Socrates uncovered his face – for he had covered it up – and said (they were his last words): 'Crito, we ought to offer a cock to Asclepius. See to it, and don't forget.'

'No, it shall be done,' said Crito. 'Are you sure that there is nothing else?'

Socrates made no reply to this question, but after a little while he stirred; and when the man uncovered him, his eyes were fixed. When Crito saw this, he closed the mouth and eyes.

Such, Echecrates, was the end of our comrade, who was, we may fairly say, of all those whom we knew in our time, the bravest and also the wisest and most upright man.

From PLATO: THE LAST DAYS OF SOCRATES. *Translated by Hugh Tredennick*

The Clock Strikes Twelve for Doctor Faustus

FAUSTUS: Ah, Faustus,
Now hast thou but one bare hour to live,
And then thou must be damn'd perpetually!
Stand still, you ever-moving spheres of Heaven,
That time may cease, and midnight never come;
Fair Nature's eye, rise, rise again and make
Perpetual day; or let this hour be but
A year, a month, a week, a natural day,
That Faustus may repent and save his soul!
O lente, lente, currite noctis equi![1]
The stars move still, time runs, the clock will strike,
The Devil will come, and Faustus must be damn'd.
O, I'll leap up to my God! Who pulls me down?
See, see where Christ's blood streams in the firmament!
One drop would save my soul – half a drop: ah, my Christ!
Ah, rend not my heart for naming of my Christ!
Yet will I call on him: O spare me, Lucifer! –
Where is it now? 'Tis gone; and see where God
Stretcheth out his arm, and bends his ireful brows!
Mountains and hills come, come and fall on me,
And hide me from the heavy wrath of God!
No! no!
Then will I headlong run into the earth;
Earth gape! O no, it will not harbour me!
You stars that reign'd at my nativity,
Whose influence hath allotted death and hell,
Now draw up Faustus like a foggy mist
Into the entrails of yon labouring clouds,
That when they vomit forth into the air,
My limbs may issue from their smoky mouths,
So that my soul may but ascend to Heaven.

The watch strikes.

Ah, half an hour is past! 'Twill all be past anon!
O God!
If thou wilt not have mercy on my soul,

1. 'Run softly, softly, horses of the night.' – Ovid's *Amores*.

Yet for Christ's sake whose blood hath ransom'd me,
Impose some end to my incessant pain;
Let Faustus live in hell a thousand years –
A hundred thousand, and at last be sav'd!
O, no end is limited to damned souls!
Why wert thou not a creature wanting soul?
Or why is this immortal that thou hast?
Ah, Pythagoras' metempsychosis! were that true,
This soul should fly from me, and I be chang'd
Unto some brutish beast! All beasts are happy,
For, when they die,
Their souls are soon dissolv'd in elements;
But mine must live, still to be plagu'd in hell.
Curst be the parents that engender'd me!
No, Faustus: curse thyself: curse Lucifer
That hath depriv'd thee of the joys of Heaven.

The clock striketh twelve.

O, it strikes, it strikes! Now, body, turn to air,
Or Lucifer will bear thee quick to hell.

Thunder and lightning.

O soul be chang'd into little water-drops,
And fall into the ocean – ne'er be found.
My God! my God! look not so fierce on me!

Enter DEVILS.

Adders and serpents, let me breathe awhile!
Ugly hell, gape not! come not, Lucifer!
I'll burn my books! – Ah Mephistophilis!

Exeunt [DEVILS *with* FAUSTUS.

From THE TRAGICAL HISTORY OF DOCTOR FAUSTUS,
by Christopher Marlowe (1564–1593)

On the Death of an Epicure

At length, my friends, the feast of life is o'er;
I've eat sufficient – and I'll drink no more:
My night is come; I've spent a jovial day;
'Tis time to part: but oh! what is to pay?

Richard Graves (1715–1804)

HENRY GARNETT

The Night they came for Guy Fawkes

(Contemporary accounts of the apprehension of Guy Fawkes in the vaults of Westminster on the night of 4th/5th November 1665 are confused and conflicting. Here is a picture of it by Henry Garnett in his 'Portrait of Guy Fawkes: An Experiment in Biography.')

GUY RODE directly to the Westminster house and, booted and spurred as he was, made his usual inspection of the cellar. All was as before. Not a log had been moved and every faggot was in place. He mounted again and ambled up Whitehall and the Strand to make his report to Mr Catesby. It was the evening of November 4th.

That night Robert Catesby and Guy Fawkes sat late over their food and wine. Across the table they remembered their difficulties with the mine and laughed at the recollection of the labour. There had been so many set-backs, so many fears, and now the way seemed clear before them. A few short hours remained and those men who had brought untold misery to so many Catholic families in England would be no more. Robert Catesby raised his glass to Guy and drank to the success of their enterprise. There was a little doubt in Guy's mind about the countrywide rising that Catesby foresaw, but even he thought that the shock of the explosion would so numb the minds of Englishmen that there would be time for the initiative to be seized.

It was near midnight when Guy parted from his leader and friend, Robert Catesby. He mounted his horse and sat for a moment in the soft glow of candlelight that flowed from Catesby's open door. Robert stood with his hand on Guy's knee. Guy was prompted to remove his hat and in the glow of candlelight, and the flicker of torches set in their sconces outside the doors of the great houses in the Strand, the two saluted one another. It was the last time they met. Guy paced his horse through the ruts and rubbish back to the livery stables.

At Mr Percy's house in Westminster, Guy unlocked the outer door, struck fire with flint and steel, and with lighted candle made his way to his own room. He would have everything in readiness, he thought, for the morrow. In his pockets he stowed his touchwood, which he had calculated would burn for fifteen minutes before the powder was ignited, and lit his lantern. With the feeble glimmer illuminating the treads of the stairway he made his way downstairs to the passage and door that led to the cellar.

What it was that made him hesitate he did not know. There was a faint gleam of light beneath the door, but he had seen that before. It meant no more than one of those who rented other partitioned rooms was seeking fuel. Or the Lord Keeper of the Wardrobe was after some trappings for the ceremony on the next day. Yet there was an uneasiness and a sound that was not a sound, but a sense of living bodies standing tensed. Guy's jaw set. He put down his lantern on the stone flags and softly drew his sword. Then, slowly, inch by inch, he opened the door silently on its new-oiled hinges. The light he had seen came from far away at the other end of the vast room, filtering through ill-fitting and cracked wooden partitions. He picked up his lantern and held it high. Dimly he could see a deeper blackness that was his orderly pile of wood and faggots and nothing more. All seemed to be as he had left it, and yet. . . .

Then, without warning, and with a gentle brushing noise as of men's feet passing through dried reeds, they were on him. His sword was useless. He smashed the hilt into yielding flesh, was rewarded by a gasping for breath, and flung the weapon from him. Hands seemed to be everywhere. Human hands at his throat, grasping at his arms and legs, and even clawing at his face. A man's hoarse voice shouted for light and as he struggled towards his hidden powder, lantern still in his left hand, his heels were kicked from under him and he fell on the stone flags with a crash that jarred the teeth in his head.

The bodies of men were all over him, pressing him down. The lantern was forced from his hand, and he was roughly heaved over on to his face. His arms were wrenched behind his back. A torch flared, and another and another. A knee between his shoulder blades drove the breath from his body and an arrow of pain shot through him as a cord was passed round his arms and hauled tight. Rough hands jerked him to his feet.

The cellar seemed full of armed men and more were coming through the partition. A richly dressed gentleman was directing those who were throwing down Guy's pile of logs. The first barrel came into view. A triumphant 'Ah' came from a dozen throats. An accident with one of the torches, Guy thought, and . . . He struggled with his guards. A blow from a sword hilt full in the mouth sent him staggering against the wall and brought the salt taste of blood to his tongue.

The gentleman rapped out a sharp order and Guy was marched through the partition door and out into the street. Hemmed in on every side by soldiers he was dragged away into Whitehall.

Soliloquy of a Misanthrope

Whenever I am got under my gravestone,
Sending my flowers up to stare at the church-tower,
Gritting my teeth in the chill from the church-floor,
I shall praise God heartily, to see gone,

As I look round at old acquaintance there,
Complacency from the smirk of every man,
And every attitude showing its bone,
And every mouth confessing its crude shire;

But I shall thank God thrice heartily
To be lying beside women who grimace
Under the commitments of their flesh,
And not out of spite or vanity.

From THE HAWK IN THE RAIN, *the early poems of Ted Hughes*

REMEMBER, REMEMBER, *by Bert Hardy*

ANOTHER DAY: Early morning worker, West Hartlepool, *by Donald McCullin*

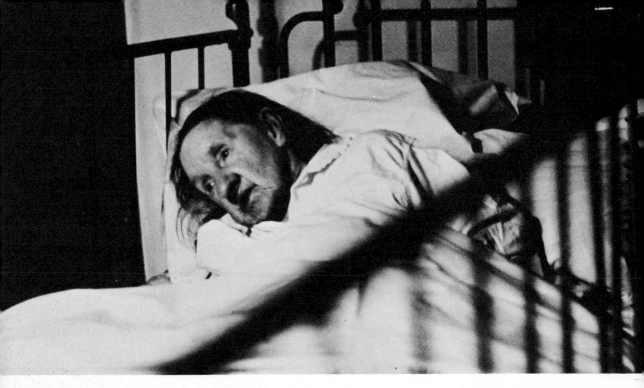

HOSPITAL BED, *by Roger Mayne*

Uphill

Does the road wind uphill all the way?
   Yes, to the very end.
Will the day's journey take the whole long day?
   From morn to night, my friend.

But is there for the night a resting-place?
   A roof for when the slow, dark hours begin.
May not the darkness hide it from my face?
   You cannot miss that inn.

Shall I meet other wayfarers at night?
   Those who have gone before.
Then must I knock, or call when just in sight?
   They will not keep you waiting at that door.

Shall I find comfort, travel-sore and weak?
   Of labour you shall find the sum.
Will there be beds for me and all who seek?
   Yea, beds for all who come.

Christina Georgina Rossetti (1830–1894)

So, we'll go no more a roving
 So late into the night,
Though the heart be still as loving,
 And the moon be still as bright.

For the sword outwears its sheath,
 And the soul wears out the breast,
And the heart must pause to breathe,
 And love itself have rest.

Though the night was made for loving,
 And the day returns too soon,
Yet we'll go no more a roving
 By the light of the moon.

Lord Byron (1788–1824)

When thou must home to shades of underground

When thou must home to shades of underground,
 And there arrived, a new admirèd guest,
The beauteous spirits do ingirt thee round,
 White Iope, blithe Helen and the rest,
To hear the stories of thy finished love
From that smooth tongue whose magic hell can move;

Then wilt thou speak of banqueting delights,
 Of masks and revels which sweet youth did make,
Of tourneys and great challenges of knights,
 And all these triumphs for thy beauty's sake.
When thou hast told these honours done to thee,
Then tell, oh, tell how thou didst murder me!

Thomas Campion (1567?–1619)

JOHN STEINBECK

The Night they Buried Grampa

PA SAID: 'We got to figger what to do. They's laws. You got to report a death, an' when you do that, they either take forty dollars for the undertaker or they take him for a pauper.'

Uncle John broke in: 'We never did have no paupers.'

Tom said: 'Maybe we got to learn. We never got booted off no land before, neither.'

'We done it clean,' said Pa. 'There can't no blame be laid on us. We never took nothin' we couldn' pay; we never suffered no man's charity. When Tom here got in trouble we could hold up our heads. He only done what any man would a done.'

'Then what'll we do?' Uncle John asked.

'We go in like the law says an' they'll come out for him. We on'y got a hundred an' fifty dollars. They take forty to bury Grampa an' we won't get to California – or else they'll bury him a pauper.' The men stirred restively, and they studied the darkening ground in front of their knees.

Pa said softly: 'Grampa buried his pa with his own hand, done it in dignity, an' shaped the grave nice with his own shovel. That was a time when a man had a right to be buried by his own son an' a son had the right to bury his own father.'

'The law says different now,' said Uncle John.

'Sometimes the law can't be foller'd no way,' said Pa. 'Not in decency, anyways. They's lots a times you can't. When Floyd was loose an' goin' wild, law said we got to give him up – an' nobody give him up. Sometimes a fella got to sift the law. I'm sayin' now I got the right to bury my own pa. Anybody got somepin to say?'

The preacher rose high on his elbow. 'Law changes,' he said, 'but "got to's" go on. You got the right to do what you got to do.'

Pa turned to Uncle John. 'It's your right too, John. You got any word against?'

'No word against,' said Uncle John. 'On'y it's like hidin' him in the night. Grampa's way was to come out a-shootin'.'

Pa said ashamedly: 'We can't do like Grampa done. We got to get to California 'fore our money gives out.'

Tom broke in: 'Sometimes fellas workin' dig up a man an' then they raise hell an' figger he been killed. The gov'ment's got more interest in a dead man than a live one. They'll go hell-scrapin' tryin' to fin' out who he was and how he died. I offer we put a note of writin' in a bottle an' lay it with Grampa, tellin' who he is an' how he died, an' why he's buried here.'

Pa nodded agreement. 'That's good. Wrote out in a nice han'. Be not so lonesome too,

312

knowin' his name is there with 'im, not jus' a old fella lonesome underground. Any more stuff to say?' The circle was silent.

Pa turned to Ma. 'You'll lay 'im out?'

'I'll lay 'im out,' said Ma. 'But who's to get supper?'

Sairy Wilson said: 'I'll get supper. You go right ahead. Me an' that big girl of yourn.'

'We sure thank you,' said Ma. 'Noah, you get into them kegs an' bring out some nice pork. Salt won't be deep in it yet, but it'll be right nice eatin'.'

'We got a half sack a potatoes,' said Sairy.

Ma said: 'Gimme two half-dollars.' Pa dug in his pocket and gave her the silver. She found the basin, filled it full of water, and went into the tent. It was nearly dark in there. Sairy came in and lighted a candle and stuck it upright on a box and then she went out. For a moment Ma looked down at the dead old man. And then in pity she tore a strip from her own apron and tied up his jaw. She straightened his limbs, folded his hands over his chest. She held his eyelids down and laid a silver piece on each one. She buttoned his shirt and washed his face.

Sairy looked in, saying: 'Can I give you any help?'

Ma looked slowly up. 'Come in,' she said. 'I like to talk to ya.'

'That's a good big girl you got,' said Sairy. 'She's right in peelin' potatoes. What can I do to help?'

'I was gonna wash Grampa all over,' said Ma, 'but he got no other clo'es to put on. An' 'course your quilt's spoilt. Can't never get the smell a death from a quilt. I seen a dog growl an' shake at a mattress my ma died on, an' that was two years later. We'll wrop 'im in your quilt. We'll make it up to you. We got a quilt for you.'

Sairy said: 'You shouldn't talk like that. We're proud to help. I ain't felt so – safe in a long time. People needs – to help.'

Ma nodded. 'They do,' she said. She looked long into the old whiskery face, with its bound jaw and silver eyes shining in the candlelight. 'He ain't gonna look natural. We'll wrop him up.'

'The ol' lady took it good.'

'Why, she's so old,' said Ma, 'maybe she don't even rightly know what happened. Maybe she won't really know for quite a while. Besides, us folks take a pride holdin' in. My pa used to say: "Anybody can break down. It takes a man not to." We always try to hold in.' She folded the quilt neatly about Grampa's legs and around his shoulders. She brought the corner of the quilt over his head like a cowl and pulled it down over his face. Sairy handed her half a dozen big safety pins, and she pinned the quilt neatly and tightly about the long package. And at last she stood up. 'It won't be a bad burying,' she said. 'We got a preacher to see him in, an' his folks is all aroun'.' Suddenly she swayed a little, and Sairy went to her and steadied her. 'It's sleep – ' Ma said in a shamed tone. 'No, I'm awright. We been so busy gettin' ready, you see.'

'Come out in the air,' Sairy said.

'Yeah, I'm all done here.' Sairy blew out the candle and the two went out.

A bright fire burned in the little gulch. And Tom, with sticks and wire, had made supports from which two kettles hung and bubbled furiously, and good steam poured out under the lids. Rose of Sharon knelt on the ground out of range of the burning heat, and she had a long spoon in her hand. She saw Ma come out of the tent, and she stood up and went to her.

'Ma,' she said. 'I got to ask.'

'Scared again?' Ma asked. 'Why, you can't get through nine months without sorrow.'

'But will it – hurt the baby?'

Ma said: 'They used to be a sayin', "A chile born outa sorrow'll be a happy chile." Isn't that so, Mis' Wilson?'

'I heard it like that,' said Sairy. 'An' I heard the other: "Born outa too much joy'll be a doleful boy?" '

'I'm all jumpy inside,' said Rose of Sharon.

'Well, we ain't none of us jumpin' for fun,' said Ma. 'You jes' keep watchin the pots.'

On the edge of the ring of firelight the men had gathered. For tools they had a shovel and a mattock. Pa marked out the ground – eight feet long and three feet wide. The work went on in relays. Pa chopped the earth with the mattock and then Uncle John shovelled it out. Al chopped and Tom shovelled, Noah chopped and Connie shovelled. And the hole drove down, for the work never diminished in speed. The shovels of dirt flew out of the hole in quick spurts. When Tom was shoulder-deep in the rectangular pit, he said: 'How deep, Pa?'

'Good and deep. A couple feet more. You get out now, Tom, and get that paper wrote.'

Tom boosted himself out of the hole and Noah took his place. Tom went to Ma, where she tended the fire. 'We got any paper an' pen, Ma?'

Ma shook her head slowly. 'No-o. That's one thing we didn' bring.' She looked toward Sairy. And the little woman walked quickly to her tent. She brought back a Bible and a half pencil. 'Here,' she said. 'They's a clear page in front. Use that an' tear it out.' She handed book and pencil to Tom.

Tom sat down in the firelight. He squinted his eyes in concentration, and at last wrote slowly and carefully on the end-paper in big clear letters: 'This here is William James Joad, dyed of a stroke, old old man. His fokes bured him becaws they got no money to pay for funerls. Nobody kilt him. Jus a stroke and he dyed.' He stopped. 'Ma, listen to this here.' He read it slowly to her.

'Why, that soun's nice,' she said. 'Can't you stick on somepin' from Scripture so it'll be religious? Open up an' git a-sayin' somepin outa Scripture.'

'Got to be short,' said Tom. 'I ain't got much room lef' on the page.'

Sairy said: 'How 'bout "God have mercy on his soul"?'

'No,' said Tom. 'Sounds too much like he was hung. I'll copy somepin.' He turned the pages and read, mumbling his lips, saying the words under his breath. 'Here's a good short one,' he said. ' "An' Lot said unto them, Oh, not so, my Lord" '

'Don't mean nothin',' said Ma. 'Long's you're gonna put one down, it might's well mean somepin'.'

314

Sairy said: 'Turn to Psalms, over further. You kin always get somepin outa Psalms.'

Tom flipped over the pages and looked down the verses. 'Now here *is* one,' he said. 'This here's a nice one, just blowed full a religion: "Blessed is he whose transgression is forgiven, whose sin is covered." How's that?'

'That's real nice,' said Ma. 'Put that one in.'

Tom wrote it carefully. Ma rinsed and wiped a fruit jar and Tom screwed the lid down tight on it. 'Maybe the preacher ought to wrote it,' he said.

Ma said: 'No, the preacher wan't no kin.' She took the jar from him and went into the dark tent. She unpinned the covering and slipped the fruit jar in under the thin cold hands and pinned the comforter tight again. And then she went back to the fire.

The men came from the grave, their faces shining with perspiration. 'Awright,' said Pa. He and John and Noah and Al went into the tent, and they came out carrying the long, pinned bundle between them. They carried it to the grave. Pa leaped into the hole and received the bundle in his arms and laid it gently down. Uncle John put out a hand and helped Pa out of the hole. Pa asked: 'How about Granma?'

'I'll see,' Ma said. She walked to the mattress and looked down at the old woman for a moment. Then she went back to the grave. 'Sleepin',' she said. 'Maybe she'd hold it against me, but I ain't a-gonna wake her up. She's tar'd.'

Pa said: 'Where at's the preacher? We oughta have a prayer.'

Tom said: 'I seen him walkin' down the road. He don't like to pray no more.'

'Don't like to pray?'

'No,' said Tom. 'He ain't a preacher no more. He figgers it ain't right to fool people actin' like a preacher when he ain't a preacher. I bet he went away so nobody wouldn' ast him.'

Casy had come quietly near, and he heard Tom speaking. 'I didn' run away,' he said. 'I'll he'p you folks, but I won't fool ya.'

Pa said: 'Won't you say a few words? Ain't none of our folks ever been buried without a few words.'

'I'll say 'em,' said the preacher.

Connie led Rose of Sharon to the graveside, she reluctant. 'You got to,' Connie said. 'It ain't decent not to. It'll jus' be a little.'

The firelight fell on the grouped people, showing their faces and their eyes, dwindling on their dark clothes. All the hats were off now. The light danced, jerking over the people.

Casy said: 'It'll be a short one.' He bowed his head, and the others followed his lead. Casy said solemnly: 'This here ol' man jus' lived a life an' jus' died out of it. I don' know whether he was good or bad, but that don't matter much. He was alive, an' that's what matters. An' now he's dead, an' that don't matter. Heard a fella tell a poem one time, an' he says: "All that lives is holy." Got to thinkin', an' purty soon it means more than the words says. An' I would'n pray for a ol' fella that's dead. He's awright. He got a job to do, but it's all laid out for 'im an' there's on'y one way to do it. But us, we got a job to do, an' they's a thousan' ways, an' we don' know which one to take.

An' if I was to pray, it'd be for the folks that don' know which way to turn. Grampa here, he got the easy straight. An' now cover 'im up and let him get to his work.' He raised his head.

Pa said 'Amen', and the others muttered 'A-men'. Then Pa took the shovel, half filled it with dirt, and spread it gently into the black hole. He handed the shovel to Uncle John, and John dropped in a shovelful. Then the shovel went from hand to hand until every man had his turn. When all had taken their duty and their right, Pa attacked the mound of loose dirt and hurriedly filled the hole. The women moved back to the fire to see to supper. Ruthie and Winfield watched, absorbed.

Ruthie said solemnly: 'Grampa's down under there.' And Winfield looked at her with horrified eyes. And then he ran away to the fire and sat on the ground and sobbed to himself.

Pa half filled the hole, and then he stood panting with the effort while Uncle John finished it. And John was shaping up the mound when Tom stopped him. 'Listen,' Tom said. ' 'F we leave a grave, they'll have it open in no time. We got to hide it. Level her off an' we'll strew dry grass. We got to do that.'

Pa said: 'I didn't think a that. It ain't right to leave a grave unmounded.'

'Can't he'p it,' said Tom. 'They'd dig 'im right up, an' we'd get it for breakin' the law. You know what I get if I break the law.'

'Yeah,' Pa said. 'I forgot that.' He took the shovel from John and levelled the grave. 'She'll sink, come winter,' he said.

'Can't he'p that,' said Tom. 'We'll be a long ways off by winter. Tromp her in good, an' we'll strew stuff over her.'

From THE GRAPES OF WRATH, *by John Steinbeck*

The Night has a Thousand Eyes

The night has a thousand eyes,
  And the day but one;
Yet the light of the bright world dies
  With the dying sun.

The mind has a thousand eyes,
  And the heart but one;
Yet the light of a whole life dies
  When love is done.

Francis William Bourdillon (1852–1921)

GRAVEYARD, *by Godfrey Macdomnic*

Acknowledgements

The Young Visitors by Daisy Ashford. Copyright, © 1919 by George H. Doran Company. Selection reprinted by permission of Doubleday & Company, Inc., and Chatto & Windus, Ltd.

"The Night has a Thousand Eyes" by F. W. Bourdillon. Reprinted by permission of Mr. F. B. Bourdillon, CBE.

The Complete Poems of Cavafy by C. P. Cavafy, translated by Rae Dalven. Selection reprinted by permission of Harcourt, Brace & World, Inc.

The Canterbury Tales by Geoffrey Chaucer, translated into modern English by Nevill Coghill. Selection reprinted by permission of Penguin Books, Ltd.

A Roving Commission: My Early Life by Winston Churchill. (Chap. XXI, pp. 268-285) Copyright, © 1930 by Charles Scribner's Sons; renewal copyright © 1958 Winston Churchill. Selection reprinted by permission of Charles Scribner's Sons and Odhams Books, Ltd.

Rape of the Fair Country by Alexander Cordell. Selection reprinted by permission of Doubleday & Company, Inc. and Victor Gollancz, Ltd.

Poems 1923-1954 by E. E. Cummings. Copyright, © 1925, 1944 by E. E. Cummings. Selections reprinted by Harcourt, Brace & World, Inc.

"The Stuff that Sleep is made of" by John Davy, from *The Observer*. Reprinted by permission of the publishers.

"Silver" by Walter de la Mare. Reprinted by permission of The Literary Trustees of Walter de la Mare and the Society of Authors.

Wind, Sand and Stars by Antoine de Saint-Exupéry. Copyright, © 1939 by Antoine de Saint-Exupéry, translated by Lewis Galantière. Selection reprinted by permission of Harcourt, Brace & World, Inc.

"Impression de Nuit" by Lord Alfred Douglas. Reprinted by permission of The Hutchinson Publishing Group.

The Philosophy of the Bed by Mary Eden and Richard Carrington. Selections reprinted by permission of the Hutchinson Publishing Group.

Collected Poems 1909-1962 by T. S. Eliot. Copyright 1936 by Harcourt, Brace & World, Inc.; copyright © 1963, 1964, by T. S. Eliot. Selection reprinted by permission of Harcourt, Brace & World, Inc., and Faber & Faber, Ltd.

Murder in the Cathedral by T. S. Eliot. Copyright, © 1935 by Harcourt, Brace & World, Inc.; renewed, 1963, by T. S. Eliot. Selection reprinted by permission of Harcourt, Brace & World, Inc., and Faber & Faber, Ltd.

Thrilling Cities by Ian Fleming. Copyright, © 1959, 1960, 1962, 1963, 1964 by Gildrose Productions, Ltd. Selection reprinted by arrangement with the New American Library, Inc., New York, and Jonathan Cape, Limited.

The Golden Bough by Sir James Frazer. Selection reprinted by permission of St. Martin's Press, Inc., and Macmillan, Ltd.

Complete Poems of Robert Frost by Robert Frost. Copyright, © 1930, 1949 by Henry Holt and Company, Inc. Copyright © 1936, 1948 by Robert Frost. Copyright renewed 1944, 1951, © 1956, 1958, 1962 by Robert Frost. Copyright renewed © 1964 by Lesley Frost Ballantine. Selections reprinted by permission of Holt, Rinehart & Winston, Inc., and Jonathan Cape, Ltd.

Portrait of Guy Fawkes by Henry Garnett. Selection reprinted by permission of Robert Hale, Ltd.

A Book of Anecdotes by Daniel George. Selections reprinted by permission of Mr. John M. Bunting.

The Two Deaths of Christopher Martin by William Golding. Copyright, © 1956 by William Golding. Selection reprinted by permission of Harcourt, Brace & World, Inc., and Faber & Faber, Ltd.

Mr. Ludwig Goldscheider for the photograph of Michelangelo's "Night."

Oblomov by Ivan A. Goncharov, translated by Natalie Duddington. Selection reprinted by permission of E. P. Dutton & Co., Inc., and J. M. Dent & Sons, Ltd.

Diary of a Nobody by George Grossmith and Weedon Grossmith. Everyman's Library. Selection reprinted by permission of E. P. Dutton & Co., Inc., and J. M. Dent & Sons, Ltd.

My Sad Captains by Thom Gunn. Selection reprinted by permission of Faber & Faber, Ltd.

"The Origin of the Milky Way" from *The National Gallery* by Philip Hendy. Selection reprinted by permission of Harry N. Abrams, Inc., and Thames and Hudson.

No Boats on the River by A. P. Herbert. Selection reprinted by permission of Sir Alan Herbert and Methuen & Company, Ltd.

Hiroshima by John Hersey. Copyright, © 1946 by John Hersey. *Hiroshima* originally appeared in *The New Yorker*. Selection reprinted by permission of Alfred A. Knopf, Inc.

KON-TIKI: *Across the Pacific by Raft* by Thor Heyerdahl. Published in the U.S.A. by Rand McNally & Company. Selection reprinted by permission of Rand McNally & Company and George Allen and Unwin, Ltd.

Birds as Individuals by Len Howard. Selection reprinted by permission of Curtis Brown, Ltd., and William Collins Sons & Co., Ltd.

Hawk in the Rain by Ted Hughes. Copyright, © 1957 by Ted Hughes. Selections reprinted by permission of Harper & Row, Publishers.

Music at Night by Aldous Huxley (pp. 40-42). Copyright, © 1931 by Aldous Huxley. Selection reprinted by permission of Harper & Row, Publishers, and Chatto & Windus, Ltd.

"On the Nightmare" by Ernest Jones. Reprinted by permission of the Liveright Publishing Corporation, New York, and The Hogarth Press, Limited.

Three Men in a Spaceship by Konarov, Egorov and Feoktistov. Selection reprinted by permission of Opera Mundi-Novosti.

The Poems of Vachel Lindsay by Vachel Lindsay. Copyright 1914 by The Macmillan Company. Copyright renewed by Elizabeth C. Lindsay. Selection reprinted by permission of The Macmillan Company.

A Doomsday Book by George MacBeth. Selection reprinted by permission of Scorpion Press.

Absolute Beginners by Colin MacInnes. Copyright, © 1959 by Colin MacInnes. Selection reprinted by permission of The Macmillan Company and MacGibbon and Kee, Limited.

The Dream World by R. L. Megroz. Selections reprinted by permission of The Bodley Head, Limited.

The Collected Poems of Wilfred Owen by Wilfred Owen. Copyright, © 1963 by Chatto & Windus, Ltd. Selection reprinted for the U.S.A. by permission of the publisher, New Directions Publishing Corporation.

Plato: The Last Days of Socrates, translated by Hugh Tredennick. Selection reprinted by permission of Penguin Books, Ltd.

The Republic by Plato, translated by B. Jowett, M.A. Selection reprinted by permission of The Clarendon Press, Oxford.

Mr. Graham Rees for his translation of "The Vision of the Cross."

The Year of the Gorilla by George Schaller. Copyright, © by the University of Chicago. Selection reprinted by permission of the publishers.

The Grapes of Wrath by John Steinbeck. Copyright, © 1939 by John Steinbeck. Selection reprinted by permission of The Viking Press, Inc.

Under Milk Wood by Dylan Thomas. Copyright, © 1954 by New Directions. Selection reprinted by permission of New Directions Publishing Corp., and J. M. Dent & Sons, Ltd.

My Life and Hard Times by James Thurber, published by Harper & Row and Hamish Hamilton, Ltd. (*Vintage Thurber*). Copyright, © 1933, 1961 by James Thurber. Selection reprinted by permission of Mrs. Helen Thurber.

The Stuff of Dreams by Alison Uttley. Selection reprinted by permission of Faber & Faber, Limited.

Victoria and Albert Museum for "Tobias and Sara," Piranesi's "Dream," and "Night" by Hogarth.

While Berlin Burns by Hans Georg von Studnitz. Copyright, © 1964 by George Weidenfeld & Nicholson, Ltd., published by Prentice-Hall, Inc. Selection reprinted by permission of the publishers.

Permission to include the extracts from the 1938 Macmillan edition of the Greville Diaries was granted by the present copyright-holders who are the beneficiaries under the Will of the Countess of Strafford and John W. Ogilvie.

The editor wishes especially to thank the photographers whose work appears here: So many of them have taken a friendly interest in *Night* and have given much care to the selection and printing of their pictures.

His warm thanks, too, to Miss Ann Newman and her colleagues of the Muswell Hill Public Library: They have been unfailingly gracious and helpful.